INTERPERSONAL SKILLS
TRAINING

INTERPERSONAL SKILLS
TRAINING

A Sourcebook of Activities for Trainers

PHILIP BURNARD

KOGAN PAGE

First published in 1992

Apart from any fair dealing for the purposes of research or private study, or criticism or review, as permitted under the Copyright, Designs and Patents Act, 1988, this publication may only be reproduced, stored or transmitted, in any form or by any means, with the prior permission in writing of the publishers, or in the case of reprographic reproduction in accordance with the terms of licences issued by the Copyright Licensing Agency. Enquiries concerning reproduction outside those terms should be sent to the publishers at the undermentioned address:

Kogan Page Limited
120 Pentonville Road
London N1 9JN

© Philip Burnard, 1992

Although this book remains subject to copyright, permission is granted free of charge to photocopy for instructional purposes the pages which are required for the activities. This may be done within the purchasing institution, organization, school or college only.

British Library Cataloguing in Publication Data

A CIP record for this book is available from the British Library.

ISBN 0 7494 0708 5

Typeset by DP Photosetting, Aylesbury, Bucks
Printed and bound in Great Britain by
Biddles Ltd, Guildford and Kings Lynn

Contents

List of activities	7
Introduction	11

Part I Skills training 17

1	Interpersonal skills training	19
2	Managing interpersonal skills training: facilitation and group dynamics	53
3	Evaluating interpersonal skills workshops	73
4	A guide to running an interpersonal skills workshop	83
5	Interpersonal skills training checklists	90

Part II Training activities 97

6	Icebreakers and introductions	99
7	Pairs activities	118
8	Small group activities	142
9	Exploring eye contact	163
10	Exploring feelings	182
11	Gestalt activities	204
12	Evaluation activities	228
13	Counselling skills activities	248
14	Assertiveness skills activities	270
15	Interviewing skills activities	290
16	Facilitation skills activities	314

Topics for Discussion 340

References 342

Bibliography 345

Index of activities 352

Index 356

List of activities

Icebreakers and introductions

Opening round **Activity number 1**	100
Brief interviews **Activity number 2**	101
Pairs introductions **Activity number 3**	104
Introductory handout **Activity number 4**	105
Milling and pairing **Activity number 5**	108
Blind walk **Activity number 6**	109
Inventory **Activity number 7**	111
Good and new **Activity number 8**	114
Formal introductions **Activity number 9**	115
Prepared sheets **Activity number 10**	116

Pairs activities

Introductory pairs **Activity number 11**	119
Brainstorming **Activity number 12**	121
Co-counselling **Activity number 13**	124
Listening **Activity number 14**	126
Using questions **Activity number 15**	129
Pairs interview **Activity number 16**	132
Exploration of topic **Activity number 17**	134
Snowballing **Activity number 18**	136
Silent pairs **Activity number 19**	138
Don't listen **Activity number 20**	140

Small group activities

Rogerian listening **Activity number 21**	143

Brainstorming **Activity number 22** 145
No chairperson **Activity number 23** 147
Fishbowl **Activity number 24** 148
Ground rules **Activity number 25** 150
Free for all **Activity number 26** 153
Alternating chair **Activity number 27** 155
Hotseat **Activity number 28** 157
Quaker group **Activity number 29** 159
Body language **Activity number 30** 161

Exploring eye contact

No eye contact **Activity number 31** 164
Centring **Activity number 32** 166
Sustained eye contact **Activity number 33** 168
Group eye contact **Activity number 34** 170
Talking and eye contact **Activity number 35** 172
Silent gazing **Activity number 36** 173
What the eyes say **Activity number 37** 174
Eye contact in everyday life **Activity number 38** 176
Recording **Activity number 39** 178
Eye movements **Activity number 40** 180

Exploring feelings

Brainstorming feelings **Activity number 41** 183
Feeling words **Activity number 42** 185
Expressing feelings **Activity number 43** 187
Giving permission **Activity number 44** 189
Exaggeration **Activity number 45** 191
Paradox **Activity number 46** 193
Earliest experience **Activity number 47** 195
Focusing **Activity number 48** 197
Childhood **Activity number 49** 200
Future **Activity number 50** 202

Gestalt activities

Immediate awareness **Activity number 51** 207
Shifting awareness **Activity number 52** 209
Noticing **Activity number 53** 211
Describing **Activity number 54** 213

Self and object **Activity number 55**	215
Self-description **Activity number 56**	217
Self-not self **Activity number 57**	219
Meditation **Activity number 58**	221
Stream of consciousness **Activity number 59**	224
Here and now **Activity number 60**	226

Evaluation activities

Pairs evaluation **Activity number 61**	229
Nominal group evaluation **Activity number 62**	232
Self and peer evaluation **Activity number 63**	234
Journal **Activity number 64**	236
Least and best **Activity number 65**	238
Things learned **Activity number 66**	239
Brainstorming **Activity number 67**	240
Future planning **Activity number 68**	241
Questionnaire **Activity number 69**	243
Personal evaluation **Activity number 70**	246

Counselling skills activities

Simple listening **Activity number 71**	250
Using open questions **Activity number 72**	252
Using closed questions **Activity number 73**	254
Using empathy-building statements **Activity number 74**	256
Checking for understanding **Activity number 75**	258
Exploring silence **Activity number 76**	260
Using probes **Activity number 77**	262
Summarizing **Activity number 78**	264
Putting it all together **Activity number 79**	266
Perverse role play **Activity number 80**	268

Assertiveness skills activities

Yes/No activity **Activity number 81**	272
Saying no **Activity number 82**	274
Saying yes **Activity number 83**	276
Contradictory body language **Activity number 84**	278
Congruent body language **Activity number 85**	280
Role play **Activity number 86**	282
Submissive role play **Activity number 87**	284

10 List of activities

Exaggerated role play **Activity number 88** 285
Psychodrama **Activity number 89** 286
Real life practice **Activity number 90** 288

Interviewing skills activities

Preparing for an interview **Activity number 91** 292
Interview checklist **Activity number 92** 294
Identifying key issues **Activity number 93** 297
Writing a CV **Activity number 94** 299
Role-play interview **Activity number 95** 302
Perverse role play **Activity number 96** 304
Confidence building **Activity number 97** 306
Practising interviewing **Activity number 98** 308
Devil's advocate **Activity number 99** 310
Putting it all together **Activity number 100** 312

Facilitation skills activities

Identifying facilitation skills **Activity number 101** 320
Self-assessment **Activity number 102** 322
Planning **Activity number 103** 326
Meaning **Activity number 104** 327
Confronting **Activity number 105** 329
Dealing with feelings **Activity number 106** 331
Structuring **Activity number 107** 333
Valuing **Activity number 108** 335
Listening to the group **Activity number 109** 337
Putting group facilitation into practice
  Activity number 110 338

Introduction

This book is all about all aspects of interpersonal skills training. It is written as a sourcebook for those who want useful ideas about how to run interpersonal skills workshops. Its aim is practical. It is a manual to be used in the training field. While the early chapters are about theory - it is important to be clear about the theory behind training - the bulk of the book is a series of easy-to-use training activities.

Most trainers will have been to workshops and on courses themselves. Sometimes an activity will be remembered but the detail of it forgotten. When this has happened, this book can serve as a jog to the memory. For others it can act as a source of ideas of ways of helping people to reflect on their interpersonal skills. There are lots of ways of using the book; this introduction illustrates some of those ways.

WHO THE BOOK IS FOR

This book is for anyone who trains others in interpersonal skills. It is a sourcebook of activities - as well as theory - and is aimed at a broad audience. The sorts of trainers who may find it useful will include those in:

- business and administration training;
- management training;
- staff development;

- further and higher education;
- workshop facilitation;
- the human potential field;
- post-basic education and training;
- the health professions;
- personal growth development;
- customer relations training;
- quality circles;
- personnel training.

We all need to communicate and we all need to develop our interpersonal skills. The activities in this book have all been used in counselling, assertiveness and management training – and they work. Also, you can adapt them to suit your own situation. The main aim is to provide a diverse and varied range of simple activities that allow professional people to explore their own skills.

I have often used the term 'professional' to describe the person who is undertaking interpersonal skills training. I have used the term 'client' to describe the person with whom the professional has an interpersonal relationship. Such clients may be any of the following:

- students;
- managers;
- researchers;
- colleagues;
- clients;
- residents;
- customers;
- patients;

and many others.

The question of the label is a difficult one and I am writing for any trainers, students, clients and customers who want practical ways to enhance their communication skills. In the end, interpersonal skills are pertinent to everyone. Anyone who works and lives with other people and who interacts with others as part of their job is going to benefit from reviewing and enhancing interpersonal performance.

WHAT IS IN THE BOOK

The first part of the book offers a theoretical context. It deals with issues such as:

- What are interpersonal skills?
- What sort of training methods are available?
- How do I run an interpersonal skills course?
- How do I evaluate such a course?

The emphasis throughout is on practice. The first part is referenced to other literature so that the reader who wants a more detailed exposition can find the details in other books and papers. I have also included a detailed bibliography.

Part II of the book contains the activities themselves. These are broken up into manageable sections:

- icebreakers;
- pairs activities;
- small group activities;
- activities for exploring eye contact;
- activities concerned with feelings;
- gestalt activities;
- evaluation activities;
- counselling activities;
- assertiveness activities;
- interviewing activities;
- facilitation activities.

I have tried to avoid some of the more 'therapy' oriented activities that were popular in similar books in the 1960s, some of which are not very clear in their aims, nor always based on sound theory. Some are embarrassing for people to take part in. I feel that adult learners should never have their dignity compromised in the process of trying to develop interpersonal skills. In the interpersonal skills business, we all have a lot to learn, and we should respect each other's feelings as we engage in this learning process.

I have also tried to avoid taking a particular theoretical stance. I would not identify myself with the behavioural, psychodynamic or humanistic schools of psychology and training. What I do feel to be important is that we acknowledge that different people view the world in ways that we do not. In interpersonal skills training we need to accommodate those different perspectives. My influences in this field have been the personal construct psychologist, George Kelly, the existential writings of Sartre, Camus and others and the psychological writings of Carl Rogers, Gerard Egan, Guy Claxton and John Heron.

A consistent theme throughout the book is the importance of the individual reflecting on his or her behaviour, beliefs and values. I do not believe that effective interpersonal skills training can merely be a drilling in a range of required behaviours. All the activities listed here ask the person to think about what they already do. This approach is justified through reference to experiential learning theory, curriculum design and approaches to adult learning. The approach is also based on my own experience of training a variety of professionals in a range of interpersonal and communication skills. It is not, of course, the only approach; but it is a pragmatic and useful one.

Throughout the book I have raised questions that you might want to ask of yourself. The aim of these is to encourage you to reflect on your own experience. More than anything, you should be critical of what you read for change comes through critical awareness. Also, such critical ability should be encouraged in interpersonal skills workshops. I have found a tendency for some trainers (particularly those trained in the client-centred approach) to be rather bland. Some feel it important not to argue with their students. My feeling is that lively argument can push things forward. Interpersonal skills, like all other aspects of human life, are constantly changing. There is room for a range of views and opinions about what does and what does not constitute effective interpersonal behaviour. I think it is particularly important to avoid 'cloning'. This occurs when the trainer demonstrates a particular style of interaction with others which is then adopted by his workshop participants. After such workshops, it is not unusual to see 10 to 20 people all looking and sounding like the person who ran the workshop! This does not strike me as the best way of helping in the enhancement of interpersonal skills.

HOW TO USE THE BOOK

People use books differently. Personally, I rarely read one from cover to cover. While you *can* do that with this one, I would advise you not to. Instead, if you want ideas for activities for interpersonal skills workshops, go straight to the activities section. If you are thinking of setting up an interpersonal skills workshop and don't know how to do it, read the first three chapters.

Part II offers a wide range of activities for a considerable array of interpersonal workshops. These can be used in various ways, for example they can be used as the basis of 'theme workshops' on assertiveness or on counselling. They can also be used as part of a tailored programme designed by the trainer to suit the needs of a particular group. Alternatively, workshop participants themselves can choose the activities that they take part in as part of a co-operative training venture. All the activities contain explicit details of how best to use them and many have worksheets that can be photocopied and used as handouts.

There are three ways of finding the activities that you want to use: you can browse through and pick out the ones you need, you can use the straightforward listing of all of the activities at the front of the manual or you can use the index of activities that sits alonside the main index at the back.

Above everything, the point it to *use* the book and not just to read it. The activities may be read through, memorized and used in a workshop; alternatively, you may want to take the book into the workshop and work from it directly. Feel free to write in the margins and to make notes about what does and does not work for you and your style of workshop management.

The activities in this book are not guaranteed to make other people interpersonally skilled. They will make people think about what they do and why they do it. That seems to me to be the basis of working in the interpersonal domain. Also, as you read through the activities, reflect on your own skills or lack of them. I have noticed an unnerving tendency for interpersonal skills workshops to be run by people who are, strangely, without these skills in everyday life. In the end, we must offer ourselves as role models. While we will not always achieve this goal, we must, at least, try.

PART I
SKILLS TRAINING

Chapter 1:

Interpersonal skills training

INTERPERSONAL SKILLS

We all use interpersonal skills every day of our lives and we have been using them almost from the day we were born. The territory is already familiar. The range of what constitutes interpersonal skills is vast. A short list of such skills would include at least the following: counselling, group membership skills, assertiveness, social skills, interviewing skills of various sorts, writing skills, using the telephone and group facilitation skills. Examples of how such skills are used in a range of settings are also numerous and would include the following among many others:

- counselling skills: counselling colleagues, friends, clients and customers;
- assertiveness skills: returning faulty goods, saying 'no', keeping to contracts and agreements;
- social skills: introducing yourself, attending meetings, working with the general public, with customers and clients;
- facilitation skills: running meetings and groups, chairing discussions and organizing planning meetings.

All professional people need and use a variety of interpersonal skills in every aspect of their work. The difficult thing, however, is to teach these skills to other people. Very often, they are learned through the process known as 'sitting with Nellie': the new professional is supposed to pick up various skills through observing older and more experienced colleagues at work. The problem arises when those colleagues demonstrate that they do not have particular interpersonal skills! Arguably, this situation has arisen because those colleagues were given no formal training either and so the cycle of events is continued. This chapter explores how interpersonal skills may be taught to professionals.

However, skills alone will not suffice. Behind and alongside the practice of interpersonal skills must be a set of values, a series of attitudes, all of which contribute to the 'human' element of interpersonal behaviour. We cannot afford to train ourselves and others in a range of skills alone. While the skills are being used, there must be a reflection of the human being that lies behind them. In fact it can be stated more strongly: the interpersonally skilled person is one who *demonstrates* humane, caring qualities. Therefore, before we explore different sorts of skills, it is important to explore some of these core qualities.

PERSONAL QUALITIES FOR INTERPERSONAL EFFECTIVENESS

Certain personal qualities are a prerequisite of effective interpersonal relationships. A basic cluster of such necessary qualities may be identified as: warmth, genuineness, empathy, and unconditional positive regard (Rogers 1967). This cluster of qualities occurs again and again in both the literature and the research into interpersonal skills (Truax and Carkuff 1967, Schulman 1982, Burnard and Morrison 1989). These personal qualities cannot accurately be described as 'skills' but they are necessary if we are to use interpersonal skills effectively and caringly. They form the bedrock of all effective human relationships, and are worthy of discussion in any workshop or course on interpersonal skills training. It is inappropriate merely to teach people a range of interpersonal skills without first discussing attitudes and personal qualities.

The question always arises as to whether or not you can *train* people in these qualities or even if they are discrete qualities at all.

In the end, it would seem that some people have a greater disposition towards these personal qualities than others (ie, some are just better at getting on with people than others). However, we cannot leave it at that. We must make some attempt at developing the qualities that people have. Facilitators of interpersonal skills workshops should return again and again to these core qualities as the focus of their discussions.

Warmth

Warm people are likely to get on better with others than frosty ones. Warmth, in a relationship, means an ability to be approachable and open to the client. Schulman (1982) argues that the following considerations are involved in demonstrating the concept of warmth:

- equal worth;
- absence of blame;
- nondefensiveness;
- closeness.

Warmth is as much a frame of mind as a skill and perhaps one developed through being honest with oneself and being prepared to be open with others. It also involves treating the other person as an equal.

Warmth must be offered by the professional but the feeling may not necessarily be reciprocated by the client. If we are offering a professional service of some kind, we should show warmth but we cannot expect that the recipient of that service will necessarily return it. Professional relationships, unlike friendships, are not necessarily reciprocal.

There is another problem with the notion of warmth. We all perceive personal qualities in different ways. One person's warmth is another person's sickliness or sentimentality. We cannot guarantee how our warmth will be perceived by the other person. In a more general way, however, warmth may be compared with 'coldness'. It is clear that the cold person would not be the ideal one to undertake helping another person in a professional setting. It is salutary, however, to reflect on the degree to which there are cold people working in the professional arena and to question why this may be so. It is possible that interpersonal skills training may help this situation for it may be that some cold people are unaware of their coldness. Personal warmth cannot easily be faked. Notice the degree to which other professionals that you come in contact with *try* to be warm and then notice the degree to which you feel they really *are* warm.

To a degree, however, our relationships with others tend to be self-monitoring: as we go on with a relationship we anticipate the effect we are having on others and modify our self-presentation accordingly. Thus we soon get to know if our warmth is too much for the client or is being perceived in a negative way. This ability constantly to monitor ourselves and our relationships is an important part of the process of developing interpersonal and counselling skills.

KEY QUESTIONS:

- **What do you understand by warmth in interpersonal relationships?**
- **To what degree can warmth be taught to another person?**
- **How central is it in the relationships that you have with others?**
- **Are you a warm person? If you are to facilitate interpersonal skills workshops, it would seem reasonable that you role model the quality.**

Genuineness

Genuineness is another important aspect of the professional interpersonal relationship. In one sense, the issue is clear: we either genuinely care for the person in front of us or we do not. We cannot easily fake professional interest. We must *be* interested. Some people, however, will interest us more than others. Often, those clients who remind us of our own problems or our own personalities will interest us most of all. This is not so important as our having a genuine interest in the fact that the relationship is happening at all.

We have all been on the receiving end of 'assumed genuineness', for instance in some hotel and service staff there is sometimes a rather insincere attempt at being genuine. It is not difficult for most people to discern the difference. The *real* professional – almost despite being such – will also genuinely want to help or care for the other person.

On the surface, there may appear to be a conflict between the concept of genuineness and the self-monitoring alluded to above. Self-monitoring may be thought of as 'artificial' or contrived and therefore not genuine. The 'genuineness' discussed here relates to the professional's interest in the relationship that is developing between the two people. Any ways in which that relationship can be enhanced must serve a valuable purpose. It is quite possible to be genuine and yet aware of what is happening, genuine and yet committed to increasing interpersonal competence.

Sometimes, the question of being genuine is tied up with role. I remember a conversation, quite recently, with a member of staff in a hotel in the north of England. I was feeling quite chatty and expansive. He, on the other hand, was playing the 'professional hotel member' role, called me 'sir' and did not readily join in the conversation. Perhaps, for some, being 'genuine' also means being able to play out a particular role with a high degree of professionalism. On the other hand, perhaps the true professional is the one who can be really genuine and who has the ability to demonstrate this quality to others.

KEY QUESTIONS:

- **What sort of people do you find it difficult to be genuine with?**
- **To what extent are you genuine in your professional work?**
- **How, if at all, can you teach other people to be genuine?**

Learning warmth and genuineness
I have claimed that personal warmth and genuineness are important elements of the interpersonal relationship. Can a person learn

to be warm and genuine? It is arguable that we have learned all our personal qualities so why should we imagine that a person is somehow 'naturally' warm and genuine or not as the case may be? Clearly these qualities cannot be learned in the same way as skills. They can, however, be developed through the person's awareness of them as qualities at all and through that person striving to pay attention to others to forgo artifice and the adoption of a 'professional veneer'. If we are truly to help others, we cannot do so if we are trying to maintain a particular posture or trying too hard to be professional. We must, instead, come to the client as we are. Ironically, we must learn to be ourselves.

Empathic understanding

We need to be able to empathize with other people in order to understand them at all. Empathy is the term usually used to convey the idea of the ability to enter the perceptual world of the other person: to see the world as they see it. It also suggests an ability to convey this perception. Kalisch (1971) defines empathy as 'the ability to perceive accurately the feelings of another person and to communicate this understanding to him'.

To empathize is not to sympathize. Sympathy suggests 'feeling sorry' for the other person, perhaps identifying with how they feel. If a person sympathizes they imagine themselves as being in the other person's position. With empathy one tries to imagine how it is to *be* the other person. Feeling sorry for them does not really come into it.

There are, of course, limitations to the degree to which we can truly empathize. Because we all live in different 'worlds' based on our particular culture, education, physiology, belief systems and so forth, we all view things slightly differently. Thus, truly to empathize with another person would involve actually becoming that person! We can, however, strive to get as close as possible to the perceptual world of the other by listening and attending and by suspending judgement. We can also learn to forget ourselves temporarily and give ourselves as completely as we can to the other person. There is an interesting paradox involved here. First, we need self-awareness to enable us to develop empathy. Then we need to forget ourselves in order to give our full empathic attention to the other person.

> **KEY QUESTIONS:**
>
> - What sort of people do you find it difficult to empathize with?
> - Would you describe yourself as an empathic person?
> - What role does empathy play in your professional life?
> - What sorts of things *stop* you empathizing?

Unconditional positive regard

This rather awkward phrase conveys a particularly important predisposition towards other people (Rogers 1967). Rogers also called it 'prizing' or even just 'accepting'. It means that the client is accorded dignity and valued as a worthwhile and positive human being. The 'unconditional' prefix refers to the idea that such regard is offered without any preconditions. Often in relationships, some sort of reciprocity is demanded: I will like you (or love you) as long as you return that liking (or loving). Rogers is asking the feelings the professional holds for the client should be undemanding and not require reciprocation.

It seems likely that unconditional positive regard will matter more in some professional situations than in others. It will be relevant, for example, in counselling and health care settings. It may be less important in business and administration. On the other hand, showing regard for people, unconditional or otherwise, is likely to be an asset in *any* setting.

Learning unconditional positive regard
Learning not to judge others sometimes comes through accepting ourselves. We judge others more harshly when we have not resolved various personal problems. We judge even more readily when we do not know what our personal problems are. One route to learning unconditional positive regard may begin with the development of self-awareness. While we cannot hope to sort ourselves out totally, as professionals it seems reasonable that we begin by at least becoming aware of some of our own problems.

In the end, though, this is the quality that most reflects personal value systems and personality traits. We cannot have unconditional regard for everyone. Sometimes, we just don't like other people. Sometimes, too, the idea of having unconditional regard conflicts with being genuine. We cannot, on the one hand, be ourselves - prejudices and all - and on the other have unconditional positive regard for everyone.

> **KEY QUESTIONS:**
>
> - **What are your feelings about the notion of unconditional positive regard?**
> - **Does it apply to your professional situation?**
> - **Can it be learned?**
> - **For whom do you hold unconditional positive regard?**

EXPERIENTIAL LEARNING

All the qualities and interpersonal skills referred to in this book arise out of human experience. We are learning about such skills by using them every day. All this leads, appropriately, to the main mode of learning interpersonal skills: experiential learning. As we noted right at the beginning of this chapter, we have all been using interpersonal skills for a long time, so it would seem odd not to draw on that experience. Experiential learning methods call directly on people's previous experience.

Experiential learning is learning through doing; but it is also more than that. It is learning through *reflecting* on the doing. In all aspects of our actions, we have at least two choices: to just act or to notice how we act. It is only through noticing what it is that we do that we can hope to learn about ourselves and our behaviour. To 'just act' is to act blindly, unawares. This is what happens when we do not learn from experience. In a sense, it is as simple as that: if we are to learn from what we do, we must notice what we do and reflect on it. To notice what we do is to allow ourselves to evaluate action and to choose the next piece of behaviour. This is living in a more precise way. There need not be anything cold and calculating about this; simply, we are being asked to pay attention: to observe ourselves in action. Paying attention in this way is also part of caring for others. It teaches us, not only about ourselves, but about others.

We cannot notice our behaviour and actions all the time. But in terms of the relationships we have with our clients, we owe it to them to notice our behaviour more frequently than we may be doing at present. To do this is to engage in what Heron (1973) calls 'conscious use of the self': using behaviour and the self in a conscious, therapeutic manner. To make conscious use of the self during interpersonal relationships is to enhance the likelihood of our relationships being therapeutic.

There is a second meaning of the term 'experiential learning'. We all learn through experience, whether directly, through taking action by being involved in a situation, or by observing others. In this sense, every situation is an experiential learning situation. To describe experiential learning in such broad terms would be rather fruitless, however, as it would make the concept so huge as to render it unmanageable. To make things a little clearer, we may identify three aspects of experiential learning: (1) personal experience, (2) reflection on that experience, and (3) the transformation of knowledge and meaning as a result of that reflection.

First, something happens to us (personal experience). If we choose, we can then reflect on that experience. As a result of that experience and reflection, we can, if we wish, reorder and restructure the way in which we think about ourselves, other people and the world in general. The process is likely to be both cumulative and ongoing. We continue to learn and we continue to change throughout life.

Experiential knowledge is necessarily idiosyncratic. Indeed, it may be difficult to convey to another person in words. Words tend to be loaded with personal (often experiential) meanings and thus to understand each other we need to understand the nature of the way in which the people with whom we converse use words. It is arguable, however, that such experiential knowledge is sometimes conveyed to others through gesture, eye contact, tone of voice, inflection and all the other non-verbal and paralinguistic aspects of communication (Argyle 1975). Indeed, it may be experiential knowledge that is passed on when two people become very involved with each other in a conversation, a learning encounter or counselling. It may also be experiential knowledge that is passed on in workshops and groups that make use of the sort of experiential learning activities contained in this book. For in the end, the activities as they are written here are only a small part of the story. The real learning comes from the interplay of different people's perceptions, experiences and views and from the *sharing* of all of those things.

All the activities in this manual call upon the notion of experiential learning. First, none of them involves lecturing or formal 'talking' methods of teaching; all of them involve activity. Second, they all acknowledge that people respond to situations differently and often idiosyncratically. Therefore, an important part of these activities are the reflection and the sharing stages. Reflection comes after doing the 'active' part of the activity. Here, each individual in the group considers what has happened to his or her reactions. In the sharing phase, all of the group participants share those experiences. In this way, new learning about interpersonal skills can occur. All that the activities in this book can offer is a vehicle for exploring interpersonal skills. What those activities are *not* is an attempt to drill people in a particular style of personal presentation.

A note of caution needs to be sounded. In some research I have done into experiential learning, including methods such as role play, psychodrama, pairs exercises, group activities and so on, I found that trainers were much more keen to undertake these activities than were students (Burnard 1991). Indeed, many students in my study said that such activities made them feel uncomfortable and some described acute embarrassment at being asked to do role play. For that reason, I find it helpful to introduce experiential learning activities slowly. I also make a point of keeping the atmosphere in workshops light. Once the workshop becomes heavy and 'meaningful', people seem to become uncomfortable. In the end, this is a question of goals and of contracts. In my view, the aim of an interpersonal workshop is to explore interpersonal skills, not to do therapy of any sort. This too is the contractual element: the people who enrol in interpersonal skills workshops are usually there for training rather than therapy. My feeling is that it is important to be clear about your intentions in any educational or training activity. The intention in setting up an interpersonal skills training course or workshop is to enhance interpersonal skills. It is not, necessarily, to engage in soul searching.

There are other conflicts of interest. In one sense, any interpersonal skills trainer is seeking to change the behaviour of others. Otherwise, he would not be engaged in the enterprise at all. Sometimes, that change is spelt out clearly – in keeping with company or organizational policy. How, then, can we incorporate, on the one hand, the idea of personal learning with, on the other, the idea of specific training? Perhaps a certain compromise is called for. While interpersonal skills training should never simply be drilling in a range of specific behaviours, neither can it be a free for all, with everyone deciding for themselves what sorts of behaviours they adopt. As with most things in life, we have to weigh our own beliefs and values against those of the people with whom we live and work.

Examples of experiential learning methods

If experiential learning is learning from personal and life experience, there are a number of teaching and learning methods that can be described as experiential learning methods. Many of them are used as the basis of the exercises and activities included in this book. Read through the list below and see which ones you are familiar with, which ones you are comfortable in using and those which you need more training in. Consider, too, any other methods that you might add to this list:

- role play;
- small group activities;
- pairs exercises;
- meditation and stress reduction activities;
- project work;
- work-related projects;
- discussion groups;
- psychodrama;
- sociodrama;
- gestalt exercises;
- counselling skills activities;
- listening exercises;
- icebreakers;
- games;
- simulations.

> **KEY QUESTIONS:**
>
> - What are your feelings about taking part in experiential learning activities?
> - What are your views on using personal experience as the key to enhancing interpersonal skills?
> - What else do you need to learn in order to be an effective interpersonal skills trainer?

SUMMARY

The following checklist offers a summary of the points that have been discussed, so far, on teaching interpersonal skills:

- Personal qualities are almost as important as interpersonal skills themselves.
- Warmth, the ability to empathize and the tendency to be non-judgemental appear to be important attitudinal qualities when using interpersonal skills.
- Interpersonal skills are unlike other sorts of skills in that they are personal and involve two or more people meeting each other. Therefore, experiential learning methods have been advocated for teaching and learning interpersonal skills.
- Experiential learning involves drawing on a person's real life experiences, reflecting on them and then modifying behaviour in the light of that reflection.
- We probably learn most about our own interpersonal skills when we begin to notice what it is we do and say.

TYPES OF INTERPERSONAL SKILL

There are certain core interpersonal skills and it is possible to offer clear descriptions of the stages of training that may be used in workshops aimed at developing those skills. The style of training advocated in this book is that based on the notion of experiential learning, discussed above. The argument is that the only way to learn interpersonal skills is to engage in them. They can be lectured upon, discussed and generally dissected but they will not be learned effectively until the learner uses them. The recurrent theme throughout this chapter (and throughout this book) is how to offer people experiences that will help them to develop their own particular but effective style of interacting with others.

It will be noted that counselling skills are argued to be the bedrock upon which all other interpersonal skills are built. It is asserted that the professional who can learn to use a wide range of effective counselling skills is well on the way to being interpersonally competent. The fact that the person who is counselling has to deal with so many different aspects of the human condition suggests that the one who can counsel effectively is likely to be able to transfer those skills to a variety of other interpersonal situations. It is important to state what I am *not* saying here. I am not suggesting that all professionals have to work as counsellors but merely that counselling skills can usefully serve as a paradigm for interpersonal skills training.

To broaden the argument just a little and to demonstrate the breadth of skills involved in the interpersonal domain, it will be useful to consider three clusters of skills. These are counselling skills, assertiveness skills and the skills of group facilitation. They are all relevant to both the professional and the trainer who is facilitating interpersonal skills workshops. If the principles of all three of these clusters of skills can be grasped, then the person will already be demonstrating a considerable level of interpersonal skill.

Counselling skills

Counselling skills can be used in a variety of settings. They may be used to help the person who is suffering from a temporary emotional crisis or they may be useful in helping the person who has longer-term problems in living. Counselling skills are also useful in everyday business and administration situations when dealing with colleagues, clients or customers. They may also be practical and useful as a set of interpersonal skills for everyday use in every client–practitioner situation. Counselling skills, after all, are not skills to be turned on and off according to the need, but a way of being with the client to enable them to communicate their thoughts and feelings more effectively. Counselling skills form the basis of all effective interpersonal relationships between the professional and the consumer, whatever that relationship is. Further, the skills are essential ones for helping colleagues. A short list of situations in which counselling skills are useful in all professions includes:

- Helping people to make career changes.
- Helping people to make business decisions.
- Enabling people to make life decisions for themselves.
- Helping relatives to cope with bereavement.
- Working with children and adolescents.
- Helping families to work through problems.
- Discussing psychiatric difficulties and making decisions about when to 'refer on' to other professionals.
- Helping colleagues.
- Teaching students to become counsellors.

It may be noted that the term 'counselling' has different connotations for different people. In an everyday sense, the term seems to mean advising, helping, giving guidance and so forth. In a more 'professional' sense, it is often used to describe a particular sort of helping relationship which tends to eschew advice-giving in favour of helping the other person to stand on their own feet and make their own decisions. In my view, the debates about what counselling is and is not are sometimes rather sterile. The important thing is to be clear about how *you* are using the term when you engage in any sort of interpersonal skills or personnel training.

Counselling skills may be divided into two sub-groups: (a) listening and (b) counselling interventions. Listening involves not only giving full attention to the person being listened to, but also being seen to be listening by the other person. Gerard Egan (1990) argues that in Western countries, the following behaviours are often associated with effective listening and may be practised in order to enhance listening ability:

- **Sit squarely** in relation to the person being listened to. This can be taken both literally and metaphorically. If we are truly to listen to the other person we need to be able to see them and for

them to see us; thus it is better that we sit facing them rather than beside them. We also need to 'face' them in the sense of not being put off by them nor daunted by them.
- **M**aintain an **o**pen position. Crossed arms and legs can often suggest defensiveness. It is better to sit comfortably and in a relaxed 'uncrossed' position.
- **L**ean slightly towards the person being listened to. Egan argues that this is usually perceived as a warm and interested gesture. On the other hand, it is important that the other person does not feel crowded by the listener.
- Maintain reasonable **e**ye contact. The eyes are a potent means of interpersonal communication. It is important that our gaze is 'available' for the other person.
- **R**elax while listening. Listening does not have to involve rehearsing the next thing to be said. All that is needed is the listening itself. The relaxed listener helps the person being listened to, to relax.

Egan suggests the acronym SOLER as a means of remembering these basic listening behaviours. The letters in the acronym are used to remember key words in the cycle.

Listening forms the basis of all good counselling and, arguably, of all interpersonal relationships. If the professional can learn to enhance listening ability there will be an improvement in other interpersonal skills, too. Not that listening can ever be a mechanical set of behaviours. It also requires that we are 'present' for the other person: that we are with them as fellow human beings and not purely as professionals doing a job.

The other sub-group of counselling skills is that of counselling interventions: the things that the counsellor says in the counselling relationship. Before specific counselling interventions are discussed, consideration needs to be given to our disposition towards counselling or our 'philosophy' of counselling. Perhaps the most familiar type of professional counselling is that known as client-centred counselling and it is that sort that we now turn to as a practical example of interpersonal skills in action.

The term 'client-centred' refers to the notion that it is the client who is best able to decide how to find the solutions to their problems in living. Client-centred, in this sense may be contrasted with the idea of counsellor-centred or professional-centred, both of which may suggest that someone other than the client is the 'expert'. While this may be true when applied to certain real-life problems – housing, surgery, legal problems and so forth – it is difficult to see how it can apply to personal-life issues. In such cases, it is the client who identifies the problem and the client who, given time and space, can find their way through the problem to the solution.

Client-centred counselling is a process rather than a particular set of skills. It evolves through the relationship that the counsellor has with the client and vice versa. In a sense, it is a period of growth for both parties, for both learn from the other. It also involves the exercise of restraint. The counsellor must refrain from offering advice and resist the temptation to 'put the client's life right for them'. The outcome of such counselling cannot be predicted nor can concrete goals be set (unless they are devised by the client, at their request). In essence, client-centred counselling involves an act of faith: a belief in the other person's ability to find solutions through the process of therapeutic conversation and through the act of being engaged in a close relationship with another human being.

Certain, basic client-centred skills may be identified, although as we have noted, it is the total relationship that is important. Skills exercised in isolation amount to little; warmth, genuineness and positive regard must also be present. On the other hand, if basic skills are not considered, then the counselling process will probably be shapeless or it will degenerate into the counsellor becoming prescriptive. The skill of standing back and allowing the client a free rein is a difficult one to learn. The following interventions or skills may help in the process:

- questions;
- reflection;
- selective reflection;
- empathy building;
- checking for understanding.

Each of these skills can be learned. In order for that to happen, each must be tried and practised. There is a temptation to say 'I do that anyway!' when reading a description of some of these skills. The point is to notice the doing of them and to practise doing them better. While counselling often shares the characteristics of everyday conversation, if it is to progress beyond that it is important that some, if not all, of the following skills are used effectively and tactfully.

A debatable point is whether or not it is appropriate to learn a series of very specific sorts of behaviours as part of learning to counsel. Carl Rogers, the well-known humanistic psychologist, started his career as a counselling trainer by focusing particularly on skills training (Kirschenbaum 1978). He soon found that what was far more important than the specific skills was the quality of the relationship; a point we have discussed in the preceding paragraphs. It is recommended that, throughout interpersonal skills training programmes, the tension between skills training and personal qualities is emphasized repeatedly.

Questions

Two main sorts of questions may be identified in the client-centred approach: closed and open. A closed question is one that elicits a 'yes', 'no' or similar one-word answer. Or it is one to which the counsellor can anticipate an approximation of the answer when asking it. Examples of closed questions are: What post do you hold at the moment? Are you married? What is your salary? Are you living at home?

Too many closed questions can make the counselling relationship seem like an interrogation! They also inhibit the development of the client's telling of his story and place the locus of responsibility in the relationship firmly with the client.

Open questions are those that do not elicit a particular answer: the counsellor cannot easily anticipate what an answer will 'look like'. Examples of open questions include: What did you do when that happened? How did you feel then? How are you thinking right now? What do you feel will happen?

Open questions encourage the client to say more, to expand on their story or to go deeper. They are generally preferable in counselling to closed ones. They encourage longer, more expansive answers and are rather more free of value judgements and interpretation than are closed questions. All the same, the counsellor has to monitor the 'slope' of intervention when using open questions. It is easy, for example, to become intrusive by asking too piercing questions, too quickly. As with all counselling interventions, the timing of the use of questions is vital.

Questions can be used in counselling relationships for a variety of purposes. The main ones include:

- Clarification: 'I'm sorry, did you say you are to move or did you say you're not sure?'; 'What did you say then?'
- Encouraging the client to talk: 'Can you say more about that?'; 'What are your feelings about that?'
- Obtaining further information: 'How many children have you got?'; 'What sort of work were you doing before you retired?'
- Exploration: 'What else happened?'

Reflection

Reflection (sometimes called 'echoing') is the process of reflecting back the last few words, or a paraphrase of the last few words, that the client has used, in order to encourage them to say more. It is as though the counsellor is echoing the client's thoughts and as though that echo serves as a prompt. It is important that the reflection does not turn into a question and this is best achieved by the counsellor making the repetition in much the same tone of voice as the client used. An example of the use of reflection is as follows:

> *Colleague:* I was working at the Edinburgh office for a number of months. Then we moved and I suppose that's when things started to go wrong...
> *Manager:* Things started to go wrong...

Note that the 'reflection' is not a question. The counsellor's tone of voice does not rise at the end of the reflected fragment. If it does, the client's answer is likely to be a simple 'Yes'!

Used skilfully and with good timing, reflection can be an important method of helping the client. On the other hand, if it is overused or used clumsily, it can appear stilted and is very noticeable. Unfortunately, it is an intervention that takes some practice and one that many people anticipate learning on counselling courses. As a result, when people return from counselling courses, their friends and relatives are often waiting for them to use the technique and may comment on the fact! This should not be a deterrent as the method remains a useful and therapeutic one.

Selective reflection

Selective reflection refers to the method of repeating back to the client a part of something they said that was emphasized in some way or which seemed to be emotionally charged. Thus selective reflection draws from the middle of the client's utterance and not from the end. An example of the use of selective reflection is as follows:

> *Colleague:* I had just started work. I didn't earn very much and I hated the job. Still, it was better than being unemployed, I suppose. It's very difficult these days ...
> *Manager:* You hated the job ...
> *Colleague:* It was one of the worst periods of my life. I'll never forget working there ...

The use of selective reflection allowed the client in this example to develop further an almost throwaway remark. Often, these 'asides' are the substance of very important feelings and the counsellor can often help in the release of some of these feelings by using selective reflection to focus on them. Clearly concentration is important, in order to note the points on which to selectively reflect. Again, the tone of voice does not rise at the end of the reflected statement, so the phrase does not become a question.

The counselling relationship is a flowing, evolving conversation which tends to be 'seamless'. Thus, it is little use the counsellor storing up a point which he feels would be useful to selectively reflect. By the time a break comes in the conversation, the item will probably be irrelevant! This points up the need to develop 'free floating attention': the ability to allow the ebb and flow of the conversation to go where the counsellor takes it and for the counsellor to trust his own ability to choose an appropriate intervention when a break occurs.

Empathy building

Empathy has been described in an earlier part of this chapter. Here, it refers to the counsellor making statements to the client that indicate that he has understood the feeling that the client is experiencing. A certain intuitive ability is needed here, for often empathy-building statements refer more to what is implied than what is overtly said. An example of the use of empathy-building statements is as follows:

Colleague: People at the factory are the same. They're all tied up with their own friends and families... they don't have a lot of time for me... though they're friendly enough...
Manager: You sound angry with them...
Colleague: I suppose I am! Why don't they take a bit of time to ask me how I'm getting on? It wouldn't take much!...
Manager: It sounds as though you are saying that people haven't had time for you for a long time...
Colleague: They haven't. My family didn't bother much... I mean, they looked as though they did... but they didn't really...

The empathy-building statements, used here, are ones that read between the lines. Now, sometimes such reading between the lines can be completely wrong and the empathy-building statement is rejected by the client. It is important, when this happens, for the counsellor to drop the approach altogether and to pay more attention to listening. Inaccurate empathy-building statements often indicate an overwillingness on the part of the counsellor to become involved with the client's perceptual world – at the expense of accurate empathy! Used skilfully, however, empathy-building statements help the client to disclose further and to feel that they are understood.

Empathy would seem to be a central plank of all interpersonal skills training. We encountered it earlier as a quality and here it is offered as a type of skill. Central to the whole process of getting on with other people is the ability to see the world as they do. In a more general way, what seems most important of all is the realization that people are individuals, and do not necessarily see things as we do. Unfortunately, we all have a tendency to want others to share our views. This can be turned to our advantage in interpersonal skills training. People actually want us to understand them. If we allow them to talk, we can hear them telling us how the world looks to them. That means that we have to be prepared to suspend judgement and to hold back our own picture of the world so that the other person's can emerge for us.

Checking for understanding
If we do not know what the other person is talking about, we are failing to communicate. Checking for understanding involves either asking the client if you have understood them correctly or occasion-

ally summarizing the conversation in order to clarify what has been said. The first type of checking is useful when the client covers a lot of topics quickly and seems to be 'thinking aloud'. It can be used to focus the conversation further or as a means of ensuring that the client really stays with what the counsellor is saying. The second type of checking should be used sparingly or the counselling conversation can get to seem rather mechanical and studied. The following two examples illustrate the two uses of checking for understanding.

1. *Client:* I don't know what to do really... money's O.K. and I can cope at home... then there's the job. I mean, what do you do?
   Counsellor: Let me just get things a little more clear. You say that you don't always cope at home and you don't cope all that well at work...?
   Client: Yes... My parents treat me as though I'm still about fourteen and people at work aren't much better!

2. *Counsellor:* Let me see if I can just sum up what we've talked about this morning. We talked about your financial problems and the question of seeing the bank manager. You said you may ask for a loan. Then you went on to say how you felt you could organize your finances better in the future...?
   Client: Yes, I think that covers most things...

Some counsellors prefer to use the second type of checking at the end of each counselling session and this may help to clarify things before the client leaves. On the other hand, there is much to be said for not 'tidying up' the end of the session in this way. If the loose ends are left, the client continues to think about all the issues that have been discussed, while walking away from the session. If everything is summarized too neatly, the client may feel that the problems can be closed down for a while or even worse, that they have been solved! Personal problems are rarely simple enough to be summarized in a few words and the practice of checking at the end of a session should be used sparingly.

These are some of the particular skills that encourage self-direction on the part of the client and can be learned and used by the counsellor. They form the basis of all good counselling and can always be returned to as a primary way of working with the client in the counselling relationship.

Learning counselling skills

Counselling skills can be developed in a variety of ways. Perhaps, for the beginner they are best learned in a small group setting such as the workshop. The essential ingredients of interpersonal skills workshops are:

- An adequate theoretical framework. This can be supplied by the workshop trainer either in the form of a handout, a short lecture or, preferably, through group discussion.
- Discrimination between different sorts of counselling intervention. The neophyte counsellor needs to be able consciously to choose between different sorts of counselling interventions. Here an analysis such as the Six Category Intervention Analysis (Heron, 1986) can be useful.
- Examples or role models of effective counselling interventions are required. These may be supplied in various ways:
  - the workshop trainer may model them in front of the group, with one of the group acting as client;
  - the trainer may do a monodrama and play both ends of a role play as a demonstration of effective use of counselling interventions;
  - short video films may be used which offer exemplars to the group of effective use of interventions; or
  - the trainer may only describe the interventions and leave the group members to improvise from the descriptions.
- The opportunity for group members to practise using the interventions. Initially, this practice may take place within the workshop itself. Increasingly, however, practice should be moved away from the workshop setting to encourage reinforcement of the new behaviour in the 'real' situation: the client/professional relationship.

Counselling skills are the basic building blocks for skilled interpersonal living. The professional who can learn expertise in a range of counselling skills will find the development of the other interpersonal skills discussed here considerably easier. Also, the elements of training described above are common to most sorts of interpersonal skills training. In these senses, as we have seen, counselling skills training can be considered a paradigm for all other sorts of interpersonal skills training.

It is worth noting, of course, that not all counselling is necessarily client-centred. Although the Rogerian style of counselling has been the most widely used form in the helping professions for the past 20 years, there are other, more prescriptive methods of counselling.

John Heron (1990) offers a useful framework for considering all possible approaches to therapeutic intervention. He calls this 'Six Category Intervention Analysis' and his six categories are described below. Heron argues that if a professional/client intervention is therapeutic, then it will fit under one of the following six headings:

1. Prescriptive interventions (giving advice, making suggestions).
2. Informative interventions (giving information).
3. Confronting interventions (challenging what the other person says).
4. Cathartic interventions (helping the other person to express emotion).
5. Catalytic interventions (drawing the other person out: encouraging them to talk more about themselves and their problems).
6. Supportive interventions (encouraging and validating the other person).

Arguably, the Rogerian or client-centred approach to counselling calls only for catalytic interventions. Heron is arguing that there is room in the therapeutic and helping relationship for a wider range of interventions. I have described both research and training methods in the six-category approach elsewhere (Burnard 1990, Morrison and Burnard 1991). The approach has been widely used in the health care and other sorts of helping professions and has, at least, the following applications:

- An assessment and evaluation tool in interpersonal skills training.
- A training guide for training people in a wide range of therapeutic skills.
- A guide to practice in therapy and counselling.
- A framework for research.
- A means of monitoring personal progress in counselling skills.

As a closing thought to this section, it often occurs to me, both as a counsellor and as a trainer, that I do not stick to any particular framework of counselling. Often, I make it up as I go along. This seems to be true of other counsellors too. There are at least two possible reasons for this. First, it is just possible that we pay too much attention to the specific skills of counselling and try to break them down into too small chunks. Second, it is possible that as we develop more experience in counselling, we break the rules. It seems likely that most professionals know how to break the rules effectively and the expert counsellor may just be illustrating this fact. Either way, it is important to consider the degree to which we expect other people to use a particular array of skills. I suspect that such skills are useful as a way of learning the basics of counselling and are always useful as a 'first-aid kit' when we find ourselves wondering what to say. Otherwise, I suspect that counselling is a much more fluid and dynamic process than can ever be conveyed by the listing of such skills.

Also, what seems to come through every research account in the field, is that what counts most of all is the *quality of the relationship* between the two people. A person can be highly skilled and yet lack the commitment, personality and genuine delight in other people's company that would make him or her a good counsellor. Throughout interpersonal skills training it is important to keep an eye on the fundamental relationship issue. This can be explored throughout a workshop by inviting participants to question their relationships both with each other and with themselves. I suspect that if we do not get on with ourselves, we are unlikely to find other people all that rewarding.

KEY QUESTIONS:

- **What role does counselling play in your job?**
- **If you were running a counselling skills workshop, what would be the key elements of it?**
- **What do you need to learn in order to become an effective counsellor?**

Assertiveness

Assertiveness is often confused with being aggressive. A friend of mine once referred to assertiveness workshops as 'courses for learning how to be rude to other people'! The assertive person is the one who can state clearly and calmly what they want to say, does not back down in the face of disagreement and is prepared to repeat the point if necessary. A continuum may be drawn for a range of types of behaviour ranging from the submissive to the aggressive, with assertive behaviour being the mid-point on such a continuum. Heron (1986) has argued that when we have to confront another person, we tend to feel anxiety at the prospect. As a result of that anxiety we tend to either 'pussyfoot' (and be submissive) or 'sledgehammer' (and be aggressive).

So it is with being assertive: most people, when they are learning how to assert themselves experience anxiety and as a result tend to be either submissive or aggressive. Other people handle that anxiety by swinging right the way through the continuum. They start submissively, then develop a sort of confidence and rush into an aggressive attack on the other person. Alternatively, some deal with their anxiety by starting an encounter very aggressively and quickly back off into submission. The level and calm approach of being assertive takes practice, nerve and confidence.

Examples of how assertiveness can be useful include the following situations:

- when used by a colleague who feels he is being exploited by another colleague;
- when used by a person who has never been able to express her wants and needs in a marriage;
- when used by the professional, when facing bureaucratic processes in trying to get help for another person;
- in everyday situations (in shops, offices, restaurants, etc.) where a stated service being offered is not actually being given.

Arguably, the assertive approach to living is the much clearer one when it comes to dealing with other people. The submissive person often loses friends because they come to be seen as duplicitous, sycophantic or as a 'doormat'. On the other hand, the aggressive person is rarely popular perhaps, simply, because most of us don't particularly like aggression. The assertive person comes to be seen as an 'adult' person who is able to treat other people reasonably and without recourse to either childish or loutish behaviour. Much has been written about the topic of assertiveness and the reader is referred to the bibliography at the end of this volume.

Examples of assertiveness skills

While assertiveness is as much a confident frame of mind as a particular interpersonal approach, there are some particular assertiveness skills that can be demonstrated in workshops. Two frequently cited skills are 'broken record' and 'fogging'. Broken record refers to the skill of repeating a particular response without either getting aggressive or becoming submissive. Here is an example of the use of the broken record technique in practice:

'... but I only want to borrow five pounds – that's not a lot to ask, is it?'
'No, but I am still not going to lend it to you ...'
'You always have in the past.'
'But not this time.'
'You really won't lend me the money?'
'No.'
'There is nothing I can do to make you change your mind?'
'No.'

Using the method takes courage and a certain presence of mind. More particularly, it takes practice and such practice should be available in the form of role play in any assertiveness workshop.

Fogging is a method of accepting the other person's feelings and acknowledging their request but still sticking to your guns. An example of this sort of approach is as follows:

'But we would consider that, as you have used the computer, it is now second-hand.'
'I appreciate that that is how you see it but my rights as a consumer mean that I can return it to you.'
'And what if I don't see it that way?'
'I realize that you might not, but these are my rights.'
'Well, perhaps I could send someone to look at it for you?'
'Thank you for offering, but I want it replaced.'
'You want me to replace the whole computer?'
'Yes. I would appreciate your doing that. Thank you.'

The fogging technique allows the assertive person to help the other person retain dignity but also ensures that the other person hears what has to be said. Like 'broken record', it takes practice and this can take place through the role-play activities described in the second part of this book.

Alberti and Emmons (1982), the well-known writers on assertiveness training, identified four major elements in assertive behaviour:

- Intent: the assertive person does not intend to be hurtful to others by stating his own needs and wants.
- Behaviour: behaviour classified as assertive would be evaluated by an 'objective observer' as honest, direct, expressive and non-destructive of others.
- Effects: behaviour classified as assertive has the effect on the other of a direct and non-destructive message by which that person would not be hurt.
- Socio-cultural context: behaviour classified as assertive is appropriate to the environment and culture in which it is demonstrated and may not necessarily be considered 'assertive' in a different socio-cultural environment.

Alberti and Emmons thus suggest that there are some ethical dimensions to the issue of assertiveness. They further suggest that assertive behaviour can be broken down into at least the following components:

- Eye contact. The assertive person is able to maintain eye contact with another person to an appropriate degree.
- Body posture. The degree of assertiveness that we use is illustrated through our posture, the way in which we stand in relation to another person and the degree to which we face the other person squarely and equally.
- Distance. There seems to be a relationship between the distance we put between ourselves and another person and the degree of comfort and equality we feel with that person. If we feel overpowered by the other person's presence, we will tend to stand further away from them than we would do if we felt equal to them. Proximity in relation to others is culturally dependent but, in a commonsense way, we can soon establish the degree to which we, as individuals, tend to stand away from others or feel comfortable near to them.

- Gestures. Alberti and Emmons suggest that appropriate use of hand and arm gestures can add emphasis, openness and warmth to a message and can thus emphasize the assertive approach. Lack of appropriate hand and arm gestures can suggest lack of self-confidence and lack of spontaneity.
- Facial expression and tone of voice. It is important that the assertive person is congruent in their use of facial expression (Bandler and Grinder 1975). Congruence is said to occur when what a person says is accompanied by an appropriate tone of voice and by appropriate facial expressions. The person who is incongruent may be perceived as unassertive. An example of this is the person who says he is angry but smiles as he says it; the result is a mixed and confusing communication.
- Fluency. A person is likely to be perceived as assertive if she is fluent and smooth in the use of her voice. This may mean that those who frequently punctuate their conversation with 'ums' and 'ers' are perceived as less than assertive.
- Timing. The assertive person is likely to be able to pay attention to his 'end' of a conversation. He will not interrupt the other person excessively, nor be prone to leaving long silences between utterances.
- Listening. As was noted about the effective counsellor, the assertive person is likely to be a good listener. The person who listens effectively not only has more confidence in her ability to maintain a conversation but also signals her interest in the other person. Being assertive should not be confused with being self-centred.
- Content. It is important that what is said is appropriate to the social and cultural situation in which a conversation is taking place. Any British person who has been to America will know about the unnerving silence that is likely to descend on a conversation if words such as 'fag' or 'lavatory' are used in certain settings! So will the person who uses slang or swear words in inappropriate situations. To be perceived as assertive, it is important that a person learns to use appropriate words and phrases.

A paradox emerges from all these dimensions of assertive behaviour. The assertive person also has to be genuine in their presentation of self. Now if that person is too busy noticing their own behaviour and verbal performance, they are likely to feel distinctly self-conscious and contrived.

There is also a cultural dimension to assertiveness. Much of the literature on assertiveness emanates from the USA where the culture supports and encourages a more assertive style of behaviour than is the norm in the UK and which would be completely out of keeping with life in some Far Eastern countries. Assertiveness training is not simply a question of rehearsing certain behaviours. It is important to take into account the cultural norm for the society in which that training is occurring. It is also vital to respect individual participants' personal preferences in this field. Not everyone chooses to be assertive and this, paradoxically, seems like a reasonably assertive choice!

It would seem that assertiveness training, like other forms of interpersonal skills training tends to go through three stages and an understanding of those stages can help to resolve that paradox. In stage one the person is unaware of his or her behaviour and unaware of the possible changes that they may bring about in order to become more assertive; in stage two the person begins to appreciate the various aspects of assertive behaviour, practises them and temporarily becomes clumsy and self-conscious in their use; finally, in stage three, the person incorporates the new behaviours into their personal repertoire of behaviours and 'forgets' them but is perceived as more assertive. The new behaviours have become a 'natural' characteristic.

If behaviour change in interpersonal skills training is to become relatively permanent, the client must learn to live through the rather painful second stage of the above model. Once through it, the new skills become more effective as they are incorporated into that person's everyday presentation of self.

KEY QUESTIONS:

- **Would you describe yourself as an assertive person?**
- **To what degree is assertiveness a necessary part of your professional role?**
- **Could you teach assertiveness?**

48   Interpersonal skills training

Learning to be assertive
In developing assertiveness in others, the trainer clearly must be able to role model assertive behaviour. The starting point in this field, then, is personal development (if it is required). This can be gained initially through attendance at an assertiveness training course and later through undertaking a 'training-the-trainers' course. There are an increasing number of colleges and extramural departments of universities which offer such courses and they are also often included in the list of topics offered as evening courses.

Once the trainer has developed some competence in being assertive, the following stages need to be followed in the organization of a successful training course for others:

1. A theory input which explains the nature of assertive behaviour, including its differentiation from submissive and aggressive behaviour.
2. A discussion of the participants' own assessment of their assertive skills or lack of them. This assessment phase may be enhanced by volunteers role playing typical situations in which they find it difficult to be assertive.
3. Examples of assertive behaviour from which the participants may role model. These may be offered in the form of short video film presentations, demonstrations by the trainer with another trainer, demonstrations by the trainer with a participant in the workshop or through demonstrations offered by skilled people invited into the workshop to demonstrate assertive behaviour. This option is perhaps the least attractive as too good a performance can often lead to group participants feeling deskilled. It is easy for the less confident person to feel 'I could never do that'. For this reason, too, it is important that the trainer running the workshop does not come across as being too assertive but allows some 'faults' to appear. Paradoxically, a certain amount of lack of skill in the trainer can be reassuring to course participants.
4. Selection by participants of situations that they would like to practise in order to become more assertive. Commonly requested situations here may include:

    - responding assertively to a marriage partner;
    - dealing with colleagues at work more assertively;
    - returning faulty goods to shops or returning unsatisfactory

food in a restaurant;
- not responding aggressively in a discussion;
- being able to speak in front of a group of people or deliver a short speech.

These situations can then be rehearsed using role play method, described above. At each stage of the role play, the participants are encouraged to reflect on their performances and adopt assertive behaviour if they have slipped into being either aggressive or submissive. Sometimes, this means repeating the role play several times.

5. Carrying the newly learned skills back into the 'real world'. Sometimes, the very act of having practised being assertive is enough to encourage the person to practise being assertive away from the workshop. More frequently, however, there needs to be a follow-up day or a series of follow-up days in which progress, or lack of it, is discussed and further reinforcement of effective behaviour is offered.

Reviewing the literature on the topic, it is not difficult to see how assertiveness training grew from a number of sources: the individualism of the 1960s brand of humanistic psychology, the American business schools and the feminist movement. In the 1990s, however, we seem more open to pluralism in the way we think about relationships. People always have the option *not* to be assertive, and it seems reasonable to assume that assertiveness will not be a choice for everyone.

The assertiveness training approach described here is similar to the one for counselling training described above. It offers subtle variations on the original theme but maintains the need to reflect on, share and utilize personal experience.

Group facilitation

Another type of interpersonal skill is group facilitation – the process of enabling groups to run effectively. The discussion of such skill serves two purposes here. First, it is another illustration of the use of interpersonal skills in a professional context. Second, all the aspects of facilitation discussed have relevance for the interpersonal skills trainer. Read this section on two levels: both for the content and also with an eye to your own performance in this domain.

John Heron (1989) has described six dimensions of 'trainer style' that may help here. It is not suggested that a potential trainer must use one particular aspect of a dimension rather than another but rather that such a decision will arise out of the *type* of group that is to be facilitated. The analysis of trainer styles is particularly useful in identifying the range of possible options open to the group leader. The six styles of group facilitation can also be used in teaching others about facilitation.

The sorts of questions that may be asked in relation to the six dimensions before attempting to facilitate a group are as follows:

- Does this group need to be led or can it be free flowing and open ended (the directive–non-directive dimension)?
- Do I need to explain what is happening in the group? Do I need to offer theories and frameworks for understanding what is going on or can the group 'explain itself' (the interpretative–non-interpretative dimension)?
- Do I need to challenge the group and to point out rigidities and repetitions in group and individual behaviour or can I let the group sort these issues out for themselves (the confronting–non-confronting dimension)?
- Will I be able to handle the expression of laughter, tears, anger or fear or will I need to divert it through lighter topics (the cathartic–non-cathartic dimension)?
- Should I use exercises, games, plans and set procedures to bring structure to the group or should I let the group organize itself (the structuring–unstructuring dimension)?
- Am I going to let the group share my own thoughts and feelings as they occur or will I play a more neutral role (the disclosing–non-disclosing dimension)?

Sometimes the aim and purpose of the group meeting will help to determine the style to be used. Consider, for example, the following types of groups. What would be examples of *inappropriate* styles of group facilitation in each one?

- a planning meeting
- a quality circle
- a working party meeting
- a group therapy meeting

- a meeting of friends in the pub
- a political meeting
- a discussion group in a school or college
- an interpersonal skills training group

Consideration of such issues will develop the conscious use of self alluded to earlier. If these issues are clarified the trainer will be in a better position to act knowingly rather that blindly or unawares. We cannot change our behaviour until we know what our behaviour is. Going to a group prepared in this way means that you have considered the group's needs. Not all groups are the same and not all groups will require the same sorts of facilitation.

A useful rule-of-thumb for working with interpersonal skills groups is to begin with a directive, structured and lightly confronting approach and gradually to help the group take more and more responsibility for itself. As the group progresses, the trainer becomes, on the one hand, increasingly non-directive, unstructuring and non-confronting and on the other, increasingly cathartic and disclosing. Whether or not to be interpretative of other people's behaviour is a moot point. As a rule (and adopting a phenomenological point of view) such interpretations are probably best made by the individual.

It is often better to be descriptive rather than interpretative. For instance, a group may be discussing a point which causes one member to begin to move around in her seat and to stop talking. The group trainer who is being *descriptive* says: 'I notice that you are quieter than you were and that you are shifting around in your seat quite a lot.' The group trainer who is *interpretative* says: 'I think you are finding this discussion a bit difficult and that it is making you anxious.' The description allows the group member to interpret their own behaviour and to report their own feelings if they so choose. The interpretation pre-empts the individual's perception of what he or she is doing and why.

The general points that may be made about facilitating a well-established group is that the group should not be over-directed but should be allowed to develop for itself. Do not depend too much on structured exercises but allow the group to develop its own structure. Consider allowing the free expression of emotion where it is appropriate and do not be in a hurry in a try to rescue people or 'explain' their emotions to them. Do not rush to interpret other people's behaviour but encourage individuals to make their own sense of what happens to them. These points are generally in line with the philosophy of experiential learning so far discussed (although the list contains rather too may 'shoulds' and 'nots' for my liking!). Experiential learning is, after all, about reflection on personal experience and about the personal ownership and transformation of meaning. We can never create meaning for other people: in the end each person finds it for himself.

KEY QUESTIONS:

- **What else do you need to learn in order to function as an effective trainer?**
- **To what degree is facilitation an important part of your professional job?**
- **Could you teach other people facilitation skills?**

INTERPERSONAL SKILLS TRAINING CHECKLIST

- Are you clear about the SORTS of interpersonal skills that you want to teach?
- What personal values do you bring to your training programme?
- Are you clear about the theoretical framework *behind* your training programme?
- What educational theories do you need to consider in order to help other people to change their interpersonal behaviour?
- Are you engaged in *education* or *training* when you run interpersonal skills workshops?

Chapter 2:

Managing interpersonal skills training: facilitation and group dynamics

The previous chapter explored some examples of interpersonal skills and discussed some of the issues for training that were thrown up by them. In this chapter, we examine the actual process of interpersonal skills training.

PLANNING INTERPERSONAL SKILLS TRAINING

All educational activities are underpinned by certain philosophical beliefs about the nature of education. This chapter explores the *facilitative* approach to education and offers practical guidelines for putting this approach into action. In discussing the broad principles behind the experiential learning approach and considering the work of adult educators, you will be able to make decisions about how to plan workshop and course programmes *with* rather than *for* the participants.

> **KEY QUESTIONS:**
>
> - How would you set up an interpersonal skills programme?
> - To what degree can interpersonal skills be taught?
> - How did you learn to become interpersonally effective?
> - What other ways (apart from the ones discussed in this book) are there for training people in interprersonal skills?

Before you begin to facilitate your own workshops or training courses you need to think hard about a number of issues, including:

- Your own educational philosophy.
- Your own experience of teaching and learning.
- Your views on the aims of interpersonal skills training.
- The overall aims of the organization or institution for which you work.

PLANNING WORKSHOPS

Running interpersonal skills workshops, then, involves facilitation rather than teaching. Put simply, teaching is about the passing on of a body of knowledge, while facilitation is more concerned with helping people to examine and reflect on what they know and to enable them to restructure that knowledge. Elizabeth King (1984) offers the following suggestions about the nature of the trainer's role, with regard to the facilitative approach to education and training:

- They must believe students should make their own decisions and think for themselves.
- They must refrain from assuming an authoritative role and adopt a more facilitative and listening position.

- They must accept diversity of race, sex, values, etc. amongst their students.
- They must be willing to accept all viewpoints unconditionally and not impose their personal values on the students. The ability to entertain alternatives and to negotiate no-lose solutions to problems often leads to group decisions that are more beneficial for both the individual and the group.

Certain stages in the facilitation process can be described and the trainer needs to be aware of the processes that can occur in groups. The stages described here are modified from those offered by Malcolm Knowles (1975) in his discussion of facilitating learning groups for adults. (It is anticipated that most of the people using this manual will be working with adults.)

It is arguable that facilitation of learning has more in common with group therapy than it does with teaching. It is recommended that the person who sets out to become a group trainer should gain experience as a member of a number of different sorts of groups before leading one. In this way you will not only learn about group processes experientially but will also see a number of trainer styles. As Heron (1989) points out, in the early stages of becoming a trainer, it is often helpful to base your style on a trainer that you have seen in action. Later, the style becomes modified in the light of your own experience and you develop your own approach, in the end relearning to *be yourself*. This is a central paradox of facilitation training. First you have to learn a set of skills, then you have to become 'natural' again.

Stages in the facilitation process

Setting the learning climate
The first aspect of helping adults to learn is the creation of an atmosphere in which adult learners feel comfortable and thus able to learn. This is particularly important when it comes to developing interpersonal skills through experiential learning. Unlike more formal classroom learning, the experiential approach asks learners to try things out, take some risks and experiment. If this is to happen at all, it needs to be undertaken in an atmosphere of mutual trust and understanding.

The first aspect of setting a learning climate is to ensure that the environment is appropriate. Rows of desks and chairs are reminiscent of schooldays. For the adult experiential learning group it is often better and certainly more egalitarian if learners and trainer sit together in a closed circle of chairs. Experiential learning workshops rarely involve a great deal of note-taking, so desks or tables rarely serve as anything more than a barrier between learners and trainer.

In the early stages of a workshop or learning group it is useful too if the group members spend time getting to know each other. 'Icebreakers' are sometimes used for this purpose by many trainers in the experiential learning field. An icebreaker is a simple group activity that is designed to relax people and allow them to 'let their hair down' a little, thus creating a more relaxed atmosphere, arguably more conducive to learning interpersonal skills. A further gain is that they encourage group participation and the learning of names. Chapter 6 offers a range of icebreaker activities, and other examples can be found elsewhere (Heron 1973, Brandes and Phillips 1984, Burnard 1990).

Some people (including the author) feel more comfortable with a more straightforward form of introduction. The argument here is that learners coming to a new learning experience are already apprehensive. Many carry with them memories of past learning experiences which may or may not have been of the 'formal' sort. To introduce those people to icebreakers too early may alienate them before they start. The icebreaker, by its very unorthodoxy, may surprise and upset them. A simpler form of introductory activity is to invite each person in turn to tell the rest of the group their name, place of work, job description, hobbies, etc.

It is helpful if the trainer sets the pace for the activity by providing a similar introduction. A precedent is thus set and the group members have some idea of both what to say and how much to say. I recall forgetting this principle when running a workshop in The Netherlands. As a result, each group member talked for about ten minutes and what was intended to be a short introductory activity turned into a lengthy exercise! The golden rule, perhaps, is keep the activity short and sharp and keep the atmosphere light and easygoing.

Once group members have begun to get to know each other, either through the use of icebreakers or by the introductory activity described above, the trainer should deal with domestic issues regarding the group itself. These will include:

- when the group will break for refreshments and meal breaks and when it will end;
- a discussion of the aims of the group;
- a discussion of the 'voluntary principle': that learners should decide for themselves whether or not they will take part in any given activity suggested by the trainer and that no one should feel pressurized into taking part in any activity by either the trainer or by the rest of the group. It is worth pointing out that if a person finds themselves to be the only one not participating in a particular activity, they should not feel under any further obligation either to take part or to justify their decision not to take part;
- issues relating to smoking in the group, when smokers are present;
- any other issues identified by either the trainer or group members.

This early discussion of group rules is an important part of the process of setting the learning climate. The structure so engendered helps everyone to feel part of the decision-making and learning process.

Identifying learning resources
Most interpersonal skills workshops run for people in the professions are attended by adults who have considerable life experience, learning experience and work skills. The aim of the next stage of group development is to identify skills within the group that may serve as resources for further learning. Examples of such skills include: specific counselling skills; skills with particular client groups, eg customers and clients, students, the elderly, adolescents, people with AIDS etc, previous experience in groups, and so on.

Once such skills have been identified, they can be made use of by the group as and when opportunities arise. They can also be more formally 'written in to' the aims of the learning group by setting aside time for those people with skills to demonstrate them or through their conducting teaching sessions with the rest of the group. It is at this stage that the trainer needs to retain some humility. It is often difficult to appreciate, when you are running a group, that other people in that group may be more skilled than you in various respects!

Running the learning group
Once the learning climate has been established and resources within the group have been identified, all that remains is for the trainer to establish the smooth running of the group throughout the use of various activities aimed at enhancing learning. In Part II of this book, a variety of exercises are offered as examples of the group activities that can be used to encourage the learning of specific interpersonal skills. Following the pattern laid down by the experiential learning cycle discussed earlier, the following stages may be used in this part of the workshop:

1. Brief theory input (this can be omitted and the activity becomes the central focus of the learning session. I have indicated in Part II where a theory input might be useful).
2. Description of the activity to be undertaken.
3. Setting up of the activity with group members.
4. Running the activity.
5. Discussion of group members' experiences following the activity (including debriefing).

Thus, for example, the first part of a workshop on counselling skills may be prefaced by a short theory input by the trainer or by another member of the group, on the subject of listening. This input need not be a lecture but is often best treated as a fairly informal discussion, drawing on group members' experiences. Following this theory input, an activity taken from the second part of this book is described to the group and instructions given as to pairing, timing and so on. The group then performs the activity. After this, two options present themselves for 'processing' the outcome. Group members may either stay in their pairs and discuss the activity, before returning to a larger plenary session with the rest of the group, or return to the group for a discussion led by the trainer.

Whichever format is used, the trainer may choose to discuss either the process of the activity or the content of it. The process of an activity refers to what it felt like to undertake that activity and what learning followed as a result of those feelings. A discussion of the content is one that analyses what was talked about. In interpersonal skills training, it may be more productive to spend more time discussing the process of any given activity than the content. In this way, group members develop the skill of noticing their own behaviour in interpersonal situations. Indeed, it is sometimes helpful to suggest that the content of pairs and small group activities remains confidential to those people taking part, and that such content does not become part of the general discussion of the group. In this way, the group can quickly learn to handle true self-disclosure in a safe atmosphere – a situation that closely resembles many real life interpersonal encounters that the professional will have to face.

It is useful to spend a good deal of time in this post-activity discussion. Referring back to the experiential learning cycle discussed in the previous chapter, it was noted that Kolb (1984) asserts that new learning occurs when people reflect on their behaviour. The discussion following an activity is an example of such reflection and the reflective process takes time. It should not be rushed by the trainer nor should any attempt be made to suggest what outcomes the group members may have discovered through performing the activity. It is common in more traditional educational settings for a teacher to ask questions that begin 'Did you notice how...?' or 'Most people find ... when they do this sort of activity.'

Such questions have little relevance in this sort of educational experience. The aim is not to lead the group participants in a particular direction but to enable them to undertake the reflective process themselves and then decide whether or not to share their experience with other people. More useful questions, from a facilitation point of view, would be: 'What did you notice...?' or 'Does anyone want to talk about what they experienced during that activity...?' or 'What else happened...?'

Debriefing

All the activities in this manual call upon people's personal experience. Whenever we disclose things about ourselves (beyond the obvious), we invest some emotion in what we are doing. It often takes courage to talk about ourselves and our experience in the company of other people. Sometimes, too, feelings get stirred up. It is important, therefore, that at the end of each activity, some time is spent in discussing how people felt about doing the activity. This period is known as debriefing time. In role play, the term has a slightly different function. The debriefing time following role play is a time in which people disassociate themselves from the roles they have been playing. For example, the student who has been role playing a senior manager is allowed to return to his everyday, real role.

Sometimes, people find this difficult. The following advice can help: 'Just spend a few moments coming back from your role as . . . to who you are in everyday life. It may help if you just tell us your name and what you normally do, when you are not attending workshops like this.'

Different trainers have different views about the importance of the debriefing period. Some feel that it is useful to allow a person to continue to muse over the role that they have been playing and not particularly helpful to make sure that a person is 'brought back'. Others feel just as strongly that it is vital that a person is returned to their normal role. Give this issue careful thought and decide, in the light of your own experience, on which side you come down. You may decide that sometimes you need to use a debriefing approach, while on other occasions, it is not necessary. If you can, attend other trainers' workshops and see what they do.

Closing the group
You will probably develop your own style of closing the group at the end of the day or at the end of a workshop. A traditional way is through summary of what the day has been about. There are two drawbacks to this method. First, you are restating group members' thoughts, opinions, etc. in your own words. Second, while closing in this way, group members are often silently closing off their thoughts about the day or the workshop in much the same way that schoolchildren begin to put their books away as soon as a teacher sums up at the end of a lesson. It may be far better to leave the session open-ended and to avoid any sort of summing up. Alternatively, rather than allowing the day or the workshop to end abruptly, the trainer may choose to use one or more of the following closing and evaluating activities.

1. Each person in turn makes a short statement about what they liked least about the day or about the workshop. Each then makes a short statement about what they liked most about the day or the workshop. No one has to justify what they say for their statement is taken as a personal evaluation of their feelings and experience.
2. Each person in turn briefly states three things that they feel they have learned during the day or the workshop. This may or may not be followed by a discussion on the day's learning.
3. The group has an 'unfinished business' session. Group members are encouraged to share any comments they may have about the day or the workshop, of either a positive or negative nature. The rationale for this activity is that such sharing helps to avoid bottled-up feelings and increases a sense of group cohesion.

These, then, are the stages of a typical interpersonal skills workshop and they may be adapted to suit the particular needs of the group and of the trainer. The last activity, 'unfinished business' can also be used at periods throughout a training session when the trainer judges that the atmosphere of the session has become emotionally charged. The skilled trainer can suggest, at such times, that the next 15 minutes be designated an 'unfinished business session' and that people should be free to say what is on their minds. Each of the activities in Part II has a closing activity.

Group dynamics and processes

All groups are different just as all people are different. However, certain group processes crop up sufficiently often that it is possible to make some general statements about them. Apart from considering the stages of group facilitation that are involved in planning a group learning session or a workshop, the trainer also needs to know something about the dynamics or processes that can occur in such a group. Forewarned is forearmed. In this section, some of those processes are described and suggestions offered as to how they can be coped with as they occur. In the end, there can be no one correct way of coping with a particular process; everything is dependent upon the people concerned, the context, the perceptions of the trainer and of group members and so on.

Pairing
In groups, pairing refers to one of two phenomena. First, the word

can refer to two group members who talk quietly to each other, ignoring the rest of the group. It is arguable that such a manoeuvre is a defensive one in that the pair are avoiding issues being discussed in the larger group by talking to each other. Pairing of this sort can be distracting to the trainer and disruptive to the group because it means that the group is not operating as a single unit but is divided. The second type of pairing is when two group members (and one is sometimes the trainer) tend to discuss issues with each other across the group, rather than sharing a 'whole group' discussion. This sort of pairing is less distracting than the previous sort but can cause problems if the trainer consistently pairs with another person in the group and tends to ignore other group members.

A variety of options are available to the trainer for dealing with pairing when it occurs. Some of these are:

— Confront the two persons concerned. This must be done carefully if it is not to cause reminders of schooldays and bossy teachers!
— Ignore it and see what happens. Sometimes, pairing takes care of itself.
— Draw attention to the fact that pairing has occurred and allow the group to resolve the issue.
— Set a contract with the group, prior to the group's development, that all members will be on the lookout for the occurrence of such dynamics.
— Engage one of the pair in discussion so that the pairing is at least temporarily broken up.

Scapegoating
Scapegoating is the situation where one person in the group becomes the one who the group attacks, for whatever reason. Sometimes only one or two people are involved in the attack, sometimes everyone is involved. Again, it is arguable that this is a defensive manoeuvre in that the scapegoat becomes a focal point for the pent-up aggression of the collective group. Sometimes the scapegoat is a particularly strong person who is well able to cope with the hostility. At other times, a weaker member becomes the focus. The trainer has at least the following options when scapegoating occurs:

— Draw attention to it and allow the group to deal with it.

- Stop it. This is particularly important when a weaker member of the group is under attack.
- Suggest a short break in the group's activities.
- Ask the scapegoated person how he or she is feeling about what is happening and take the cue for what to do from them.
- Switch the discussion suddenly to another topic so as to reduce tension. This is usually only a temporary measure.

Projection
Projection is where one or more of the group members identifies a mood or a quality in the group that is, in fact, a mood or a quality of that person. For example, a group member who is projecting his own anxiety may say 'I find this a very tense group', when all the other group members feel relaxed. It is clearly important to distinguish between descriptive comments about the group and examples of projections! Sometimes a group member will be offering a useful description of what is happening in the group and this should not be too readily written off as projection.

Another version of projection is when the group as a whole comes to view an aspect of the world outside the group in a hostile or aggressive way. For example, common group projection is the 'group moan', where members get caught up in a circular discussion about how dreadful the 'organization' or 'management' is and how helpless the group is given these circumstances. Again, it is important for the trainer to be able to distinguish between the group describing an accurate situation and a group projection.

When projection occurs, the trainer can try one or more of the following interventions:

- Ask the group to consider what *they* think may be happening and allow it to make its own interpretations.
- Ignore it and see what happens.
- Offer the idea of projection to the group as a group 'interpretation' and see what the group does with the idea.

'League of Gentlemen'
This expression was used by John Heron (1973) and refers to a variant of pairing, whereby a small sub-group of people disrupt a group by forming a hostile and often sarcastic body whose aim is to make life difficult. Often such a league is formed by one central and

dominant figure who draws into quiet discussion, by use of sub-vocal 'asides', the members of the group sitting either side of him. It is recommended that the league of gentlemen is always dealt with quite quickly, for otherwise its effects can be very detrimental to the life of the group. Confronting the league of gentlemen is nearly always difficult. Some suggestions of how this can be achieved include:

— Direct confrontation. The sub-group leader is challenged about what is happening. This nearly always leads to a power struggle between the trainer and the leader of the 'league of gentlemen'.
— The trainer asks members to notice what is happening in the group and allows the 'league of gentlemen' to surface as an issue. Unfortunately, it may not!
— The trainer expresses discomfort at what is happening within the group. This intervention is often disarming to the league.

Of course the 'league of gentlemen' may equally well be a 'league of ladies' or a mixture of both!

Wrecking

This is a one person version of the league of gentlemen. Here, an individual member, for whatever reason, attempts to sabotage the group. This can take place in a variety of ways. The person may, for instance, consistently disagree with everything the trainer says or does; may refuse to take part in any activities and encourage others to do the same; may always be late in coming to the group or suddenly walk out of it. On the other hand, they may offer non-verbal resistance by remaining silent but indicating constant displeasure by use of facial expression. Wrecking as a group process often occurs when people are 'sent' to interpersonal skills training groups rather than coming of their own volition. A number of interventions are available:

— The person may be confronted directly. As with direct confrontation of the league of gentlemen, the confrontation is likely to be met with direct denial followed by a power struggle between the wrecker and the trainer.
— The group's attention may be drawn to the fact that something is happening within the group and comments invited.
— The trainer may choose to talk to the person on one side and try

to reach an understanding of what is happening. Sometimes, wrecking behaviour can be a cover for deep unhappiness or distress on the part of the wrecker. Whether or not the trainer chooses to investigate the deeper meanings of the wrecking behaviour will depend on the trainer's beliefs about the aims of the group and on his or her expertise and training in that sort of work.

Flight

Sometimes the intensity of a group becomes too much for an individual member or for the entire group. Emotions have been aroused, people are feeling threatened, it seems likely that someone will openly express emotion. At such times, it is not uncommon for the individual or the group to 'take flight'. They do this by changing the subject, injecting humour into the discussion, or by becoming silent. If the trainer is unaware of what is happening, they too may (inadvertently) have taken flight, and find that the discussion has quickly moved away from its original subject. There are various ways of handling flight, including the following:

— Point out to the group that it is happening and allow the group to take its own course.
— Ignore it and see what happens.
— Encourage it. The paradoxical intervention (one that is apparently the completely wrong intervention at the right time), by encouraging the behaviour that is happening, takes a step towards changing that behaviour. An example from a therapeutic context may help here. The normal response to someone who is suffering from extreme anxiety is to help them to calm down. They may be asked to take deep breaths or to try to relax. Yet these are the very things that they cannot do! The paradoxical approach is to suggest that they become even more anxious. Frequently, when a person is encouraged (or 'allowed') to do this, they laugh and find the anxiety beginning to drain away. Arguably what has happened is that they have been encouraged and allowed to do the very thing that they are good at doing. In the process, they have found the means to reverse their problem. So it is with encouraging flight in a group. As the group is encouraged to change tack or to laugh so they quickly come to acknowledge what they have been doing.

It is usually not long before someone in the group picks up the fact that the group has been running away from itself.

The paradoxical approach to working with groups and interpersonal skills training workshops is an interesting and varied one. The method of encouraging a group activity that you want to change is always an option (Heron 1986, Fay 1987).

— Gently bring the group or the individual back on track and away from the flight. Afterwards, it is useful to go back and discuss what has happened.

Shutting down
This is a particular sort of internal flight that can occur when an individual is threatened by what is happening in the group. When a person shuts down, they become silent and withdrawn and appear to be taking little interest in what is going on in the group. Shutting down usually only occurs in groups where emotions are running high or where 'hidden agenda' (see below) have suddenly been made explicit. The shut-down person needs gentle handling and some of the options are:

— Offering simple, physical support, if the person is sitting next to the trainer. If the trainer reaches out and merely touches the person or holds their hand or arm, it can help them to feel acknowledged. It may also trigger off the release of pent up emotion, even tears. In this case it is often helpful if the trainer can allow the emotional release and thus enable the shut-down person to gently 'thaw out'.
— Acknowledging, verbally, that the trainer is aware of the shut-down person. Here, the trainer allows the person to express some of the things that they are feeling. Again, pent-up emotion may be expressed.
— Moving on to new topics. If the shut-down person is finding the group heavy going, it is sometimes kinder to change the subject that is under discussion to a more emotionally neutral one. Arguably, however, this is merely putting off the time when the issues that have caused the person to become shut down, are discussed.
— Asking the group to support the shut-down person. Here, the group is made aware that one of its members is cut off from the group's activities and the group is asked for suggestions for

helping that person. This intervention, if it is used badly, can slip rapidly into group patronage!

Rescuing

Rescuing is the opposite of scapegoating. Here, a member of the group is always being protected by one or more other members. Sometimes, the person sets themselves up to be rescued. They may, for example, offer to the group a presentation of self which says 'I can't cope and need help'. Clearly a degree of rescuing is reasonable in that we all need to be helped out sometimes when the going gets rough. On the other hand, persistent rescuing disallows the person being rescued the chance to make their own decisions or to find ways of coping with difficult situations within the group. In the health care professions, there are often a number of people who are 'compulsive carers' and who always want everything to work out well. When a group contains a number of such people, it is usually inevitable that considerable rescuing will take place. The trainer can use one or more of the following interventions when rescuing occurs:

— Ignore it and see what happens.
— Ask the person being rescued what they would like to do.
— Confront the rescuer directly.
— Consult the group about what they think is going on.
— Ask the person being rescued to speak for themselves.

Hidden agenda

In all groups, at least two things are happening: the group is following an overt or obvious agenda – the activities that they are engaged in. At another level, however, all sorts of 'hidden' or undisclosed agenda are being played out. These are the issues and problems that group members bring to the group that lay outside the main or overt agenda. Kilty (1987) makes a useful set of distinctions between three sorts of hidden agenda that are frequently at work in an interpersonal skills learning group: work agenda, interpersonal agenda and personal agenda. Work agenda are those concerned with perceived competence and relationships at work. The group member who is hiding an agenda about work may be thinking 'What do my colleagues think of my performance so far?' or 'Have I damaged my reputation at work?' Interpersonal agenda are concerned with rivalries, competition, conflicts and so forth. The person who is working from an interpersonal hidden agenda may be wondering 'Does the group leader still like me?' or 'Do people in this group think themselves more intelligent than me?' and so forth. Personal agenda are to do with the individuals' own concerns about themselves and their lives. The person who is working with a personal agenda may be wondering 'Can I cope with the emotional intensity of this group?' or 'Will I get very upset if I take part in this role play... and then what will happen?'

Hidden agenda affect the life of the group in that issues from such agenda are 'playing in the background' at all times. Sometimes, too, they emerge and become part of the regular or overt agenda. For example, when two group members disagree in a group discussion, the hidden agenda may emerge when one says to the other 'That's typical. You always thought you were better than me, anyway – you're always like that at work!' Here, the issue is no longer confined to what is happening in the group but has become an issue of personal disagreement and disharmony that may have been simmering in the background for days, months or years and has suddenly surfaced. When hidden agenda become overt in this way, the trainer has at least two options:

— To allow the hidden agenda issue to play itself out between the members of the group.
— To invite the group to explore the hidden agenda that is emerging.

The first option is the 'softer' one and may be useful when there is neither time nor a contract with the group to explore personal issues. The second option is the more confronting and needs to be handled tactfully and non-judgementally by the trainer and by the rest of the group.

In a mature group (either in terms of age or of experience) an interesting (and confronting) practice is to explore the hidden agenda that are lurking beneath the surface. One means of doing this is to invite group members to pair off and to verbalize, in those pairs, what they perceive to be the hidden agenda that they bring to the group. Such an activity can be rewarding in terms of the growth of the group but it is not recommended for the faint hearted! Even if group members do not make explicit all of the hidden agenda that they bring to the group, the very act of taking part in the pairs activity will bring those agenda nearer to the surface.

Group discussions

All these group processes commonly occur in groups of all sorts. They are, perhaps, more common in therapy and self-awareness groups but also crop up in learning groups. A useful way of exploring such processes is to use an activity which involves the ground rules indicated below. A discussion held using these ground rules will often enhance the development of group processes and will also make them more noticeable to the group. After the discussion has been run for about an hour using the rules, they can be dropped and a discussion encouraged about what happened. The ground rules can also be adopted on a regular basis as a means of enhancing clear and assertive communication between group participants. The ground rules are:

— Say 'I', rather than 'you', 'we' or 'people' when discussing. Rather than say 'people in this group are getting a bit edgy', say 'I am getting a bit edgy'.
— Speak directly to other people rather than speaking about them. For example, rather than say 'I think what John is saying is ...', say 'John, you seem to me to be saying that ...'
— Avoid theorizing about what is happening in the group. Theorizing can often lead to a dry 'academic' discussion and can lead the group away from discussing how they are feeling as the group unfolds.
— Try to stay in the present tense: discuss what you are thinking and feeling *now*.

Gendlin and Beebe (1968) offer another set of ground rules which may either be used as an alternative to the ones already cited, or they may be used alongside them. These have a broader application than the previous ones and are not value-free – they presuppose a particular view of groups. It is interesting to ponder of the degree to which you agree with their use in a professional/interpersonal skills training context. Gendlin and Beebe's ground rules are:

1. Everyone who is here belongs here just because he is here and for no other reason.
2. For each person what is true is determined by what is in him,

what he directly feels and finds making sense in himself and the way he lives inside himself.
3. Our first purpose is to make contact with each other. Everything else we might want or need comes second.
4. We try to be as honest as possible and to express ourselves as we really are and really feel – just as much as we can.
5. We listen for the person inside – living and feeling.
6. We listen to everybody.
7. The group leader is responsible for two things only: he protects the belonging of every member and he protects their being heard if this is getting lost.
8. Realism: if we know things are a certain way, we do not pretend they are not that way.
9. What we say here is 'confidential': no one will repeat anything said here outside the group, unless it concerns only himself. This applies not just to obviously private things, but to everything. After all, if the individual concerned wants others to know something, he can always tell them himself.
10. Decisions made by the group need everyone taking part in some way.
11. New members become members because they walk in and remain. Whoever is here belongs.

It is interesting to reflect on the degree to which you could use this set of ground rules in your own area of training. It is sometimes helpful to negotiate this second set of rules with the particular group and they can then serve as a group contract – to be adhered to by all group members for the life of the group.

KEY QUESTIONS:

- Do you recognize the group processes described above?
- What else do you need to learn about groups?
- What style of group facilitation do you prefer?
- Where did you learn your own style?

INTERPERSONAL SKILLS TRAINING CHECKLIST

- What else do you need to learn about group dynamics?
- Are you happy that you can handle group conflict?
- Are you clear about the differences between interpersonal skills training and therapy?
- How will you respond if someone in your group tries to turn the workshop into a therapy session?

Chapter 3:
Evaluating interpersonal skills workshops

SELF AND PEER EVALUATION

The two most obvious methods of monitoring progress in interpersonal skills development have been discussed already: practising the skills involved and noticing our changing and developing reactions. The practice element often comes with the job. We are involved in interpersonal relationships every day of our professional lives so there is plenty of time for trying out new behaviour. It has to be noted, however, that the decision to try out new interpersonal behaviour must be a conscious one. It is very easy to attend a workshop on counselling skills and to believe that a lot was gained from it. The truth is of course that the workshop will only have been successful if the learning gained in it is transferred to the real situation. There is always a danger of an interpersonal skills workshop being an 'island' in the middle of a busy working life – something that was interesting at the time, but of little practical value.

The practical value of an interpersonal skills training course will only be evident if a transfer of learning occurs. This point is an important one for those who facilitate experiential learning workshops. They must attempt to ensure that learning is carried over into real life and does not remain within the confines of the comfortable atmosphere of the workshop. To this end, some trainers use homework as a means of reinforcing learning. Others ask workshop participants to set personal contracts with themselves to try out new learning. Still others have follow up days on which all the participants meet again and discuss their progress or lack of it.

The second point is a reminder about the concept of 'noticing'. We need not only to practise new behaviour but also to reflect on what effect it has both on ourselves and on its recipients. As we noted in the previous chapters, it is important to practise the skill of noticing – of having our attention rooted firmly in the present, of paying attention to ourselves and to our surroundings. As with many of these personal skills, the only way to develop the skill of noticing is to do it! Try it now and continue to notice throughout the day. If you forget and your attention wanders, slowly allow it to return and keep trying!

In summary, there are three basic requirements for 'formally' developing interpersonal competence: (1) attendance at a training course or workshop; (2) practice of new interpersonal skills in the real situation; and (3) continuing ability to notice what happens to us and other people when we use interpersonal skills. Additionally, we learn new skills incidentally through a trial and error process.

We also need to monitor our progress of interpersonal growth. The two methods for undertaking that monitoring – keeping a journal and using the mentor system – are now described. These methods can help us to maintain and evaluate both formal and informal learning.

Keeping a journal

There is a growing literature on the use of self and peer assessment in the interpersonal skills field (Kilty 1976, 1983, Burnard 1987). With the increase in interest in experiential learning is coming the realization that those taking part in interpersonal workshops and in various forms of experiential learning need to be able to develop their own criteria for checking and evaluating their own learning (Knowles 1975, 1978, 1980). In this section, the use of one such student-centred approach is discussed: the journal as a method of self-assessment and evaluation.

It is acknowledged that the two concepts of assessment and evaluation are inextricably linked. To assess is to identify a particular state at a particular time, usually with a view to taking action to change or modify that state. To evaluate is to place a value on a course of action, to identify the success or otherwise of something that has happened. Thus assessment is often seen as something that needs to occur at the outset of an educational encounter and evaluation as something that occurs at the end. In fact, evaluation necessarily leads on to reassessment and thus to another educational encounter. In this way the journal described here can be used both as an assessment tool and as an evaluation instrument.

The instructions for completion of the journal are simple. Participants are required to make weekly entries in a suitable book under the following headings:

- Problems encountered and resolution of those problems.
- Application of new skills and difficulties with them.
- New skills required to be learned.
- Personal growth issues/self awareness development.
- Application of new learning to the business or organization.
- Other comments.

These headings can be varied according to the needs and wants of a particular group using the journal approach. No guidelines need to be given regarding the amount that is written under each heading. To prescribe a particular number of words would be over-structuring, although it may be possible to negotiate maxima and minima with the group.

Participants are encouraged to make regular entries and this regularity tends to make the process of keeping the diary easier. Participants who try to 'catch up' and complete the whole thing in one last go tend to have difficulty in remembering what has happened and generally the process is less valuable.

There are several methods of using the diary as an assessment/ evaluation tool. The first is to use it as a continuous focus of discussion between the trainer and an ongoing group. In this way, the participants' experience is constantly being monitored and they are able to discuss their progress or lack of it as they continue with day-to-day field work.

The second method is to use it as a means of summative evaluation at the end of a period of field work. In this case, the following procedure may be used:

- Both trainer and student sit down and individually 'brainstorm' criteria for assessing the journal. Examples of items brainstormed may be:
  - quality of writing,
  - clarity of expression,
  - ability to problem-solve,
  - level of self-disclosure, etc.
- After this brainstorming session, both trainer and participant identify three criteria that they wish to use for assessing the journal.
- Each then uses those criteria to write notes on their assessment of the journal and they then compare those notes.

Out of this activity comes a shared view of the journal which incorporates elements of both self and trainer evaluation. The discussion that follows can be useful to both participants and trainer as a means of offering further feedback on performance. This method can also be used to focus on another important communication skill, the written word. This is a particularly fruitful area if the participant is, in this case, a student or trainee in the health-care field. At this stage, too, a mark for the diary can be negotiated if the journal is to form part of a continuous assessment procedure.

A third method of using the journal is as part of a weekly discussion. This can serve as a means of focusing on shared problems and also as a method of disseminating new information and learning. The journal can also form the basis of a seminar group, with each member in turn taking the chair.

Probably the most democratic method of deciding how to use the journal is to negotiate its use with the group. This should be done prior to the journal being started so that all participants are clear as to who will and who will not have access to it. Journal writing calls for a considerable degree of self-disclosure and it is important, in adult learning groups, that the participants' dignity is maintained (Jarvis: 1983). Jarvis maintains that the maintenance of personal dignity is at the heart of adult education. This has particular relevance for interpersonal skills training. Some exercises advocated in the interpersonal skills field are embarrassing and even humiliating to take part in. If Jarvis is right, it would seem vital that we remember to respect the dignity of the people attending our courses.

The journal as part of a total assessment and evaluation system in an interpersonal skills training course, or as part of a larger training course can be a valuable and very personal means of allowing participants to maintain a constant check on their own learning and development. The approach can be modified in a variety of ways to reflect different emphases. For instance, the bias can be towards practical skills development, or towards self-awareness. Alternatively, participants can be encouraged to develop their own headings for the journal in order to reflect their own needs and wants.

It is interesting to consider the various levels of assessment and evaluation that take place when this method is used. First, the participants have to reflect on their experience before they write. Second, they have to convert their thoughts into words and write an entry in the journal. Yet another level of assessment occurs when the journal is discussed between other group members or in a tutorial. In this way, participants are completing part of the experiential learning cycle discussed in Chapter 1. They are also fulfilling the conditions of self-disclosure and feedback from others that Luft (1969) considers necessary for the development of self-awareness. Thus the method offers a valuable educational tool on a number of levels.

KEY QUESTIONS:

- Are peers able to evaluate each other?
- Who evaluates *your* performance?
- How do you evaluate other people's performance?

Supervision and the mentor system

In learning and developing interpersonal skills we all need help at times. Sometimes it is useful if the help regularly comes from the same person and we can develop a lasting relationship with that helper. It is here that we find the basis of the notion of mentoring. The idea of having a mentor during interpersonal skills training received considerable attention in the American press (May *et al.* 1982) and two writers go as far as to say that 'everyone who makes it has a mentor' (Collins and Scott 1979). Burton (1975) notes that many of the famous American playwrights and poets revealed that they had mentors at some stage in their careers. In this country, the notion has been less written about but is gaining momentum in the health-care professions as a format for developing interpersonal skills in professionals. It is also used in the training of new teachers in Bachelor of Education and certificate and diploma courses.

What, then, is a mentor? Why do we need them and how do we train them? A mentor is usually someone older than the student and who has considerable experience of the job for which the student is being prepared. The idea of having a mentor also usually contains the idea of continuity and of the student staying with the mentor for some time. This is in contrast to more traditional approaches to professionals' education, where continuity with teaching staff is necessarily interrupted by field experience and where students work with a qualified person for only a short period of time. With the mentor system, trainees negotiate who their mentor will be and then stay 'allocated' to that person for the length of their training. Necessarily, then, a close relationship is likely to develop between the mentor and student.

Darling (1984) found in her research that there were three 'absolute requirements for a significant mentoring relationship'. These were attraction, action and affect.

In the first requirement, attraction, it is deemed vital that both people respect and like each other. Arguably, as the relationship develops, a transference relationship will evolve (Burton 1977). The term transference is usually reserved as a descriptor for the nature of the relationship which develops between psychotherapist and client. It signifies that the client comes to see the therapist as having personal characteristics (usually positive ones) that are reminiscent of one of the client's parents. All this normally takes place at a pre- or unconscious level so the client does not readily see that this is happening. The net result is usually that the client 'idealizes' the therapist and becomes very dependent on them. One of the aims of therapy is often to help the client to try to resolve this transference relationship and thus live a less dependent and more interdependent life (Burnard 1989). It seems likely that the relationship between student and mentor will also invoke transference, particularly as the mentor is already cast in the role of 'expert' by the very fact of being a mentor at all. All this suggests that mentors should be chosen very carefully. Who should do this choosing remains a question for debate!

In terms of the 'action' role of the mentor, the student is likely to want to use the mentor as a role model. Again, by definition, the mentor is seen as an expert: someone who has achieved the various skills that are deemed necessary for effective practice and who is able to use and pass on those skills. In a sense, this aspect of mentoring may be equivalent to the 'sitting with Nellie' approach to training office staff in some organizations referred to in Chapter 1. Clearly, though, it is to be hoped that this will not be the only way that skills are passed on. Traditionally, there has been an element of this approach in previous student-training methods. Just being with a qualified person was sometimes seen as enough to encourage and enable students to develop skills. Whether or not this was ever the case is another debatable point! A certain skill in coaching seems to be a requirement of the skilled mentor. The ability to break down skills into component parts, teach them and demonstrate their use with the appropriate, accompanying affect, seems to be another skill to aim for. Mentoring, it would seem, is not for the faint hearted!

From the 'affective' point of view, the mentor needs to act in a supportive role: encouraging, enhancing his self-confidence and teaching the student to be constructively critical of events. Again, this aspect of the role may well re-open the debate about the likelihood of a transference relationship occurring. If transference does occur, it is important that the mentor can cope with it. He or she will also need to know how to close the relationship and be skilled in 'saying goodbye'. This is unlikely to be easy because of the possible 'counter-transference' that may occur: the mentor's complicated network of feelings for the student! At best, however, the relationship may come to mirror the best aspects of the truly therapeutic relationship that the student will develop with his or her own clients. Hopefully, then, the mentor will be able to initiate and sustain the sort of exemplary relationship that will stand as a role model for future relationships. Again, a lot is being asked of the person who acts as mentor.

On the other hand, there are numerous problems. Because of the nature of the partnership, the student starts in a 'one-down' relationship with the mentor. The mentor is necessarily in a dominant position in the relationship. It is not and cannot be a relationship of equals. Now much of the recent writing on adult education has suggested that adult education should concern itself with negotiation, with shared learning and with meeting students' own perceived needs (Brookfield 1987). Adults, so this argument goes, need to use what they learn, as they learn it; they need to be treated as equals in a partnership that leads along a road of inquiry; they need to have their self-concept protected, as they go. Now whether such demands for equality and negotiation can exist within the constraints of the mentor/student relationship is not clear. It seems more likely that the mentor will be identified as a benign (or perhaps, not so benign!) father or mother substitute. Some may find such a portrayal overdramatic, but, as we have noted, the perfectly respectable notion of transference depends upon the 'unconscious designation' of the other person as a surrogate parent.

There is also the problem of the mentor's own development. There is nothing worse than the 'guru' who feels that he has gained enlightenment and all he needs to do is to sit back and pass on pearls of wisdom to others! (I write 'he': unfortunately, such guru figures are nearly always male!) All of us need to continue our development and education. None of us has 'arrived'; none of is skilled to the point where we cannot learn other skills. The mentor must be a convert to lifelong education, if anything.

Lifelong education is a concept that fits in well with the notion of experiential learning. With lifelong learning the assumption is that education does not and should not end with 'formal' education. Unfortunately, the preparation of many professionals is such that a 'front-end' model of education and training is offered. That is to say that there is a lengthy preparation period (often of between two and six years) followed by very little further education, apart from the occasional study day. Further and continuing education thus becomes the responsibility of the individual practitioner. This is particularly pertinent to the mentor who will be responsible for helping the newcomer to the profession. Lifelong learning commends an approach entailing personal responsibility for learning.

Lifelong learning is concerned with growth and development. There are echoes here of Whitehead's (1933) remark: 'knowledge keeps no better than fish!' The lifelong learner is one who does not hoard 'dead knowledge' but appreciates the changing nature of it. What serves us well as knowledge and skill, today, will to quite an extent, be out of date tomorrow. No professional can afford to allow their knowledge and skills base to become out of date. Interestingly, the task of being a mentor can help in the process of keeping up to date, for the mentor also learns from the protégé. This raises an interesting paradox. The mentor takes responsibility for overseeing the learner, but must also be constantly encouraging that learner's self-determination. Mentors, in other words, should always be trying to do themselves out of a job. All of these things, and no doubt plenty more, need consideration before the partnership of mentoring begins. (Alternatively, they could be faced as they occur, which may be the more painful way.)

How can mentors be trained? Should they be trained? There is a tendency, in some quarters, to be disparaging about training in the interpersonal domain. Some prefer to think of professionals as having 'natural' ability in their field. It would seem reasonable, however, to try to identify some aspects of the role of mentor that would lend themselves to training.

First, the mentor will need skills in identifying learning objectives, with the student. This involves skilful negotiation of the students objectives. Such negotiation takes two factors into account: what the *student* identifies as a need and what the *mentor* identifies as a need. Together, the two must work out a reasonable and workable programme.

Second, the mentor will need to be interpersonally competent. By this I mean that they will be able to initiate and maintain a student-centred relationship which takes full account of the possibility of transference occurring. They will be skilled as a counsellor and be regularly prepared to set aside time to talk to the student. This aspect of the role may be described as the 'befriending' aspect.

Thirdly, they will need coaching skills. They will require the ability to encourage learning described above. This is, of course, different to the skills required of a teacher, for mentors will not be teachers in the traditional sense of that term. Students will, however, by various means, learn a great deal from them!

Finally, in this tentative list of requirements, the mentor will need skills in enabling the student to self-evaluate both the student's skills and the nature of the mentor/student relationship. Thus the mentor will be encouraging the development of self-awareness in the student. Such awareness is likely to help the student in their subsequent relationships with patients or clients. All in all, the relationship needs to be an unselfish one on the part of the mentor.

KEY QUESTIONS:

- **Who were or are your mentors?**
- **Can you train mentors?**
- **Is the mentor system compatible with a student-centred approach to teaching and learning?**

Keeping a journal and the mentor system are two important methods of evaluating and monitoring experience. Both are non-traditional methods and both offer the professional who is learning to develop interpersonal competence the tools to develop their awareness and to identify new learning goals.

INTERPERSONAL SKILLS TRAINING CHECKLIST

- Why will you evaluate your courses or workshops?
- Who will see the evaluation report?
- What methods are available to you for such evaluation?
- To what degree do you need to consider mentorship training in your organization?
- How do you evaluate *your own* performance as an interpersonal skills trainer?

Chapter 4:

A guide to running an interpersonal skills workshop

So far, we have discussed many of the theoretical and practical issues related to running interpersonal skills workshops. The aim of this chapter is to summarize some of the principles and to illustrate their use. The chapter offers an account of the things to bear in mind when running a workshop. It can be used as a further checklist of considerations to be made when planning and working with groups.

BEFORE YOU START

First of all, the workshop has to be planned. You need to give consideration to the following teaching and learning issues:

- What are the aims of your workshop?
- What content will you include in your workshop?
- What teaching and learning methods will you use?
- How will you evaluate the workshop?

Once you have clarified these issues, work out a timetable of events for the day. Remember that it is easy to overestimate the amount of

84 Interpersonal skills training

Time	Activities	Notes
	INTERPERSONAL SKILLS TRAINING WORKSHOP	
9.00	Registration and coffee	• check coffee • take registration sheet • check OHP • remember handouts, OHP, acetates and notes.
9.30 - 10.00	Introduction to trainer and introductory activity	Activity no 3
10.00 - 10.30	Theory input : Interpersonal skills and their application in the health care setting.	• Handouts • OHP's • Notes
10.30 - 11.00	Coffee	Check coffee
11.00 - 12.30	Listening activity	Activity no 32
12.30 - 1.00	Lunch	Don't forget to confirm 15 extra lunches
1.00 - 2.00	Activity in using basic counselling skills	Activity no 39
2.00 - 3.00	Activity applying counselling skills to everyday working practice	Activity no 40
3.00 - 3.30	Tea	
3.30 - 4.00	Open discussion	
4.00 - 4.30	Evaluation of workshop. Distribution of booklists and handouts.	• Self and peer evaluation format • Remember handouts

Figure 4.1 Example trainer's timetable

ground that you can cover in one day. Figure 4.1 is an illustration of one possible timetable for a one-day workshop on interpersonal skills. The timetable is for use by the trainer of the workshop.

Alongside these educational issues, you will need to consider these domestic issues:

- How many people will be attending your workshop?
- Have they all had clear joining instructions?
- Have they all paid their fees?

- Have you booked rooms for the workshop?
- Have you all the equipment that you need?
- Have you made arrangements for tea, coffee and meal breaks?
- Have you had programmes printed and have they been sent to participants? Do you have some spares?

BEFORE THE PARTICIPANTS ARRIVE

On the day of the workshop, you will need to arrive early and check the following:

- The seating arrangements. It is useful to all sit in a closed circle. In this formation, everyone can see everyone else and no one dominates the proceedings.
- The heating and ventilation of the room.
- Is there a rule about smoking? If participants are to be allowed to smoke, is provision made for seating them separately to non-smokers and are there enough ashtrays?
- Does all your equipment work? If you are using an overhead projector, check that you have spare bulbs and that you know how to change them. If you are using flipchart pads, make sure that you have enough, and that your flipchart marker pens all work.
- If necessary, turn on any heating systems for tea and coffee.
- Make sure that you have a list of the participants' names and have some means of checking names as people arrive. One way to do this is to have people sign their names on a pre-printed form.

OPENING THE WORKSHOP

It is a good idea to start your workshop promptly at the time on the programme. (When latecomers arrive, greet them and ask them to assimilate themselves into the group. At the first break, invite them to introduce themselves.) Open workshop by introducing yourself. Remember that your introduction will serve as an example of the way that other people will introduce themselves. Next, use one of the introductory icebreakers or activities from Part II to enable people to get to know each other. Once you are satisfied that most people know who they are sharing the room with, clarify the aims of the workshop, announce any domestic details about breaks and then outline the structure of the day.

A theory input

Many people like to start interpersonal skills workshops with a brief theory input in order to offer a framework for participants to hang their ideas on. If you choose to do things this way, have your theory input well prepared, use plenty of visual aids and keep the presentation short and simple. Resist the tendency to lecture and try to make sure that all participants take part in the discussion of the main points of your input. Alternatively, avoid a theory input altogether and go straight into one or more of the interpersonal skills activities. You can relate practice to theory later in the day.

INTRODUCING ACTIVITIES

There are a number of factors to bear in mind when using interpersonal skills activities and exercises:

- Allow plenty of time. Do not try to cram too many activities into too short a time. The reflection period and discussion of the activity is usually more important than the activity itself. It is during this phase that the experiential learning cycle is being completed. People are making sense of what has happened to them. Allow about one hour for each activity.
- Make sure that you give clear instructions about the activity. Check that everyone in the room is clear about what you are asking them to do. If necessary, write the instructions out and give them to participants as a handout. This is particularly important if you are working with large groups.
- Stick to the activity format. Once you have given instructions, follow them yourself. Resist the temptation to modify the activity once it is underway.
- Keep to time. If you suggest that part of an activity will take five minutes to complete, remind participants when the five minutes is up.

- If you are using a pairs activity, be authoritative when you ask the group to reconvene. Sit in the larger circle of chairs and call participants to join you. Once you have called them back, remain silent until everyone else is back in the larger group.

REFLECTION AND PROCESSING

Reflection and discussion after an activity are the most important elements of the undertaking. Allow plenty of time for discussion. Begin with a broad open question such as 'What happened?' 'What did you notice?' or 'How did you feel about the activity?' Allow participants plenty of time to think about what you have asked and let people respond in their own time.

Avoid the 'schoolteacher' approach of asking each person, in turn, to respond. If people choose not to respond to the question, this should be respected. Try to avoid pre-emptive questions such as 'Did you notice how . . .' or 'Did anyone feel that . . .'

Accept the fact that participants will respond to the activities idiosyncratically. It is important that people are allowed to verbalize what happened to them and that they are not rushed to see the outcome of an activity in any particular sort of way. On the other hand, encourage participants to link their experiences with the 'real world' with questions such as 'What are the implications of all this . . .?' 'How does all this link up with your job . . .?' and 'What are the key issues here . . .?'

TAKING BREAKS

Try to gauge the atmosphere and the rhythm of the group. Do not carry on when people are obviously flagging. Take regular, short breaks. Such breaks can be an important part of the learning process as this is the time that people 'really' talk to each other. If the atmosphere flags a little, between breaks, consider running a quick icebreaker or revitalizing activity from Part II.

DEBRIEFING

As we saw in Chapter 2, some activities in interpersonal skills training involve people role playing. Some trainers feel that it is important that people who have been asked to play out a role are given time to 'return' from it. In Chapter 2 we noted that the following statement can be used to debrief or help the participant to get out of a role and to return to 'real life':

> Just spend a few moments coming back from your role as ... to who you are in everyday life. It may help if you just tell us your name and what you normally do, when you are not attending workshops like this.

HANDOUTS AND BOOKLISTS

If necessary, prepare handouts that contain further reading, booklists and other information. Try to make sure that these are professionally prepared using a wordprocessor, desktop publishing program and a laser printer. If you use a desktop publishing program, keep your design simple, do not use too many type faces and try to establish a uniform look to the handouts that you use. Do not prepare handouts that contain too much information. Three-page, closely printed handouts are rarely read. A single side of A4, on the other hand, can be read quickly and may well spark off further discussion.

CLOSING THE WORKSHOP

Consider carefully the closing activity that you use. Such activities may be of various sorts:

- Activities which help to evaluate the workshop.
- Activities which enable participants to evaluate their own performance.

Running an interpersonal skills workshop 89

- Activities which encourage people to link their learning to 'real life'.
- Activities which enable participants to say goodbye to each other.

A range of closing activities is included in the second part of this book.

Chapter 5:

Interpersonal skills training checklists

The previous four chapters have been about interpersonal skills, experiential learning methods and running interpersonal skills training groups and workshops. This chapter is a series of checklists you can use to identify what else you must do in order to function better in this field. It would seem appropriate that the theory be put into practice. I have argued in the previous chapters that what is most important in adult learning, particularly in interpersonal skills training, is that people make their own decisions about what they need to do to enhance their interpersonal competence. In the first checklist you are asked to explore your own competencies as a trainer. The other checklist provide issues for you to consider.

Checklist One

QUESTIONS TO ASK YOURSELF BEFORE YOU RUN A TRAINING GROUP

- What prior experience have you had of running training groups?
- What training have you had in group work?
- What beliefs do you hold about the nature of groups?
- If you were asked to run a group tomorrow how would you feel?
- What are the best and worst things about a group approach to training?

Checklist Two

SETTING THE ENVIRONMENT

- Is the setting appropriate to the training group that you want to run?
- Have you set out the room with a circle of similar-height chairs?
- Have you got all the teaching aids that you need (flipchart, white or blackboard, OHP, handouts etc.)?
- Have you organized coffee, lunch and tea breaks?

Checklist Three

NEGOTIATING WITH THE GROUP

- Are you clear about what you are prepared to negotiate over?
- What will you do if no one wants to negotiate?
- How much time will you spend in the negotiation process?
- Will you have the last word?

Checklist Four

STARTING THE GROUP

- Have you decided on a simple 'warm up' activity? If not, you may want to turn to 'icebreakers' in Part II.
- Are you comfortable with the activity you have chosen?
- Have you allowed some time for talking through details of the domestic arrangements (tea and coffee breaks, location of library etc.)?
- Are you prepared to arrive early and to meet each participant at the door?

Checklist Five

KEEPING THE GROUP GOING

- What will you do if things start to 'flag' a little? Some of the activities in the second part of this book are specifically recommended and marked as suitable for helping in this situation.
- What will you do if someone walks out?
- What will you do if someone gets upset?
- Are you confident that you can handle most contingencies?
- What is the worst thing that could happen?
- Have you got a clear structure in mind and on paper?
- Have you highlighted the 'negotiated' parts of the course programme?

Checklist Six

USING ACTIVITIES

- Are you familiar with the activities you have chosen?
- Have you allowed plenty of time for them?
- Do you need to take notes into the workshop room about how to run the activities?
- Have you got a few 'standby' activities up your sleeve?
- Are you going to debrief participants after an activity?
- If so, how will you do this?

Checklist Seven

WHAT TO DO WHEN THINGS GO WRONG

- Acknowledge to the group that something is not as it should be.
- Slow down and do not rush any changes to the programme.
- Consult the group.
- Make a decision with the group's help.
- Make sure that everyone who wants to say something has their say.
- Don't flap – nothing is irreparable.
- Review the incident afterwards and identify how you could have handled it differently.
- Remain in control of the group – do not give up and give in.
- If necessary, suggest that everyone has a break.
- Give a clear time for return after the break.
- Review progress at the end of the day.

Checklist Eight

CLOSING THE GROUP

- Have you planned a closing activity?
- Are you prepared to hang back and say goodbye to everyone as they leave?
- Are you going to evaluate the workshop?
- What methods are you going to use?

Checklist Nine

SOME DON'TS

- Don't overplan your workshop. Allow time for changes.
- Don't ignore process. Continue to notice what is happening in the group at all times.
- Don't ignore the group's requests.
- Don't allow one or two members to dominate the group.
- Don't rush to interpret other people's experience for them.
- Don't use the same activities in every group or workshop. Someone is bound to remember what you did at a previous one!
- Don't think that everything has to go perfectly. Allow yourself, and others, to make mistakes.

Checklist Ten

THINGS TO MAKE YOUR GROUPS BETTER

- Keep the workshop or group simple and structured.
- Consult the group before making major decisions.
- Learn people's names.
- Don't worry about including everyone. You don't studiously have to make sure that everyone speaks on every topic.
- Keep the atmosphere light; don't strive for it to become heavy and 'meaningful'.
- Keep your sense of humour and use it.
- Consider changing things a little if the workshop begins to get too predictable. Consult before you change direction.
- Surprise yourself and your groups.
- Learn some new activities.
- Be clear about the theory that informs what you do.
- Be prepared to have others challenge what you do. Learn from it.
- Have a colleague sit in on your group and ask for feedback about your performance.
- Go to groups and workshops yourself – as a participant.
- Enjoy yourself.

PART II
TRAINING ACTIVITIES

Chapter 6:

Icebreakers and introductions

USING ICEBREAKERS

The first group of activities in this section are icebreakers. These are activities that can be used at the beginning of a workshop or a course to encourage participants to get to know each other. They should be both useful and enjoyable. The aim should be to keep the atmosphere light and not reminiscent of a psychotherapy group.

Icebreakers can also have another function. They can be used as a method of restimulating a group that has become a little moribund. Most of us have sat through troughs in the life of a group. A well-chosen icebreaker can help to regenerate energy and encourage more enthusiasm and motivation. It should be said, however, that not all group participants and not all trainers like icebreakers. Some find them embarrassing and even feel them to be childish. If this is the case, it is probably better to stick to more formal methods of starting groups – the 'round' of names is one example of such an introduction procedure. To this end, I have included one or two 'formal' openers in this section.

OPENING ROUND

Activity 1

Time required 15 minutes.

Aim To encourage people in a group to get to know each other.

Group size Any number between 5 and 25.

Environment A large room in which people can sit comfortably in a group. Chairs should be of equal height and the group should remain in a closed circle throughout. The trainer should be part of the circle.

Equipment No special equipment is required.

Procedure Each person, in turn, tells the rest of the group the following things about themselves:

- name;
- job;
- home town;
- two of three personal details.

The group trainer joins in wherever possible.

Evaluation Each person in the group, in turn, says first what they liked least about the activity. Then, each person in the group says what they liked most about it. The group leader or trainer joins in too.

Closing The trainer can invite questions about any aspect of the activity.

© P. Burnard 1992, published by Kogan Page

BRIEF INTERVIEWS
Activity 2

Time required 30 minutes.

Aim To encourage all members of a workshop or course to get to know each other.

Group size Any number between 5 and 25.

Environment A large room with chairs of equal height. Space enough to allow participants to pair off and then to reconvene. Smaller rooms can be used for the pairs activity if required.

Equipment No special equipment is required.

Procedure After the trainer has introduced himself to the group, he asks the participants to pair off with someone in the room that they do not know. The pairs then interview each other for about 10 minutes. Once all the interviews have been completed, the larger group reforms. Each person, in turn, stands behind their partner and introduces that person to the group. If there is an odd number of participants the trainer makes up a pair. Otherwise, he offers more information about himself after all the feedback to the larger group has taken place. A checklist can be given out if this is required; a sample checklist is included in this section.

Evaluation The trainer invites each person in the group, in turn, to identify two things that they feel they learned from doing the activity.

Closing The trainer can invite questions about any aspect of the activity.

© P. Burnard 1992, published by Kogan Page

102 Interpersonal skills training activities

Notes This activity can be used with more than 25 participants if a certain amount of structure is used. One way of managing larger numbers is to draw up a handout that gives explicit instructions to participants. Then, sub-groups are formed from the larger group and a chairperson is elected for each of the sub-groups. The task of each chairperson is to work through the instruction sheet with their group and to ensure things run smoothly. After the activity has been completed in each of the sub-groups, the larger group reforms. The chairpeople report back to that larger group during the plenary session. Structure is essential if the serial working of subgroups is to be effective. Make sure that everyone is clear about the aims of the activity and what it is that they are supposed to be doing. Headings for an instruction sheet might be:

- Title of the activity
- Aims
- What to do
- The role of the chairperson.

This exercise can be used to sharpen group members' attention during the course of a group or workshop. The following checklist can be given to participants to enable them to structure their interviews, if required.

SHORT INTERVIEW CHECKLIST	
1. Partner's name	
2. Place of work	
3. Job	
4. Four interests away from work	
5. Best and worst personal qualities	

© P. Burnard 1992, published by Kogan Page

PAIRS INTRODUCTIONS
Activity 3

Time required 30 minutes.

Aim To ensure that people get to know each other and to encourage group cohesion.

Group size Any number between 5 and 25.

Environment A large room in which people can sit comfortably in a group. Chairs should be of equal height and the group should remain in a closed circle throughout. The trainer should be part of the circle.

Equipment No special equipment is required.

Procedure After an initial welcome by the trainer, participants are asked to stand up, mill around the room and at a given signal from the trainer stop and introduce themselves to the person nearest to them. The process is then repeated until group members have met and shaken hands with everyone else in the room. Once the larger group reconvenes, it is helpful if all members are also invited to re-introduce themselves to the group, by stating their names. The group trainer joins in wherever possible.

Evaluation The group pairs off again, and each pair discusses what they least and most liked about the activity.

Closing The trainer can invite questions about any aspect of the activity.

© P. Burnard 1992, published by Kogan Page

INTRODUCTORY HANDOUT

Activity 4

Time required 30 minutes.

Aim To enable group or workshop participants to get to know each other.

Group size Any number between 5 and 25.

Environment A large room in which people can sit comfortably in a group. Chairs should be of equal height and the group should remain in a closed circle throughout. The trainer should be part of the circle.

Equipment A whiteboard, blackboard or flipchart to allow discussion points to be jotted down. (The board should not become a focal point of the session.) Chalk or markers for the board or flipchart. Prepared handouts where necessary.

Procedure The trainer hands out a short questionnaire (see below) which is used by each person to interview another. The group participants pair off and use the questionnaire as a means of gathering information about each other. Allow each participant 10 minutes to interview their partner and then allow another 10 minutes for the partner to reciprocate. After 20 minutes, the larger group reconvenes and each person in turn introduces their partner by referring to the completed questionnaire. The group trainer joins in wherever possible.

Evaluation The trainer invites each person in the group, in turn, to identify two things that they feel they learned from doing the activity.

© P. Burnard 1992, published by Kogan Page

Closing The trainer can invite questions about any aspect of the activity.

Notes This activity can be used with more than 25 participants if a certain amount of structure is used. One way of managing larger numbers is to draw up a handout that gives explicit instructions to participants. Then, sub-groups are formed from the larger group and a chairperson is elected for each of the sub-groups. The task of each chairperson is to work through the instruction sheet with their group and to ensure things run smoothly. After the activity has been completed in each of the sub-groups, the larger group reforms. The chairpeople report back to that larger group during the plenary session. Structure is essential if the serial working of subgroups is to be effective. Make sure that everyone is clear about the aims of the activity and what it is that they are supposed to be doing. Headings for an instruction sheet might be:

- Title of the activity
- Aims
- What to do
- The role of the chairperson.

INTRODUCTORY QUESTIONNAIRE

Use this questionnaire to interview another person in the group. Allow them plenty of time to answer and jot down their responses in the right hand column.

Questions	Answers
1. What is the name that you prefer to be known by?	
2. Where do you live?	
3. What is your job?	
4. What are your feelings about being on this course?	
5. What do you hope to learn from it?	
6. What are the two things in life that you are most proud of?	
7. What is one other thing that you would like the group to know about you?	
8. If you could change something about yourself, what would it be?	
9. How old are you?	

© P. Burnard 1992, published by Kogan Page

MILLING AND PAIRING

Activity 5

Time required 15 minutes

Aim To allow group participants to 'warm up' and to get to know each other.

Group size Any number between 5 and 25.

Environment A large room with chairs of equal height. Space enough for participants to be able to stand up and move around the room.

Equipment No special equipment is required.

Procedure Group members are invited to stand up and mill slowly around the room with their eyes closed, being careful not to bump into each other. Next, they move around with their eyes open but without making eye contact with other members of the group. Third, they mill around making direct eye contact with each person they meet. Finally, they mill, meet people coming towards them with a handshake and introduce themselves by name. The group trainer joins in wherever possible.

Evaluation Each person in the group, in turn, says first what they liked least about the activity. Then, each person in the group says what they liked most about it. The group leader or trainer joins in too.

Closing The trainer can invite questions about any aspect of the activity.

Notes This can be used as a 'warm up' activity at different points during the course of a group or workshop, or to sharpen group members' attention.

© P. Burnard 1992, published by Kogan Page

BLIND WALK
Activity 6

Time required 45 minutes to 1 hour.

Aim To get to know each other by exploring the senses.

Group size Any number between 5 and 25.

Environment A large room with chairs of equal height. Space enough for participants to be able to stand up and move around the room. Allowance should be made for participants to be able to wander around the building.

Equipment Blindfolds. These can be made out of any heavy material, torn into strips.

Procedure The group participants are invited to pair off. Each pair is given a blindfold and one of the pair puts the blindfold on. Their partner then leads them around the room, out of the door and around the building or outside, into the grounds of the building. During that time, the blindfolded person is allowed to experience different atmospheres, textures, temperatures and so forth. Also, the pair should experiment with silence: part of the 'blind walk' should be carried out with neither party talking. The 'blind' person may try walking unaided for short periods.

After quarter of an hour, roles are reversed. After a further quarter of an hour, the group reconvenes and there is a discussion about the experience. The group trainer joins in wherever possible.

Evaluation The pairs reform at the end of the activity and discuss what they liked least and most about it. They also each give an evaluation of the other's performance.

© P. Burnard 1992, published by Kogan Page

Closing Participants should be encouraged to spend a few minutes talking about their plans for the immediate future: holidays, weekend trips, social events and so forth. This allows all participants to disassociate themselves from the activity and encourages them to return to their 'normal' roles.

Notes This activity can be used with more than 25 participants if a certain amount of structure is used. One way of managing larger numbers is to draw up a handout that gives explicit instructions to participants. Then, sub-groups are formed from the larger group and a chairperson is elected for each of the sub-groups. The task of each chairperson is to work through the instruction sheet with their group and to ensure things run smoothly. After the activity has been completed by each of the sub-groups, the larger group reforms. The chairpeople report back to the larger group during the plenary session. Structure is essential if the serial working of sub-groups is to be effective. Make sure that everyone is clear about the aims of the activity and what it is that they are supposed to be doing. Headings for an instruction sheet might be:

- Title of the activity
- Aims
- What to do
- The role of the chairperson.

INVENTORY
Activity 7

Time required 30 minutes.

Aim To encourage group participants to get to know each other.

Group size Any number between 5 and 25.

Environment A large room in which people can sit comfortably in a group. Chairs should be of equal height and the group should remain in a closed circle throughout. The trainer should be part of the circle.

Equipment A whiteboard, blackboard or flipchart to allow discussion points to be jotted down. (The board should not become a focal point of the session.) Chalk or markers for the board or flipchart. Prepared handouts where necessary.

Procedure The trainer hands out prepared sheets (illustrated below). Each participant works through the sheet and fills in the details about themselves. They then pair off and the pair exchange sheets. Each pair is then encouraged to ask questions of each other – questions that arise from the information on the sheets. After ten minutes, the group reconvenes and a discussion of the activity is encouraged by the trainer. The group trainer joins in wherever possible.

Evaluation The trainer hands out a prepared short questionnaire about the activity. The questionnaire should ask about:

- What it was like to take part in the activity
- What feelings were invoked by the activity
- What elements of it would be taken back to the workplace

© P. Burnard 1992, published by Kogan Page

Closing Participants should be offered a five-minute period in which to raise questions, express feelings, address particular people in the group or to talk through anything else that has arisen from the activity.

Notes This activity can be used with more than 25 participants if a certain amount of structure is used. One way of managing larger numbers is to draw up a handout that gives explicit instructions to participants. Then, sub-groups are formed from the larger group and a chairperson is elected for each of the sub-groups. The task of each chairperson is to work through the instruction sheet with their group and to ensure things run smoothly. After the activity has been completed by each of the sub-groups, the larger group reforms. The chairpeople report back to the larger group during the plenary session. Structure is essential if the serial working of sub-groups is to be effective. Make sure that everyone is clear about the aims of the activity and what it is that they are supposed to be doing. Headings for an instruction sheet might be as follows:

- Title of the activity
- Aims
- What to do
- The role of the chairperson.

© P. Burnard 1992, published by Kogan Page

PERSONAL INVENTORY

Fill in the form below. When you have finished, the trainer will invite you to pair off with another member of the group. Exchange personal inventory sheets and ask each other questions about the information contained in them.

1. Which was the best year of your life?	
2. If you did not do the job you do now, which job would you like to do?	
3. If you could meet a famous person, who would it be?	
4. If you could live anywhere, where would you live?	
5. What is your favourite piece of music?	
6. Can you name a book that you have read recently?	
7. What are your feelings about being at this workshop?	
8. If you could be *anywhere* right now, where would you choose to be?	

© P. Burnard 1992, published by Kogan Page

GOOD AND NEW
Activity 8

Time required 15 minutes.

Aim To encourage people to get to know each other and to promote a positive atmosphere at the start of a group or workshop.

Group size Any number between 5 and 25.

Environment A large room in which people can sit comfortably in a group. Chairs should be of equal height and the group should remain in a closed circle throughout. The trainer should be part of the circle.

Equipment No special equipment is required.

Procedure Each person, in turn, is asked to tell the group about something that has happened to them in the last week that is both *good* and *new*. The person begins the statement with a self-introduction. The group trainer joins in wherever possible.

Evaluation Each person in the group, in turn, says first what they liked least about the activity. Then, each person in the group says what they liked most about the activity. The group leader or trainer joins in too.

Closing The trainer can invite questions about any aspect of the activity.

Notes This can be used as a 'warm up' activity at different points during the course of a group or workshop, or to sharpen group members' attention.

© P. Burnard 1992, published by Kogan Page

FORMAL INTRODUCTIONS
Activity 9

Time required 15 minutes.

Aim To encourage group participants to remember each other's names.

Group size Any number between 5 and 25.

Environment A large room with chairs of equal height. Space enough for participants to be able to stand up and move around the room.

Equipment No special equipment is required.

Procedure Each person, in turn, simply states his or her name at normal speed. A second, 'slow' round of introductions is then carried out when participants are encouraged to remember each person's name as they hear it. If necessary, a third 'normal speed' round is used to make sure that everyone remembers names. The group trainer joins in wherever possible.

Evaluation Each person in the group, in turn, says first what they liked least about the activity. Then, each person in the group says what they liked most about the activity. The group leader or trainer joins in too.

Closing Participants should be offered a five-minute period in which to raise questions, express feelings, address particular people in the group or to talk through anything else that has arisen from the activity.

© P. Burnard 1992, published by Kogan Page

PREPARED SHEETS
Activity 10

Time required 30 minutes.

Aim To encourage participants to get to know each other.

Group size Any number between 5 and 25.

Environment A large room in which people can sit comfortably in a group. Chairs should be of equal height and the group should remain in a closed circle throughout. The trainer should be part of the circle.

Equipment A whiteboard, blackboard or flipchart to allow discussion points to be jotted down. (The board should not become a focal point of the session.) Chalk or markers for the board or flipchart. Prepared handouts where necessary.

Procedure Each person is given an instruction sheet (illustrated below). Group members are then encouraged to work through the sheet by approaching other members of the group. When all of the participants have completed their sheets, the group reconvenes and a discussion is encouraged by the trainer. The group trainer joins in wherever possible.

Evaluation A discussion is invoked by the trainer about how any learning from the activity could be carried back to the workplace.

Closing The trainer can invite questions about any aspect of the activity.

© P. Burnard 1992, published by Kogan Page

INSTRUCTION SHEET

Read through the following items and find out the information from the other people in the group by approaching them, one at a time.

Item	Answer
1. Who is the youngest person in the group?	
2. Who lives closest to this department?	
3. What are the names of the other people in the group?	
4. Has anyone been to a workshop of this sort before?	
5. Does anyone do a similar job to yours?	

© P. Burnard 1992, published by Kogan Page

Chapter 7:
Pairs activities

USING PAIRS ACTIVITIES

The use of pairs activities is a particularly good form of interpersonal skills training. It combines one-to-one training with group activity. In one sense, all of the pairs learn in isolation: it is the coming together as a group that encourages and endorses group learning. In this sense, pairs activities represent one of the best forms of experiential learning.

What is particularly important in this style of training is that plenty of time is set aside for discussion after the pairs have worked through their activity. As a rule of thumb, the discussion period should last twice as long as the pairs activity itself.

INTRODUCTORY PAIRS
Activity 11

Time required 45 minutes to 1 hour.

Aim To explore the idea and process of working in pairs.

Group size Any number between 5 and 25.

Environment A large room with chairs of equal height. Space enough to allow participants to pair off and then to reconvene. Smaller rooms can be used for the pairs activity if required.

Equipment A whiteboard, blackboard or flipchart to allow discussion points to be jotted down. (The board should not become a focal point of the session.) Chalk or markers for the board or flipchart. Prepared handouts where necessary.

Procedure The group pairs up. Each pair sit opposite one another and introduce themselves. They then share their feelings about the workshop, the experience of pairing off and about their own strengths and deficits in terms of interpersonal skills. This pairs discussion should last for about ten minutes.

After the ten minutes, the trainer invites the group to reconvene. Then, a discussion is held about the activity.

Two facets are discussed: the *process* of the activity (what it felt like to do it) and the *content* (what was talked about during the activity). As always, the process is more important than the content and, sometimes, the trainer may choose to discuss *only* the process. Also, the trainer helps the group to identify ways in which what has been learned from the activity can be related to the group members' professional or personal lives. The group trainer joins in wherever possible.

© P. Burnard 1992, published by Kogan Page

120 Interpersonal skills training activities

Evaluation The pairs reform at the end of the activity and discuss what they liked least and most about it. They also each give an evaluation of the other's performance.

Closing Participants should be offered a five-minute period in which to raise questions, express feelings, address particular people in the group or to talk through anything else that has arisen from the activity.

BRAINSTORMING

Activity 12

Time required 45 minutes to 1 hour.

Aim To encourage the generation of ideas about a particular topic.

Group size Any number between 5 and 25.

Environment A large room with chairs of equal height. Space enough to allow participants to pair off and then to reconvene. Smaller rooms can be used for the pairs activity if required.

Equipment A whiteboard, blackboard or flipchart to allow discussion points to be jotted down. (The board should not become a focal point of the session.) Chalk or markers for the board or flipchart. Prepared handouts where necessary.

Procedure This activity can be used as part of a larger learning encounter. The group divides into pairs and is given a topic on which to 'brainstorm'. Then, each person, in turn, free-associates about the topic in question while their partner jots down those associations. When one person feels that they have made as many associations as possible the roles are swapped. The figure below illustrates an example of one set of brainstormed jottings on the topic of counselling.

The trainer invites the group to reconvene. Then, a discussion is held about the activity. Two facets are discussed: the *process* of the activity (what it felt like to do it) and the *content* (what was talked about during the activity). As always, the process is more important than the content and, sometimes, the trainer may choose to discuss *only* the process. Also, the trainer helps the group to identify ways in which what has been learned from the activity can be related to

COUNSELLING

Done by professionals?

Involves listening.

Need to check my own listening skills.

Enjoy being listened to.

Eye contact is sometimes a problem for me.

I need to practise other counselling skills.

I need to consider what counselling skills there are.

I have read about counselling.

Carl Rogers.

Richard Nelson-Jones.

Counselling is not an academic topic.

More counselling skills workshops should be run by local schools and colleges.

I need to discuss the counselling process in *this* workshop.

© P. Burnard 1992, published by Kogan Page

the group members' professional or personal lives. The group trainer joins in wherever possible.

Evaluation The pairs reform at the end of the activity and discuss what they liked least and most about it. They also each give an evaluation of the other's performance.

Closing The trainer can invite questions about any aspect of the activity.

Notes This activity can be used with more than 25 participants if a certain amount of structure is used. One way of managing larger numbers is to draw up a handout that gives explicit instructions to participants. Then, sub-groups are formed from the larger group and a chairperson is elected for each of the sub-groups. The task of each chairperson is to work through the instruction sheet with their group and to ensure things run smoothly. After the activity has been completed by each of the sub-groups, the larger group reforms. The chairpeople report back to the larger group during the plenary session. Structure is essential if the serial working of sub-groups is to be effective. Make sure that everyone is clear about the aims of the activity and what it is that they are supposed to be doing. Headings for an instruction sheet might be:

- Title of the activity
- Aims
- What to do
- The role of the chairperson.

CO-COUNSELLING
Activity 13

Time required 45 minutes to 1 hour.

Aim To explore mutual support in a pairs format.

Group size Any number between 5 and 25.

Environment A large room with chairs of equal height. Space enough to allow participants to pair off and then to reconvene. Smaller rooms can be used for the pairs activity if required.

Equipment A whiteboard, blackboard or flipchart to allow discussion points to be jotted down. (The board should not become a focal point of the session.) Chalk or markers for the board or flipchart. Prepared handouts where necessary.

Procedure The group pairs off. One member of each pair begins to talk through any topic that is worrying them. The other member simply listens. The talker (or client) is encouraged to talk through any issue of their choice. The listener (or co-counsellor) only listens and does not comment, suggest, advise or even talk. After ten minutes, the pairs swap roles. The aim is to encourage the client to work through her own difficulties, in her own time and reach her own solutions. The activity can encourage the Rogerian notion of autonomy in counselling and is based on the idea of co-counselling, developed in the UK by John Heron (Heron 1977).

The trainer invites the group to reconvene. Then, a discussion is held about the activity. Two facets are discussed: the *process* of the activity (what it felt like to do it) and the *content* (what was talked about during the activity). As always, the process is more important than the content and, sometimes, the trainer may choose to discuss *only* the process. Also, the trainer helps the group to identify ways

in which what has been learned from the activity can be related to the group members' professional or personal lives. The group trainer joins in wherever possible.

Evaluation The pairs reform at the end of the activity and discuss what they liked least and most about it. They also each give an evaluation of the other's performance.

Closing Participants should be encouraged to spend a few minutes talking about their plans for the immediate future: holidays, weekend trips, social events and so forth. This allows for all participants to disassociate themselves from the activity and encourages them to return to their 'normal' roles.

Notes This activity can be used with more than 25 participants if a certain amount of structure is used. One way of managing larger numbers is to draw up a handout that gives explicit instructions to participants. Then, sub-groups are formed from the larger group and a chairperson is elected for each of the sub-groups. The task of each chairperson is to work through the instruction sheet with their group and to ensure things run smoothly. After the activity has been completed by each of the sub-groups, the larger group reforms. The chairpeople report back to the larger group during the plenary session. Structure is essential if the serial working of sub-groups is to be effective. Make sure that everyone is clear about the aims of the activity and what it is that they are supposed to be doing. Headings for an instruction sheet might be:

- Title of the activity
- Aims
- What to do
- The role of the chairperson.

This activity can usefully be prefaced by a short theory input on co-counselling (Burnard 1990, Heron 1977). In this way, the experiential learning cycle is being played out. First, the group receive some theory about the topic. Then, they test out that theory with an activity. Keep the theory input short. This can be used as a 'warm up' activity at different points during the course of a group or workshop, or to sharpen group members' attention.

© P. Burnard 1992, published by Kogan Page

LISTENING

Activity 14

Time required 45 minutes to 1 hour.

Aim To explore listening in a pairs format.

Group size Any number between 5 and 25.

Environment A large room with chairs of equal height. Space enough to allow participants to pair off and then to reconvene. Smaller rooms can be used for the pairs activity if required.

Equipment A whiteboard, blackboard or flipchart to allow discussion points to be jotted down. (The board should not become a focal point of the session.) Chalk or markers for the board or flipchart. Prepared handouts where necessary.

Procedure The group pairs off. One member of each pair is designated talker and the other listener. The trainer offers each pair a topic (a list of suggested topics is offered below). The task of the talker is to talk about the topic. The task of the listener is to listen and, occasionally, to prompt with a simple question. The aim is not to hold a conversation but to practise listening skills. After ten minutes, roles are reversed.

The trainer invites the larger group to reconvene. Then, a discussion is held about the activity. Two facets are discussed: the *process* of the activity (what it felt like to do it) and the *content* (what was talked about during the activity). As always, the process is more important than the content and, sometimes, the trainer may choose to discuss *only* the process. Also, the trainer helps the group to identify ways in which what has been learned from the activity can be related to the group members' professional or personal lives. The group trainer joins in wherever possible.

© P. Burnard 1992, published by Kogan Page

TOPICS FOR THE LISTENING ACTIVITY

Interests away from work

Music

Poetry

Things you dislike

People you like

Personal qualities

Humour

Bringing up children

Career and job prospects

Future plans

© P. Burnard 1992, published by Kogan Page

Evaluation The pairs reform at the end of the activity and discuss what they liked least and most about it. They also each give an evaluation of the other's performance.

Closing Participants should be offered a five-minute period in which to raise questions, express feelings, address particular people in the group or to talk through anything else that has arisen from the activity.

Notes This activity can be used with more than 25 participants if a certain amount of structure is used. One way of managing larger numbers is to draw up a handout that gives explicit instructions to participants. Then, sub-groups are formed from the larger group and a chairperson is elected for each of the sub-groups. The task of each chairperson is to work through the instruction sheet with their group and to ensure things run smoothly. After the activity has been completed by each of the sub-groups, the larger group reforms. The chairpeople report back to the larger group during the plenary session. Structure is essential if the serial working of sub-groups is to be effective. Make sure that everyone is clear about the aims of the activity and what it is that they are supposed to be doing. Headings for an instruction sheet might be:

- Title of the activity
- Aims
- What to do
- The role of the chairperson.

This activity can usefully be prefaced by a short theory input on listening. In this way, the experiential learning cycle is being played out. First, the group receive some theory about the topic. Then, they test out that theory with an activity. Keep the theory input short. This can be used as a 'warm up' activity at different points during the course of a group or workshop, or to sharpen group members' attention.

USING QUESTIONS
Activity 15

Time required 45 minutes to 1 hour.

Aim To explore the use of two types of questions in a pairs format.

Group size Any number between 5 and 25.

Environment A large room with chairs of equal height. Space enough to allow participants to pair off and then to reconvene. Smaller rooms can be used for the pairs activity if required.

Equipment A whiteboard, blackboard or flipchart to allow discussion points to be jotted down. (The board should not become a focal point of the session.) Chalk or markers for the board or flipchart. Prepared handouts which consist of a number of cards, all marked in the following way:

> **C.C.O.O.C.O.O.O.C.C.**

C. = Closed question;   O. = Open question

Procedure Group members pair off. The trainer hands out the prepared cards. One member of each pair acts as questioner and the other as talker. The questioner questions the talker in the above order, ie they ask a closed question, followed by another closed question, followed by an open question, and so on until the sequence of questions is completed. The sequence may be on any topic but the same topic is addressed by all of the questions. After the sequence

© P. Burnard 1992, published by Kogan Page

has been worked through, the pairs swap roles for another round of questioning, on a different topic.

For the purposes of this activity, a closed question is one to which there is a single word answer (often 'yes' or 'no') and an open question is one that allows the talker to elaborate. Here are some examples:

Closed questions
- What is your name?
- Do you live locally?
- How many children do you have?

Open questions
- What are you feeling at the moment?
- What are the best aspects of your job?
- What are your thoughts about ...?

The trainer invites the group to reconvene. Then, a discussion is held about the activity. Two facets are discussed: the *process* of the activity (what it felt like to do it) and the *content* (what was talked about during the activity). As always, the process is more important than the content and, sometimes, the trainer may choose to discuss *only* the process. Also, the trainer helps the group to identify ways in which what has been learned from the activity can be related to the group members' professional or personal lives. The group trainer joins in wherever possible.

Evaluation The pairs reform at the end of the activity and discuss what they liked least and most about it. They also each give an evaluation of the other's performance.

Closing Participants should be offered a five-minute period in which to raise questions, express feelings, address particular people in the group or to talk through anything else that has arisen from the activity.

Notes This activity can be used with more than 25 participants if a certain amount of structure is used. One way of managing larger

© P. Burnard 1992, published by Kogan Page

numbers is to draw up a handout that gives explicit instructions to participants. Then, sub-groups are formed from the larger group and a chairperson is elected for each of the sub-groups. The task of each chairperson is to work through the instruction sheet with their group and to ensure things run smoothly. After the activity has been completed by each of the sub-groups, the larger group reforms. The chairpeople report back to the larger group during the plenary session. Structure is essential if the serial working of sub-groups is to be effective. Make sure that everyone is clear about the aims of the activity and what it is that they are supposed to be doing. Headings for an instruction sheet might be:

- Title of the activity
- Aims
- What to do
- The role of the chairperson.

PAIRS INTERVIEW

Activity 16

Time required 45 minutes to 1 hour.

Aim To explore interviewing in a pairs format.

Group size Any number between 5 and 25.

Environment A large room with chairs of equal height. Space enough to allow participants to pair off and then to reconvene. Smaller rooms can be used for the pairs activity if required.

Equipment A whiteboard, blackboard or flipchart to allow discussion points to be jotted down. (The board should not become a focal point of the session.) Chalk or markers for the board or flipchart. Prepared handouts where necessary.

Procedure The group members pair off; one will act as 'interviewer', the other as 'interviewee'. They then split up for ten minutes in order to prepare an interview schedule, following which the pairs re-meet and the interviewers interview their partners for a further ten minutes. Then the pairs swap roles. After a further ten minutes, the pairs discuss their interviewing technique with each other, before rejoining the group. The aim is for both parties to give each other feedback about their interviewing style and competence.

The trainer invites the group to reconvene. Then, a discussion is held about the activity. Two facets are discussed: the *process* of the activity (what it felt like to do it) and the *content* (what was talked about during the activity). As always, the process is more important than the content and, sometimes, the trainer may choose to discuss *only* the process. Also, the trainer helps the group to identify ways in which what has been learned from the activity can be related to

the group members' professional or personal lives. The group trainer joins in wherever possible.

Evaluation The pairs reform at the end of the activity and discuss what they liked least and most about it. They also each give an evaluation of the other's performance.

Closing Participants should be offered a five-minute period in which to raise questions, express feelings, address particular people in the group or to talk through anything else that has arisen from the activity.

Notes This activity can be used with more than 25 participants if a certain amount of structure is used. One way of managing larger numbers is to draw up a handout that gives explicit instructions to participants. Then, sub-groups are formed from the larger group and a chairperson is elected for each of the sub-groups. The task of each chairperson is to work through the instruction sheet with their group and to ensure things run smoothly. After the activity has been completed by each of the sub-groups, the larger group reforms. The chairpeople report back to the larger group during the plenary session. Structure is essential if the serial working of sub-groups is to be effective. Make sure that everyone is clear about the aims of the activity and what it is that they are supposed to be doing. Headings for an instruction sheet might be:

- Title of the activity
- Aims
- What to do
- The role of the chairperson.

© P. Burnard 1992, published by Kogan Page

EXPLORATION OF TOPIC
Activity 17

Time required 45 minutes to 1 hour.

Aim To explore a topic in depth, in a pairs format.

Group size Any number between 5 and 25.

Environment A large room with chairs of equal height. Space enough to allow participants to pair off and then to reconvene. Smaller rooms can be used for the pairs activity if required.

Equipment A whiteboard, blackboard or flipchart to allow discussion points to be jotted down. (The board should not become a focal point of the session.) Chalk or markers for the board or flipchart. Prepared handouts where necessary.

Procedure The group divides into pairs. Each pair is allowed 20 minutes to explore a specific topic in depth. Their brief is to examine, in some detail, all aspects of that topic. It is important that each pair sticks to the topic and continues the exploration for the 20 minute period. They should note any tendency towards frustration, a tendency to go off the topic and towards silence. Topics can be chosen that do not appear to warrant detailed inspection of this sort. The activity then becomes one that highlights discipline and prolonged contemplation. Examples might include listening, self-awareness and prejudice.

The trainer invites the larger group to reconvene. Then, a discussion is held about the activity. Two facets are discussed: the *process* of the activity (what it felt like to do it) and the *content* (what was talked about during the activity). As always, the process is more important than the content and, sometimes, the trainer may choose to discuss *only* the process. Also, the trainer helps the group to identify ways in which what has been learned from the activity can be related to the group members' professional or personal lives. The group trainer joins in wherever possible.

Evaluation The pairs reform at the end of the activity and discuss what they liked least and most about it. They also each give an evaluation of the other's performance.

Closing Participants should be offered a five-minute period in which to raise questions, express feelings, address particular people in the group or to talk through anything else that has arisen from the activity.

Notes This activity can be used with more than 25 participants if a certain amount of structure is used. One way of managing larger numbers is to draw up a handout that gives explicit instructions to participants. Then, sub-groups are formed from the larger group and a chairperson is elected for each of the sub-groups. The task of each chairperson is to work through the instruction sheet with their group and to ensure things run smoothly. After the activity has been completed by each of the sub-groups, the larger group reforms. The chairpeople report back to the larger group during the plenary session. Structure is essential if the serial working of sub-groups is to be effective. Make sure that everyone is clear about the aims of the activity and what it is that they are supposed to be doing. Headings for an instruction sheet might be:

- Title of the activity
- Aims
- What to do
- The role of the chairperson.

This activity can be used to sharpen group members' attention during the course of a group or workshop.

© P. Burnard 1992, published by Kogan Page

SNOWBALLING
Activity 18

Time required 45 minutes to 1 hour.

Aim To explore a topic through frequent reformation of pairs.

Group size Any number between 8 and 25.

Environment A large room with chairs of equal height. Space enough to allow participants to pair off and then to reconvene. Smaller rooms can be used for the pairs activity if required.

Equipment A whiteboard, blackboard or flipchart to allow discussion points to be jotted down. (The board should not become a focal point of the session.) Chalk or markers for the board or flipchart. Prepared handouts where necessary.

Procedure The group pairs off. Each pair explores a topic in depth, as described in the previous activity. After ten minutes, one pair links up with the next nearest pair to form a group of four. After a further five minutes, the four link up with the next nearest four to form a larger group and discussion continues for a further five minutes. This process is continued until the larger group has reformed.

Then, a discussion is held about the activity. Two facets are discussed: the *process* of the activity (what it felt like to do it) and the *content* (what was talked about during the activity). As always, the process is more important than the content and, sometimes, the trainer may choose to discuss *only* the process. Also, the trainer helps the group to identify ways in which what has been learned from the activity can be related to the group members' professional or personal lives. The group trainer joins in wherever possible.

© P. Burnard 1992, published by Kogan Page

Evaluation The pairs reform at the end of the activity and discuss what they liked least and most about it. They also each give an evaluation of the other's performance.

Closing The trainer can invite questions about any aspect of the activity.

Notes This activity can be used with more than 25 participants if a certain amount of structure is used. One way of managing larger numbers is to draw up a handout that gives explicit instructions to participants. Then, sub-groups are formed from the larger group and a chairperson is elected for each of the sub-groups. The task of each chairperson is to work through the instruction sheet with their group and to ensure things run smoothly. After the activity has been completed by each of the sub-groups, the larger group reforms. The chairpeople report back to the larger group during the plenary session. Structure is essential if the serial working of sub-groups is to be effective. Make sure that everyone is clear about the aims of the activity and what it is that they are supposed to be doing. Headings for an instruction sheet might be:

- Title of the activity
- Aims
- What to do
- The role of the chairperson

© P. Burnard 1992, published by Kogan Page

SILENT PAIRS
Activity 19

Time required 45 minutes to 1 hour.

Aim To explore silence in a pairs format.

Group size Any number between 5 and 25.

Environment A large room with chairs of equal height. Space enough to allow participants to pair off and then to reconvene. Smaller rooms can be used for the pairs activity if required.

Equipment A whiteboard, blackboard or flipchart to allow discussion points to be jotted down. (The board should not become a focal point of the session.) Chalk or markers for the board or flipchart. Prepared handouts where necessary.

Procedure The group pairs off. Each pair sit opposite each other in silence for five minutes. They are encouraged to make eye contact. If required, they can be asked to sit holding each other's hands. The only rule is that everyone remain silent.

The trainer invites the larger group to reconvene. Then, a discussion is held about the activity. Two facets are discussed: the *process* of the activity (what it felt like to do it) and the *content* (what was communicated during the activity). As always, the process is more important than the content and, sometimes, the trainer may choose to discuss *only* the process. Also, the trainer helps the group to identify ways in which what has been learned from the activity can be related to the group members' professional or personal lives. The group trainer joins in wherever possible.

© P. Burnard 1992, published by Kogan Page

Evaluation The pairs reform at the end of the activity and discuss what they liked least and most about it. They also each give an evaluation of the other's performance.

Closing Participants should be encouraged to spend a few minutes talking about their plans for the immediate future: holidays, weekend trips, social events and so forth. This allows for all participants to disassociate themselves from the activity and encourages them to return to their 'normal' roles.

Notes This activity can be used with more than 25 participants if a certain amount of structure is used. One way of managing larger numbers is to draw up a handout that gives explicit instructions to participants. Then, sub-groups are formed from the larger group and a chairperson is elected for each of the sub-groups. The task of each chairperson is to work through the instruction sheet with their group and to ensure things run smoothly. After the activity has been completed by each of the sub-groups, the larger group reforms. The chairpeople report back to the larger group during the plenary session. Structure is essential if the serial working of sub-groups is to be effective. Make sure that everyone is clear about the aims of the activity and what it is that they are supposed to be doing. Headings for an instruction sheet might be:

- Title of the activity
- Aims
- What to do
- The role of the chairperson.

This activity can be used to sharpen group member's attention during the course of a group or workshop.

DON'T LISTEN
Activity 20

Time required 45 minutes to 1 hour.

Aim To explore problems in listening, in a pairs format.

Group size Any number between 5 and 25.

Environment A large room with chairs of equal height. Space enough to allow participants to pair off and then to reconvene. Smaller rooms can be used for the pairs activity if required.

Equipment A whiteboard, blackboard or flipchart to allow discussion points to be jotted down. (The board should not become a focal point of the session.) Chalk or markers for the board or flipchart. Prepared handouts where necessary.

Procedure The group pairs off. One person is nominated as 'A' and one as 'B' in each pair. 'A' then talks to 'B', for 5 minutes, about any topic, while 'B' *does not listen*. After the five minutes, the pairs swap roles and 'B' talks to 'A', while 'A' does not listen.

The trainer invites the larger group to reconvene. Then, a discussion is held about the activity. Two facets are discussed: the *process* of the activity (what it felt like to do it) and the *content* (what was talked about during the activity). As always, the process is more important than the content and, sometimes, the trainer may choose to discuss *only* the process. Also, the trainer helps the group to identify ways in which what has been learned from the activity can be related to the group members' professional or personal lives. The group trainer joins in wherever possible.

Evaluation The pairs reform at the end of the activity and discuss

© P. Burnard 1992, published by Kogan Page

what they liked least and most about it. They also each give an evaluation of the other's performance.

Closing Participants should be encouraged to spend a few minutes talking about their plans for the immediate future: holidays, weekend trips, social events and so forth. This allows for all participants to disassociate themselves from the activity and encourages them to return to their 'normal' roles.

Notes This activity can be used with more than 25 participants if a certain amount of structure is used. One way of managing larger numbers is to draw up a handout that gives explicit instructions to participants. Then, sub-groups are formed from the larger group and a chairperson is elected for each of the sub-groups. The task of each chairperson is to work through the instruction sheet with their group and to ensure things run smoothly. After the activity has been completed by each of the sub-groups, the larger group reforms. The chairpeople report back to the larger group during the plenary session. Structure is essential if the serial working of sub-groups is to be effective. Make sure that everyone is clear about the aims of the activity and what it is that they are supposed to be doing. Headings for an instruction sheet might be:

- Title of the activity
- Aims
- What to do
- The role of the chairperson.

Chapter 8:
Small group activities

USING SMALL GROUP ACTIVITIES

The small group is a frequently used vehicle for interpersonal skills training. The advantages are clear. People in groups get almost instant feedback about their ideas and behaviour. They are also able to discuss and debate what they feel about various aspects of interpersonal skills. Learning is usually easier in the company of other people – particularly when it comes to skills – and interpersonal skills are clearly about people. Thus the small group not only offers all these advantages but also can act as a microcosm of everyday life.

All the activities in this section are ones that involve the whole of the group working together. As with many of the other activities, they can be adapted to suit individual trainers and the needs of the moment. Initially, though, it is probably better to follow the instructions fairly carefully. As you become familiar with the way the activity runs, you can begin to adapt it.

ROGERIAN LISTENING

Activity 21

Time required 45 minutes to 1 hour.

Aim To enhance listening skills in a group context.

Group size Any number between 5 and 25.

Environment A large room in which people can sit comfortably in a group. Chairs should be of equal height and the group should remain in a closed circle throughout. The trainer should be part of the circle.

Equipment A whiteboard, blackboard or flipchart to allow discussion points to be jotted down. (The board should not become a focal point of the session.) Chalk or markers for the board or flipchart. Prepared handouts where necessary.

Procedure The trainer encourages a group discussion on any topic. The only ground rule for the discussion is that each participant may only speak once they have successfully summarized what the previous speaker has said. Thus, the first speaker in the discussion has complete freedom but after that each person must offer a short summing up of what was said by previous person. An example of part of such a discussion (on the development of assertiveness) might be as follows:

> 'I'm not so sure. I think that assertive people are sometimes rude. Sometimes I think that assertiveness is just another name for insulting people.'
> 'Ann has suggested that assertiveness can mean being rude to people. My feeling is that assertiveness is more often associated

with saying what you really mean and not being thrown off course by the other person.'

'Jane is saying that she thinks assertiveness is about staying on course and saying what it is you want to say. I just want to add that I think its important to . . .'

The group trainer joins in the activity wherever possible.

Evaluation The trainer hands out a prepared short questionnaire about the activity. The questionnaire should ask about:

- What it was like to take part in the activity,
- What feelings were invoked by the activity,
- What elements of it would be taken back to the workplace.

Closing Participants should be encouraged to spend a few minutes talking about their plans for the immediate future: holidays, weekend trips, social events and so forth. This allows for all participants to disassociate themselves from the activity a little and to encourage them to return to their 'normal' roles.

Notes This activity can usefully be prefaced by a short theory input on Rogerian counselling (Rogers 1967, Burnard 1989). In this way, the experiential learning cycle is being played out. First, the group receive some theory about the topic. Then, they test out that theory with an activity. Keep the theory input short.

This can be used as a 'warm up' activity at different points during the course of a group or workshop or to sharpen group members' attention.

BRAINSTORMING

Activity 22

Time required 45 minutes to 1 hour.

Aim To encourage the development of large numbers of ideas around a particular theme.

Group size Any number between 5 and 25.

Environment A large room in which people can sit comfortably in a group. Chairs should be of equal height and the group should remain in a closed circle throughout. The trainer should be part of the circle.

Equipment A whiteboard, blackboard or flipchart to allow discussion points to be jotted down. (The board should not become a focal point of the session.) Chalk or markers for the board or flipchart. Prepared handouts where necessary.

Procedure The group trainer helps in the election of a 'scribe' – a person who will write participants' contributions down on the whiteboard or flipchart sheet.

The trainer, having identified the topic for brainstorming, invites group members to call out any 'associations' that the topic invokes. Anything can be called out in this activity. The aim is to identify as many and varied contributions as possible. The role of the scribe is merely to note these down as the ideas are called out. The group should be asked to be sympathetic towards the scribe and to allow time to get the ideas on to the board or flipchart. This process can be continued either for a prescribed amount of time (perhaps 10 minutes) or until no other ideas are forthcoming.

© P. Burnard 1992, published by Kogan Page

146 Interpersonal skills training activities

After the brainstorming session, a number of options are open to the trainer and the group:

- a discussion can be held around the items generated;
- the items can be sorted into categories by the trainer with the help of the group;
- a number of 'key themes' can be pulled out of the list of items for further discussion.

This activity is particularly useful in the early stages of a workshop when basic concepts need to be explored. Here are some examples of how brainstorming may be used:

- At the start of a workshop on counselling, to explore participants definitions of what counselling might be.
- To explore feelings about an emotive topic.
- To help identify solutions to a problem that arises in a workshop.

Evaluation Each person in the group, in turn, says first what they liked least about the activity. Then, each person in the group says what they liked most about the activity. The group leader or trainer joins in too.

Closing Participants should be offered a five-minute period in which to raise questions, express feelings, address particular people in the group or to talk through anything else that has arisen from the activity.

NO CHAIRPERSON

Activity 23

Time required 45 minutes to 1 hour.

Aim To experience a leaderless group.

Group size Any number between 5 and 25.

Environment A large room in which people can sit comfortably in a group. Chairs should be of equal height and the group should remain in a closed circle throughout. The trainer should be part of the circle.

Equipment A whiteboard, blackboard or flipchart to allow discussion points to be jotted down. (The board should not become a focal point of the session.) Chalk or markers for the board or flipchart. Prepared handouts where necessary.

Procedure In this activity, the trainer points out that a discussion will take place but that she will neither chair nor facilitate it. She notes that it will start and finish at particular times and then leaves the group to fend for itself. The group has to find ways of coping with the organization of the discussion, without help from the trainer. This activity is particularly useful for exploring the role of the trainer or chairperson in a group setting. It also helps to identify and illustrate the group dynamics that can occur.

Evaluation The trainer invites each person in the group in turn to identify two things that they feel they learned from doing the activity.

Closing Participants should be offered a five-minute period in which to raise questions, express feelings, address particular people in the group or to talk through anything else that has arisen from the activity.

© P. Burnard 1992, published by Kogan Page

FISHBOWL

Activity 24

Time required 45 minutes to 1 hour.

Aim To experience a highly structured form of group discussion.

Group size Any number between 10 and 25.

Environment A large room in which people can sit comfortably in a group. Chairs should be of equal height and the group should remain in a closed circle throughout. The trainer should be part of the circle.

Equipment A whiteboard, blackboard or flipchart to allow discussion points to be jotted down. (The board should not become a focal point of the session.) Chalk or markers for the board or flipchart. Prepared handouts where necessary.

Procedure Two circles of chairs are set up, one smaller circle of six chairs within another, larger, circle. Initially, four people sit in the inner circle and the rest sit in the outer. The trainer also sits in the inner circle. A discussion on any topic is invoked among the people sitting in the inner circle.

Three rules apply to the conduct of the discussion: (1) at all times, there must be one empty chair in the inner circle; (2) in order to speak, a person must be sitting in the inner circle; (3) a person in the inner circle may leave it to sit in the outer circle at any time during the discussion. In this way, there is a fairly frequent coming and going between the two circles. Participants have to exercise judgement about when to leave and join the discussion. They can also switch between being active participants and observers. This activity is a valuable one for exploring all aspects of small group life.

© P. Burnard 1992, published by Kogan Page

Evaluation Each person in the group, in turn, says first what they liked least about the activity. Then, each person in the group says what they liked most about the activity. The group leader or trainer joins in too.

Closing Participants should be offered a five-minute period in which to raise questions, express feelings, address particular people in the group or to talk through anything else that has arisen from the activity.

© P. Burnard 1992, published by Kogan Page

GROUND RULES
Activity 25

Time required 45 minutes to 1 hour.

Aim To experience a group discussion using a set of specific ground rules.

Group size Any number between 5 and 25.

Environment A large room in which people can sit comfortably in a group. Chairs should be of equal height and the group should remain in a closed circle throughout. The trainer should be part of the circle.

Equipment A whiteboard, blackboard or flipchart to allow discussion points to be jotted down. (The board should not become a focal point of the session.) Chalk or markers for the board or flipchart. Prepared handouts where necessary.

Procedure A discussion is invoked, on any topic, and the following ground rules are observed throughout the discussion:

- Own your statements: say 'I' rather than 'you', 'we' or 'people'. For example, it is permissible to say 'I feel angry about what is happening here' but not permissible to say 'this sort of thing makes people angry'. This rule encourages people to speak for themselves.
- Speak directly to other people in the group, rather than about them. For example, it is acceptable to say 'I don't agree with you, David'. It is not acceptable to say 'I don't agree with what David is saying.' This encourages people to be more direct.
- Listen to other people and don't interrupt them.

© P. Burnard 1992, published by Kogan Page

- Try to remain in the present. Thus, 'I am feeling uncomfortable ...' is better than saying 'I have felt uncomfortable in situations like this ...' This helps people to avoid drifting into the past or speculating about the future.
- Take some risks in disclosing what you really feel about the topic.

These ground rules can be used as an end in themselves. They can bring to the surface all sorts of aspects of group dynamics and group life. Alternatively, they can be used within other group activities to sharpen the edge of the discussion and to make participants more aware of what they are saying and doing. The group trainer joins in wherever possible.

Evaluation Each person in the group, in turn, says first what they liked least about the activity. Then, each person in the group says what they liked most about the activity. The group leader or trainer joins in too.

Closing Participants should be encouraged to spend a few minutes talking about their plans for the immediate future: holidays, weekend trips, social events and so forth. This allows for all participants to disassociate themselves from the activity and encourages them to return to their 'normal' roles.

Notes This can be used as a 'warm up' activity at different points during the course of a group or workshop. The following page offers a copy of the ground rules in the format of a handout for participants.

© P. Burnard 1992, published by Kogan Page

GROUND RULES

During this activity, you are asked to observe the following ground rules which are designed to enhance communication within the group. Try to stick to them as closely as you can and notice when you or a colleague breaks them.

- Own your statements: say 'I' rather than 'you', 'we' or 'people'. For example, it is permissible to say 'I feel angry about what is happening here' but not permissible to say 'this sort of thing makes people angry'.
- Speak directly to other people in the group, rather than *about* them. For example, it is acceptable to say 'I don't agree with you, David'. It is not acceptable to say 'I don't agree with what David is saying'.
- Listen to other people and don't interrupt them.
- Try to remain in the present. Thus, 'I am feeling uncomfortable...' is better than saying 'I have felt uncomfortable in situations like this.'
- Take some risks in disclosing what you really feel.

© P. Burnard 1992, published by Kogan Page

FREE FOR ALL
Activity 26

Time required 45 minutes to 1 hour.

Aim To explore an anarchic style of group membership.

Group size Any number between 5 and 25.

Environment A large room in which people can sit comfortably in a group. Chairs should be of equal height and the group should remain in a closed circle throughout. The trainer should be part of the circle.

Equipment A whiteboard, blackboard or flipchart to allow discussion points to be jotted down. (The board should not become a focal point of the session.) Chalk or markers for the board or flipchart. Prepared handouts where necessary.

Procedure A discussion is invoked by the trainer and the only rule that applies is that group members can say what they like, when they like, and can behave as they like! It is usual, at first, for group members to act very cautiously until they realize that the usual norms of group life can be ignored. Trainers who are new to this activity might want to limit its running to about 15 minutes. The group trainer joins in wherever possible and may want to act as a 'perverse role model'.

Evaluation The trainer invites each person in the group in turn to identify two things that they feel they learned from doing the activity.

Closing Participants should be encouraged to spend a few minutes talking about their plans for the immediate future: holidays,

© P. Burnard 1992, published by Kogan Page

weekend trips, social events and so forth. This allows for all participants to disassociate themselves from the activity and encourages them to return to their 'normal' roles.

Notes This activity can be used to sharpen group members' attention during the course of a group or workshop.

ALTERNATING CHAIR
Activity 27

Time required 45 minutes to 1 hour.

Aim To encourage group participants to explore both sides of personal issues.

Group size Any number between 5 and 25.

Environment A large room in which people can sit comfortably in a group. Chairs should be of equal height and the group should remain in a closed circle throughout. The trainer should be part of the circle.

Equipment A whiteboard, blackboard or flipchart to allow discussion points to be jotted down. (The board should not become a focal point of the session.) Chalk or markers for the board or flipchart. Prepared handouts where necessary.

Procedure This is a highly structured group activity. The trainer invokes a discussion on an emotive or personal topic, after consultation with group participants. As the discussion unfolds, the trainer periodically invites group members to speak for both sides of a debatable issue, utilizing two chairs. The chair that the person is sitting on in the discussion is the chair from which that person makes the initial point. On invitation from the trainer, the person switches to another chair and makes *exactly the opposite point*. The trainer then invites the person to return to the original chair and make a decision about which of the two points of view is now preferred. An example of a typical 'dialogue' is as follows:

Client: 'I don't think that everyone needs counselling skills. Its a

professional thing. We shouldn't meddle in things we don't know much about.'
Trainer: 'Right. Swap chairs and try saying the opposite.'
Client: 'I think we should all have counselling skills. They are common-or-garden skills that come naturally to most people.'
Trainer: 'Come back to your main chair. What are your thoughts, now?'
Client: 'Odd! I think that counselling skills probably *are* common to most people!'

Evaluation Each person in the group, in turn, says first what they liked least about the activity. Then, each person in the group says what they liked most about the activity. The group leader or trainer joins in too.

Closing Participants should be encouraged to spend a few minutes talking about their plans for the immediate future: holidays, weekend trips, social events and so forth. This allows for all participants to disassociate themselves from the activity and encourages them to return to their 'normal' roles.

HOTSEAT
Activity 28

Time required 45 minutes to 1 hour.

Aim To encourage people to get to know each other better and to practise asking questions in a group setting.

Group size Any number between 5 and 25.

Environment A large room in which people can sit comfortably in a group. Chairs should be of equal height and the group should remain in a closed circle throughout. The trainer should be part of the circle.

Equipment No special equipment is required.

Procedure The participants follow these instructions:

- Each person has two minutes in the 'hotseat'.
- While in the hotseat (which may be either their own seat or one placed in the centre of the circle) they can be asked questions, on any subject, by other members of the group.
- Any question that a person does not wish to answer may be avoided with 'pass'.
- After two minutes, the person in the hotseat nominates another member of the group to take his place.
- This cycle of events continues until everyone in the group has spent two minutes in the hotseat.

The group trainer joins in wherever possible (including two minutes in the hotseat).

© P. Burnard 1992, published by Kogan Page

Evaluation Each person in the group, in turn, says first what they liked least about the activity. Then, each person in the group says what they liked most about the activity. The group leader or trainer joins in too.

Closing Participants should be offered a five-minute period in which to raise questions, express feelings, address particular people in the group or to talk through anything else that has arisen from the activity.

Notes This can be used as a 'warm up' activity at different points during the course of a group or workshop or to sharpen group members' attention.

QUAKER GROUP
Activity 29

Time required 45 minutes to 1 hour.

Aim To explore a particular style of group decision-making.

Group size Any number between 5 and 25.

Environment A large room in which people can sit comfortably in a group. Chairs should be of equal height and the group should remain in a closed circle throughout. The trainer should be part of the circle.

Equipment No special equipment is required.

Procedure This activity is specifically for use as a decision-making enterprise. The issue over which a decision needs to be reached is identified. Group participants are then invited to make suggestions as to how the issue may be resolved. Ideas are raised until no further suggestions are floated. Once this has occurred, the last idea that was raised is the one that carries as the decision. Here is an example of this democratic decision-making process. The group are trying to solve the question of whether or not there should be a follow-up workshop after the current one...

> 'I propose that we all meet, on a regular basis, every other weekend, perhaps informally.'
> 'I think we should make do with this workshop. This should be enough for most of us.'
> 'I propose that we meet at someone's house, in a couple of weeks' time.'
> 'I suggest that we have a half-day study day in six months' time, once we have had the chance of trying out some of the ideas we have picked up.'

© P. Burnard 1992, published by Kogan Page

As no one else speaks after the final contribution this last suggestion becomes the final decision. The group trainer joins in wherever possible.

Evaluation The trainer invites each person in the group, in turn, to identify two things that they feel they learned from doing the activity.

Closing The trainer can invite questions about any aspect of the activity.

BODY LANGUAGE
Activity 30

Time required 45 minutes to 1 hour.

Aim To explore body language in a group setting.

Group size Any number between 5 and 25.

Environment A large room in which people can sit comfortably in a group. Chairs should be of equal height and the group should remain in a closed circle throughout. The trainer should be part of the circle.

Equipment No special equipment is required.

Procedure While it is probably very difficult to generalize about what we are really 'saying' with our body language, it is useful to explore people's perceptions of various sorts of non-verbal communication. In this activity, the group participants sit silently in a circle. A volunteer is then invited to 'arrange' other people in the group, to make them look more comfortable; for example, the volunteer may unfold another person's arms, push their shoulders down a little or move their head to one side. After two or three 'arrangements' of this sort, the trainer invites a discussion about how those arrangements looked and felt to everybody. The group trainer joins in wherever possible.

Evaluation A discussion is invoked by the trainer about how any learning from the activity could be carried back to the workplace.

Closing Participants should be offered a five-minute period in which to raise questions, express feelings, address particular people in the group or to talk through anything else that has arisen from the activity.

© P. Burnard 1992, published by Kogan Page

Notes This activity can usefully be prefaced by a short theory input on non-verbal communication (Argyle 1975). In this way, the experiential learning cycle is being played out. First, the group receive some theory about the topic. Then, they test out that theory with an activity. Keep the theory input short.

Chapter 9:
Exploring eye contact

USING EYE CONTACT ACTIVITIES

We all use eye contact in interpersonal relationships. It seems to be one of the few universal forms of communication. It is also one of the most rarely discussed. All the activities in this section concentrate on the issue of eye contact. Necessarily, such activities can be embarrassing. For whatever reason, we usually find the idea of discussing and analysing eye contact difficult. Allow, then, for considerable nervous laughter during the initial stages of using these activities. The best way to handle this is to allow it or even to encourage it. One thing is for sure: you cannot attempt to proscribe it. As group members get more comfortable with discussing eye contact, they usually find they relax and the topic becomes less embarrassing. This is not always so: some people continue to find it difficult. As ever, the trainer needs to act as a role model here. If he or she is relaxed and reasonably comfortable with the issue, they are likely to convey this to the group.

NO EYE CONTACT
Activity 31

Time required 45 minutes to 1 hour.

Aim To explore the importance of eye contact.

Group size Any number between 5 and 25.

Environment A large room with chairs of equal height. Space enough to allow participants to pair off and then to reconvene. Smaller rooms can be used for the pairs activity if required.

Equipment A whiteboard, blackboard or flipchart to allow discussion points to be jotted down. (The board should not become a focal point of the session.) Chalk or markers for the board or flipchart. Prepared handouts where necessary.

Procedure The group members pair off. They are then instructed to hold a two-way conversation during which time they do not make eye contact.

The trainer invites the group to reconvene. Then, a discussion is held about the activity. Two facets are discussed: the *process* of the activity (what it felt like to do it) and the *content* (what was talked about during the activity). As always, the process is more important than the content and, sometimes, the trainer may choose to discuss *only* the process. Also, the trainer helps the group to identify ways in which what has been learned from the activity can be related to the group members' professional or personal lives. The group trainer joins in wherever possible.

Evaluation Each person in the group, in turn, says first what they liked least about the activity. Then, each person in the group says

what they liked most about the activity. The group leader or trainer joins in too.

Closing Participants should be encouraged to spend a few minutes talking about their plans for the immediate future: holidays, weekend trips, social events and so forth. This allows for all participants to disassociate themselves from the activity and encourages them to return to their 'normal' roles.

Notes This activity can be used with more than 25 participants if a certain amount of structure is used. One way of managing larger numbers is to draw up a handout that gives explicit instructions to participants. Then, sub-groups are formed from the larger group and a chairperson is elected for each of the sub-groups. The task of each chairperson is to work through the instruction sheet with their group and to ensure things run smoothly. After the activity has been completed by each of the sub-groups, the larger group reforms. The chairpeople report back to the larger group during the plenary session. Structure is essential if the serial working of sub-groups is to be effective. Make sure that everyone is clear about the aims of the activity and what it is that they are supposed to be doing. Headings for an instruction sheet might be:

- Title of the activity
- Aims
- What to do
- The role of the chairperson.

CENTRING

Activity 32

Time required 45 minutes to 1 hour.

Aim To explore the concepts of 'centring'.

Group size Any number between 5 and 25.

Environment A large room with chairs of equal height. Space enough to allow participants to pair off and then to reconvene. Smaller rooms can be used for the pairs activity if required.

Equipment A whiteboard, blackboard or flipchart to allow discussion points to be jotted down. (The board should not become a focal point of the session.) Chalk or markers for the board or flipchart. Prepared handouts where necessary.

Procedure The idea of 'centring' involves feeling contained, comfortable with yourself and not 'thrown' by the other person. To be centred is to be in control of yourself, to feel that you are not being manipulated by the other person, nor particularly uncomfortable in their presence. For this activity, group members pair off and sit opposite each other, with their eyes closed. They are encouraged to take stock of themselves, take some deep breaths and concentrate on settling down. It is then suggested that as they begin to feel more centred, they open their eyes and meet the gaze of their partner. If they find themselves uncomfortable, or somehow thrown off-centre by the other person, they close their eyes again and re-gather themselves. This activity continues until both parties, in each pair, is comfortable sitting quietly with their partners.

The trainer invites the group to reconvene. Then, a discussion is held about the activity. Two facets are discussed: the *process* of the

activity (what it felt like to do it) and the *content* (what was talked about during the activity). As always, the process is more important than the content and, sometimes, the trainer may choose to discuss *only* the process. Also, the trainer helps the group to identify ways in which what has been learned from the activity can be related to the group members' professional or personal lives. The group trainer joins in wherever possible.

Evaluation Each person in the group, in turn, says first what they liked least about the activity. Then, each person in the group says what they liked most about the activity. The group leader or trainer joins in too.

Closing Participants should be encouraged to spend a few minutes talking about their plans for the immediate future: holidays, weekend trips, social events and so forth. This allows for all participants to disassociate themselves from the activity and encourages them to return to their 'normal' roles.

Notes This can be used as a 'warm up' activity at different points during the course of a group or workshop.

© P. Burnard 1992, published by Kogan Page

SUSTAINED EYE CONTACT

Activity 33

Time required 45 minutes to 1 hour.

Aim To explore eye contact.

Group size Any number between 5 and 25.

Environment A large room with chairs of equal height. Space enough to allow participants to pair off and then to reconvene. Smaller rooms can be used for the pairs activity if required.

Equipment A whiteboard, blackboard or flipchart to allow discussion points to be jotted down. (The board should not become a focal point of the session.) Chalk or markers for the board or flipchart. Prepared handouts where necessary.

Procedure This is a modification of the children's game. The group pairs off and each pair sit facing each other, in silence. Their task is to sit making sustained eye contact with each other. Participants should note the point at which such sustained gazing is broken. An alternative to this activity is to allow partners to talk to each other while they make sustained eye contact.

The trainer invites the group to reconvene. Then, a discussion is held about the activity. Two facets are discussed: the *process* of the activity (what it felt like to do it) and the *content* (what was talked about during the activity). As always, the process is more important than the content and, sometimes, the trainer may choose to discuss *only* the process. Also, the trainer helps the group to identify ways in which what has been learned from the activity can be related to

the group members' professional or personal lives. The group trainer joins in wherever possible.

Evaluation The pairs reform at the end of the activity and discuss what they liked least and most about it. They also each give an evaluation of the other's performance.

Closing Participants should be encouraged to spend a few minutes talking about their plans for the immediate future: holidays, weekend trips, social events and so forth. This allows for all participants to disassociate themselves from the activity and encourages them to return to their 'normal' roles.

Notes This activity can be used with more than 25 participants if a certain amount of structure is used. One way of managing larger numbers is to draw up a handout that gives explicit instructions to participants. Then, sub-groups are formed from the larger group and a chairperson is elected for each of the sub-groups. The task of each chairperson is to work through the instruction sheet with their group and to ensure things run smoothly. After the activity has been completed by each of the sub-groups, the larger group reforms. The chairpeople report back to that larger group during the plenary session. Structure is essential if the serial working of sub-groups is to be effective. Make sure that everyone is clear about the aims of the activity and what it is that they are supposed to be doing. Headings for an instruction sheet might be:

- Title of the activity
- Aims
- What to do
- The role of the chairperson.

This activity can be used to sharpen group members' attention during the course of a group or workshop.

© P. Burnard 1992, published by Kogan Page

GROUP EYE CONTACT
Activity 34

Time required 45 minutes to 1 hour.

Aim To explore eye contact in a group context.

Group size Any number between 5 and 25.

Environment A large room in which people can sit comfortably in a group. Chairs should be of equal height and the group should remain in a closed circle throughout. The trainer should be part of the circle.

Equipment A whiteboard, blackboard or flipchart to allow discussion points to be jotted down. (The board should not become a focal point of the session.) Chalk or markers for the board or flipchart. Prepared handouts where necessary.

Procedure The trainer explains the activity to the group. One person turns their head and makes eye contact with the next person. After a few moments, that person turns *their* head and makes eye contact with the next person and so on, around the group. This 'round' of eye contact is conducted in silence and allowed to continue two of three times around the group. The group trainer joins in wherever possible.

Evaluation The trainer invites each person in the group, in turn, to identify two things that they feel they learned from doing the activity.

Closing Participants should be offered a five-minute period in which to raise questions, express feelings, address particular people

© P. Burnard 1992, published by Kogan Page

in the group or to talk through anything else that has arisen from the activity.

Notes This activity can be used to sharpen group members' attention during the course of a group or workshop.

TALKING AND EYE CONTACT

Activity 35

Time required 45 minutes to 1 hour.

Aim To explore eye contact in group discussion.

Group size Any number between 5 and 25.

Environment A large room with chairs of equal height.

Equipment A whiteboard, blackboard or flipchart to allow discussion points to be jotted down. (The board should not become a focal point of the session.) Chalk or markers for the board or flipchart. Prepared handouts where necessary.

Procedure The group trainer invokes a discussion on any topic. The only instruction that is given is for participants to become acutely aware of the eye contact they do or do not make. Particularly, people are asked to think about when they *begin* eye contact, when they *stop it* and when they *avoid* it. The trainer joins in wherever possible. After the activity is over, the trainer encourages a discussion about the use of eye contact in group and individual discussion.

Evaluation The pairs reform at the end of the activity and discuss what they liked least and most about it. They also each give an evaluation of the other's performance.

Closing The trainer can invite questions about any aspect of the activity.

© P. Burnard 1992, published by Kogan Page

SILENT GAZING
Activity 36

Time required 45 minutes to 1 hour.

Aim To explore eye contact in a group context.

Group size Any number between 5 and 25.

Environment A large room with chairs of equal height. Space enough to allow participants to pair off and then to reconvene. Smaller rooms can be used for the pairs activity if required.

Equipment A whiteboard, blackboard or flipchart to allow discussion points to be jotted down. (The board should not become a focal point of the session.) Chalk or markers for the board or flipchart. Prepared handouts where necessary.

Procedure The group sits in silence, each member trying to sustain eye contact with others through a period of ten minutes. Eye contact once established, should be acknowledged in some way (perhaps by a nod of the head) before the pair move on to pick up eye contact with other people. The group trainer joins in wherever possible.

Evaluation Each person in the group, in turn, says first what they liked least about the activity. Then, each person in the group says what they liked most about the activity. The group leader or trainer joins in too.

Closing Participants should be offered a five-minute period in which to raise questions, express feelings, address particular people in the group or to talk through anything else that has arisen from the activity.

Notes This can be used as a 'warm up' activity at different points during the course of a group or workshop.

© P. Burnard 1992, published by Kogan Page

WHAT THE EYES SAY
Activity 37

Time required 45 minutes to 1 hour.

Aim To explore how group members interpret other people's use of eye contact.

Group size Any number between 5 and 25.

Environment A large room with chairs of equal height. Space enough to allow participants to pair off and then to reconvene. Smaller rooms can be used for the pairs activity if required.

Equipment A whiteboard, blackboard or flipchart to allow discussion points to be jotted down. (The board should not become a focal point of the session.) Chalk or markers for the board or flipchart. Prepared handouts where necessary.

Procedure First, the group pairs off and pairs sit opposite one another. Then the pairs hold a discussion with one another on a topic chosen either by them or by the trainer. This continues for five minutes, after which the pairs discuss what each other's eyes were 'saying'. Thus, the discussion is about how each member of the pair perceives the other person's use of eye contact.

The trainer invites the group to reconvene. Then, a discussion is held about the activity. Two facets are discussed: the *process* of the activity (what it felt like to do it) and the *content* (what was talked about during the activity). As always, the process is more important than the content and, sometimes, the trainer may choose to discuss *only* the process. Also, the trainer helps the group to identify ways in which what has been learned from the activity can be related to the group members' professional or personal lives. The group trainer joins in wherever possible.

© P. Burnard 1992, published by Kogan Page

Evaluation The trainer invites each person in the group, in turn, to identify two things that they feel they learned from doing the activity.

Closing Participants should be offered a five-minute period in which to raise questions, express feelings, address particular people in the group or to talk through anything else that has arisen from the activity.

Notes This activity can be used to sharpen group members' attention during the course of a group or workshop.

EYE CONTACT IN EVERYDAY LIFE

Activity 38

Time required 45 minutes to 1 hour.

Aim To explore the use of eye contact in everyday life.

Group size Any number between 5 and 25.

Environment A large room with chairs of equal height. Space enough to allow participants to pair off and then to reconvene. Smaller rooms can be used for the pairs activity if required.

Equipment A whiteboard, blackboard or flipchart to allow discussion points to be jotted down. (The board should not become a focal point of the session.) Chalk or markers for the board or flipchart. Prepared handouts where necessary.

Procedure The group pairs off. Once in pairs, the members discuss the following issues:

- when people avoid making eye contact;
- when people make sustained eye contact;
- how I feel about eye contact;
- how I use eye contact.

The trainer invites the group to reconvene. Then, a discussion is held about the activity. Two facets are discussed: the *process* of the activity (what it felt like to do it) and the *content* (what was talked about during the activity). As always, the process is more important than the content and, sometimes, the trainer may choose to discuss *only* the process. Also, the trainer helps the group to identify ways

© P. Burnard 1992, published by Kogan Page

in which what has been learned from the activity can be related to the group members' professional or personal lives. The group trainer joins in wherever possible.

Evaluation The trainer invites each person in the group, in turn, to identify two things that they feel they learned from doing the activity.

Closing Participants should be offered a five-minute period in which to raise questions, express feelings, address particular people in the group or to talk through anything else that has arisen from the activity.

© P. Burnard 1992, published by Kogan Page

RECORDING
Activity 39

Time required 45 minutes to 1 hour.

Aim To explore the use of eye contact in pairs, using a structured method.

Group size Any number between 5 and 25.

Environment A large room with chairs of equal height. Space enough to allow participants to pair off and then to reconvene. Smaller rooms can be used for the pairs activity if required.

Equipment A whiteboard, blackboard or flipchart to allow discussion points to be jotted down. (The board should not become a focal point of the session.) Chalk or markers for the board or flipchart. Prepared handouts where necessary.

Procedure The group pairs off. Each person is given a handout containing a chart which allows them to record the other person's eye movements (see below). The pair hold a conversation. For the first five minutes, one of each pair records the eye movements of the other. A mark is made on the sheet every time a change of direction is made. Crosses are used to indicate that a change of direction has occurred, as illustrated in the chart. After five minutes, the pair swap roles.

The trainer invites the group to reconvene. Then, a discussion is held about the activity. Two facets are discussed: the *process* of the activity (what it felt like to do it) and the *content* (what was talked about during the activity). As always, the process is more important than the content and, sometimes, the trainer may choose to discuss *only* the process. Also, the trainer helps the group to identify ways

© P. Burnard 1992, published by Kogan Page

in which what has been learned from the activity can be related to the group members' professional or personal lives. The group trainer joins in wherever possible.

Evaluation A discussion is invoked by the trainer about how any learning from the activity could be carried back to the workplace.

Closing The trainer can invite questions about any aspect of the activity.

Eyes move up, left	Eyes move up, right
XXXXXX	XX
Eye contact made with partner XXXXXXXXXXXXXXXXXXXXXXX	
Eyes move down, left	Eyes move down, right
XXX	XXXXXXX

© P. Burnard 1992, published by Kogan Page

180 Interpersonal skills training activities

EYE MOVEMENTS
Activity 40

Time required 45 minutes to 1 hour.

Aim To explore the possible significance of eye movements.

Group size Any number between 5 and 25.

Environment A large room with chairs of equal height.

Equipment A whiteboard, blackboard or flipchart to allow discussion points to be jotted down. (The board should not become a focal point of the session.) Chalk or markers for the board or flipchart. Prepared handouts where necessary.

Procedure The trainer asks for a volunteer from the group. He then asks that person to listen to the following statements and invites the group to observe that person's eyes. The statements are as follows:

- I want you to picture yourself wearing a blue hat.
- Now I want you to imagine that someone has put her arms around you.
- I want you to 'hear' the sound of an ambulance siren.
- Picture yourself at a fair.
- Try to hear the sound of a church bell.
- Imagine the person next to you holding your hand.

The trainer then invites the group to discuss what happened to the volunteer's eyes while considering each of the statements. Modifying the work of Bandler and Grinder (1979) it is possible to offer a tentative 'map' of what happens to people's eyes when they are considering certain things. The diagram, below, illustrates such eye movement. The trainer uses this diagram, on a handout, to initiate

© P. Burnard 1992, published by Kogan Page

a discussion about whether or not this map holds true for what they have observed during this activity. A discussion is also held about how noting such eye movements might be useful in interpersonal relationships. For examples, noting the downward movement of eyes may make a person aware that someone is upset by the conversation while an upward movement of the eyes may denote that the other person is 'picturing' what is being talked about. This can help to reaffirm that the one doing the 'picturing' understands what is being talked about.

Evaluation The trainer invites each person in the group, in turn, to identify two things that they feel they learned from doing the activity.

Closing Participants should be encouraged to spend a few minutes talking about their plans for the immediate future: holidays, weekend trips, social events and so forth. This allows for all participants to disassociate themselves from the activity and encourages them to return to their 'normal' roles.

Eyes looking up : person 'picturing' things	
Eyes looking left : person 'hearing' things	Eyes looking right : person 'hearing' things
Eyes look down : person 'feeling' things	

© P. Burnard 1992, published by Kogan Page

Chapter 10:
Exploring feelings

EXPLORING FEELINGS IN A GROUP

The affective or 'feelings' domain is an important one in the interpersonal skills field. We need to remain sensitive both to our own feelings and to those of others with whom we interact. In difficult interpersonal encounters, feelings can run high. It is only by reflecting on our own feelings that we can learn to cope effectively with those of others. The activities in this chapter all encourage group members to discuss and explore their feelings. None, though, are of the 'psychotherapy' sort. It seems to me to be an important principle that interpersonal skills training is *not* therapy. Also, it is with these activities that the concept of debriefing, discussed in Chapter 2, is important. When feelings are stirred up to any degree, it is important to allow time after the activity for people to be able to discuss what they felt during, and any residual feelings left over from, the activity.

BRAINSTORMING FEELINGS

Activity 41

Time required 45 minutes to 1 hour.

Aim To explore the range of feelings in a group context.

Group size Any number between 5 and 25.

Environment A large room in which people can sit comfortably in a group. Chairs should be of equal height and the group should remain in a closed circle throughout. The trainer should be part of the circle.

Equipment A whiteboard, blackboard or flipchart to allow discussion points to be jotted down. (The board should not become a focal point of the session.) Chalk or markers for the board or flipchart. Prepared handouts where necessary.

Procedure The group trainer invites one member to act as 'scribe'. The scribe's task is to write down all of the items generated by the group throughout this activity. The group is then invited to call out words that describe 'feelings'. Nothing is to be excluded: all words are permissible. At the end of a prescribed time or when no further words are forthcoming, the trainer helps the group to organize the words into categories of feeling. In this way, a considerable range of feelings can be identified and explored in discussion. Examples of categories might be positive feelings, negative feelings, common feelings, unusual feelings, difficult feelings, etc.

Evaluation A discussion is invoked by the trainer about how any learning from the activity could be carried back to the workplace.

© P. Burnard 1992, published by Kogan Page

184 Interpersonal skills training activities

Closing Participants should be encouraged to spend a few minutes talking about their plans for the immediate future: holidays, weekend trips, social events and so forth. This allows for all participants to disassociate themselves from the activity and encourages them to return to their 'normal' roles.

Notes This can be used as a 'warm up' activity at different points during the life of a group or workshop.

FEELING WORDS
Activity 42

Time required 45 minutes to 1 hour.

Aim To explore individuals' reactions to certain feelings.

Group size Any number between 5 and 25.

Environment A large room in which people can sit comfortably in a group. Chairs should be of equal height and the group should remain in a closed circle throughout. The trainer should be part of the circle.

Equipment A whiteboard, blackboard or flipchart to allow discussion points to be jotted down. (The board should not become a focal point of the session.) Chalk or markers for the board or flipchart. Prepared handouts where necessary.

Procedure The group trainer hands out a prepared list of 'feelings'. This could be drawn from the list generated by the previous activity or developed by the trainer. Each person is invited to tick each feeling that he or she has experienced at some time. When everyone has completed this stage of the activity, group participants are asked to turn to the person next to them and compare notes. After a further five minutes, the group reconvenes and a discussion is held about the nature and expression of feelings. The group trainer joins in wherever possible.

Evaluation Each person in the group, in turn, says first what they liked least about the activity. Then, each person in the group says what they liked most about the activity. The group leader or trainer joins in too.

© P. Burnard 1992, published by Kogan Page

Closing Participants should be offered a five-minute period in which to raise questions, express feelings, address particular people in the group or to talk through anything else that has arisen from the activity.

EXPRESSING FEELINGS

Activity 43

Time required 45 minutes to 1 hour.

Aim To explore group participants' views about the release of emotion.

Group size Any number between 5 and 25.

Environment A large room in which people can sit comfortably in a group. Chairs should be of equal height and the group should remain in a closed circle throughout. The trainer should be part of the circle.

Equipment A whiteboard, blackboard or flipchart to allow discussion points to be jotted down. (The board should not become a focal point of the session.) Chalk or markers for the board or flipchart. Prepared handouts where necessary.

Procedure The trainer leads a discussion on the topic 'Coping with Feelings'. Group members are encouraged to talk about the following issues:

- What sorts of feelings is it commonly acceptable to express?
- What are the easiest feelings to cope with when another person expresses them?
- What feelings do *you* have difficulty with?

In this way, the discussion moves from the general and open to the specific and personal. No one should feel compelled to join in the discussion. An easy, light atmosphere is best – if the atmosphere gets too heavy and emotional, the discussion is likely to dry up. Group members' feelings will get in the way of the discussion.

© P. Burnard 1992, published by Kogan Page

Evaluation The trainer invites each person in the group, in turn, to identify two things that they feel they learned from doing the activity.

Closing Participants should be encouraged to spend a few minutes talking about their plans for the immediate future: holidays, weekend trips, social events and so forth. This allows for all participants to disassociate themselves from the activity and encourages them to return to their 'normal' roles.

Notes This activity can usefully be prefaced by a short theory input on emotional release. In this way, the experiential learning cycle is being played out. First, the group receive some theory about the topic. Then, they test out that theory with an activity. Keep the theory input short.

GIVING PERMISSION
Activity 44

Time required 45 minutes to 1 hour.

Aim To explore feelings in a supportive group atmosphere.

Group size Any number between 5 and 25.

Environment A large room in which people can sit comfortably in a group. Chairs should be of equal height and the group should remain in a closed circle throughout. The trainer should be part of the circle.

Equipment A whiteboard, blackboard or flipchart to allow discussion points to be jotted down. (The board should not become a focal point of the session.) Chalk or markers for the board or flipchart. Prepared handouts where necessary.

Procedure This activity is only for use once people know each other fairly well and when the trainer feels able to cope with emotional release. It simply involves the trainer allowing group members to express emotion during a discussion or another, specific activity. When group members are exploring counselling activities, for example, the trainer may preface the activity by suggesting that it become a group norm that people be allowed to laugh, cry or get angry during the activity. If this *does* happen, it is important that full support is given to the person who expresses emotion. Such support is given by allowing full release of the emotion followed by a quiet period in which the person is allowed and encouraged to 'make sense' of what has happened. This period is sometimes known as debriefing and is an essential part of any activity that involves the free expression of feelings. The group trainer always joins in and may serve as a role model in being prepared to express appropriate emotion during an activity.

Evaluation A discussion is invoked by the trainer about how any learning from the activity could be carried back to the workplace.

Closing Participants should be encouraged to spend a few minutes talking about their plans for the immediate future: holidays, weekend trips, social events and so forth. This allows for all participants to disassociate themselves from the activity and encourages them to return to their 'normal' roles.

EXAGGERATION
Activity 45

Time required 45 minutes to 1 hour.

Aim To explore feelings in a group setting.

Group size Any number between 5 and 25.

Environment A large room in which people can sit comfortably in a group. Chairs should be of equal height and the group should remain in a closed circle throughout. The trainer should be part of the circle.

Equipment A whiteboard, blackboard or flipchart to allow discussion points to be jotted down. (The board should not become a focal point of the session.) Chalk or markers for the board or flipchart. Prepared handouts where necessary.

Procedure This sounds a slightly bizarre activity when it is put down in black and white! All that is involved is that during a particular discussion of any topic related to feelings, group participants are asked to exaggerate the way they feel about what is under discussion. Thus, the person who feels slightly irritated, acts as if he is very irritated; the person who is cheered by something that is said, laughs wholeheartedly about the issue. This form of exaggeration is sometimes described as 'acting-in' to feelings. Sometimes, too, the exaggeration leads to the expression of real feeling. If it does not, it allows group participants to consider a range of ways of thinking about feelings and about helping other people who express them. This activity is a particular sort of role play and requires the debriefing period described in the previous activity. The group trainer always joins in.

Evaluation Each person in the group, in turn, says first what they liked least about the activity. Then, each person in the group says what they liked most about the activity. The group leader or trainer joins in too.

Closing Participants should be encouraged to spend a few minutes talking about their plans for the immediate future: holidays, weekend trips, social events and so forth. This allows for all participants to disassociate themselves from the activity and encourages them to return to their 'normal' roles.

PARADOX
Activity 46

Time required 45 minutes to 1 hour.

Aim To explore the paradoxical nature of feelings.

Group size Any number between 5 and 25.

Environment A large room in which people can sit comfortably in a group. Chairs should be of equal height and the group should remain in a closed circle throughout. The trainer should be part of the circle.

Equipment A whiteboard, blackboard or flipchart to allow discussion points to be jotted down. (The board should not become a focal point of the session.) Chalk or markers for the board or flipchart. Prepared handouts where necessary.

Procedure We often seem to say the exact opposite of what we really feel. For this activity, the trainer makes use of a strategy for exploring this paradox. During a discussion about feelings, the trainer occasionally asks a group member to explore the 'opposite pole' of the expressed feeling by reversing the statement they have made. Thus, the trainer will use the expression 'try saying the opposite of that' after a group member has expressed a particular feeling. Here is an example of the trainer's intervention in action.

'I'm quite relaxed about this. Nothing bothers me about it at all.'
'Try saying the opposite of that.'
'I'm not *at all* relaxed ... How odd! I'm *not* really relaxed at all!'

Evaluation The trainer invites each person in the group, in turn, to identify two things that they feel they learned from doing the activity.

© P. Burnard 1992, published by Kogan Page

194 Interpersonal skills training activities

Closing Participants should be encouraged to spend a few minutes talking about their plans for the immediate future: holidays, weekend trips, social events and so forth. This allows for all participants to disassociate themselves from the activity and encourages them to return to their 'normal' roles.

EARLIEST EXPERIENCE
Activity 47

Time required 45 minutes to 1 hour.

Aim To explore the possible genesis of some of our feelings.

Group size Any number between 5 and 25.

Environment A large room in which people can sit comfortably in a group. Chairs should be of equal height and the group should remain in a closed circle throughout. The trainer should be part of the circle.

Equipment A whiteboard, blackboard or flipchart to allow discussion points to be jotted down. (The board should not become a focal point of the session.) Chalk or markers for the board or flipchart. Prepared handouts where necessary.

Procedure The psychodynamic school of psychology argues that our feelings in adulthood are linked to early childhood experiences. For this activity, the trainer invites members to recall their earliest remembrances and encourages each one to relate that experience to the group. Then, the trainer allows each person to describe the feelings that are associated with the early memory, and encourages them to think about how those memories and feelings link with the present.

This can either be carried out as a 'round' or it can be run more informally with group members participating as they remember things. The group trainer joins in wherever possible.

Evaluation Each person in the group, in turn, says first what they liked least about the activity. Then, each person in the group says

© P. Burnard 1992, published by Kogan Page

what they liked most about the activity. The group leader or trainer joins in too.

Closing Participants should be encouraged to spend a few minutes talking about their plans for the immediate future: holidays, weekend trips, social events and so forth. This allows for all participants to disassociate themselves from the activity and encourages them to return to their 'normal' roles.

FOCUSING
Activity 48

Time required 45 minutes to 1 hour.

Aim To explore a particular type of problem solving through 'focusing'.

Group size Any number between 5 and 25.

Environment A large room in which people can sit comfortably in a group. Chairs should be of equal height and the group should remain in a closed circle throughout. The trainer should be part of the circle.

Equipment A whiteboard, blackboard or flipchart to allow discussion points to be jotted down. (The board should not become a focal point of the session.) Chalk or markers for the board or flipchart. Prepared handouts where necessary.

Procedure 'Focusing' is a simple method of problem solving through relaxation and through focusing on feelings. This is a simple process of allowing the body and mind to relax and thus enabling a 'felt sense' of one's problems to emerge. The process allows for a natural process of problem solving to occur. The focusing approach outlined here is based on that described by Eugene Gendlin (Gendlin 1981). The group trainer uses these instructions to lead the group through the process of focusing.

Evaluation Each person in the group, in turn, says first what they liked least about the activity. Then, each person in the group says what they liked most about the activity. The group leader or trainer joins in too.

© P. Burnard 1992, published by Kogan Page

Focusing

1. Sit quietly and breathe deeply for a while. Allow yourself to relax completely. Notice the thoughts and feelings that flood into your mind. Slowly, but without worrying too much, identify each one.
2. Having identified each thought or feeling that comes drifting into your mind, find some way of 'packaging up' each of those thoughts and feelings. Some people find it easiest to imagine actually wrapping each issue up into a parcel. Others imagine putting each item into a box and sealing it with tape. However you do it, allow each thought or feeling to be packaged in some way. Then imagine those thoughts or feelings, in their packages, laid out in front of you. Notice, too, the sense of calmness that goes with having packaged up your thoughts and feelings in this way.
3. Now, in your mind, look around at those packages and notice which one of them is calling for attention. Sometimes there will be more than one but try to focus on the one that is *most* in need.
4. Now unpack that one particular issue and allow it some breathing space. Do not immediately put a name to it or rush to 'sort it out'. Instead, allow yourself to immerse yourself in that particular issue.
5. When you have spent some minutes immersing yourself in this way, ask yourself: 'what is the *feeling* that goes with this issue? Don't rush to put a label to it; try one or two labels, tentatively at first. Allow the label to 'emerge' out of the issue. This feeling that emerges in this way can be described as the 'felt sense' of the issue or problem.
6. Once you have identified this 'felt sense' in this way, allow yourself to explore it for a while. What other feelings go with it? What other thoughts do you associate with it? And so on.
7. Once you have explored the felt sense in this way, ask yourself: what is the *nub of all this*? As you ask this, allow the real issue behind all your thoughts to emerge and to surface. Often, the nub or 'bottom line' is quite different an issue to the one that you started out with.
8. When you have identified the nub or the crux of the issue, allow yourself to explore that a little. Then identify what it is you have to do next. Do not do this too hastily. Again, try out a number of solutions before you settle on what has to be done. Do not rush to make up your mind but rather let the next step emerge of its own accord. Once you have identified the next thing that you have to do acknowledge to yourself that this is the end of the activity for the time being.
9. Allow yourself some more deep breaths. Relax quietly and then rouse yourself gently.

© P. Burnard 1992, published by Kogan Page

Closing Participants should be offered a five-minute period in which to raise questions, express feelings, address particular people in the group or to talk through anything else that has arisen from the activity.

Notes This can be used as a 'warm up' activity at different points during the course of a group or workshop.

CHILDHOOD

Activity 49

Time required 45 minutes to 1 hour.

Aim To explore early, formative experiences.

Group size Any number between 5 and 25.

Environment A large room in which people can sit comfortably in a group. Chairs should be of equal height and the group should remain in a closed circle throughout. The trainer should be part of the circle.

Equipment A whiteboard, blackboard or flipchart to allow discussion points to be jotted down. (The board should not become a focal point of the session.) Chalk or markers for the board or flipchart. Prepared handouts where necessary.

Procedure As we have noted, according to some psychologists, early events have a profound influence on our present feelings, values, attitudes and behaviours. This activity helps in the exploration of some of those early events. Each person in the group is encouraged to spend a few minutes reflecting on three early, positive, formative incidents. They are allowed to identify any sorts of experiences as long as they were positive ones. Then, each person in turn relates the three to the group. The group trainer joins in wherever possible. After all of the events have been described, a discussion is developed on the degree to which early incidents really *do* influence our present behaviour.

Evaluation The trainer hands out a prepared short questionnaire about the activity. The questionnaire should ask about:

- what it was like to take part in the activity;
- what feelings were invoked by the activity;
- what elements of it would be taken back to the workplace.

Closing Participants should be encouraged to spend a few minutes talking about their plans for the immediate future: holidays, weekend trips, social events and so forth. This allows for all participants to disassociate themselves from the activity and encourages them to return to their 'normal' roles.

Notes This activity can be used to sharpen group members' attention during the course of a group or workshop.

FUTURE
Activity 50

Time required 45 minutes to 1 hour.

Aim To explore plans for the future.

Group size Any number between 5 and 25.

Environment A large room in which people can sit comfortably in a group. Chairs should be of equal height and the group should remain in a closed circle throughout. The trainer should be part of the circle.

Equipment A whiteboard, blackboard or flipchart to allow discussion points to be jotted down. (The board should not become a focal point of the session.) Chalk or markers for the board or flipchart. Prepared handouts where necessary.

Procedure This activity is aimed at helping group members to identify what they need to do in the future in terms of interpersonal skills. The activity is useful towards the end of an interpersonal skills workshop. The group pairs off and one member of each pair describes their own interpersonal-skill development plans in terms of everyday life, more training, personal development, etc. After five minutes, the pairs swap roles. This activity is *not* a conversation but a structured pairs activity. The group trainer joins in wherever possible. The group then reconvenes and a discussion is held about future plans. The trainer also focuses on how the group members *feel* about their developmental plans.

Evaluation A discussion is invoked by the trainer about how any learning from the activity could be carried back to the workplace.

© P. Burnard 1992, published by Kogan Page

Closing Participants should be offered a five-minute period in which to raise questions, express feelings, address particular people in the group or to talk through anything else that has arisen from the activity.

Chapter 11:

Gestalt activities

ABOUT GESTALT ACTIVITIES

The following activities are based on activities drawn from gestalt therapy. 'Gestalt' is a German word for which there is no exact English translation. It roughly means 'form'. Gestalt therapy, an important influence in the humanistic approach to experiential learning is a true mind/body therapy, aiming to integrate both aspects of the person. This it does by helping the individual to become aware of both psychological and physiological events as they happen. Thus it has a 'here-and-now' focus. Gestalt therapy is only interested in the individual's past in as much as it affects present-moment awareness. In an important sense, the present is all there is. The past is past and cannot be brought back, the future is yet to come and can only be speculated upon. The person who can live more fully in the present is more likely to notice, live and learn more fully.

Fritz Perls (Perls 1969a, 1969b), a psychoanalyst, developed this approach of therapy, drawing from psychoanalysis itself, Reichian character analysis theory, existential philosophy and Easter philosophy. By all accounts he was a charismatic character who no doubt developed his own theory in his own idiosyncratic style. Gestalt draws from psychoanalytical theory many beliefs about unconscious or unrecognized factors at work in our minds and bodies. One of its aims, like many other therapies, is to make the unconscious, conscious. It develops Reich's (1949) work on the concept of trapped emotion in the body's musculature (or what Reich called 'character armour'). Reich believed that we carry our repressed emotions around with us in our muscle clusters. Thus the person who consistently refuses to face their own anger often carries that anger around with them in the neck and shoulder muscles. You may want to check the status of your own muscle clusters and notice to what degree you continually tense certain muscle groups.

Gestalt is an existential approach in that it encourages the individual to take full self-responsibility, and acknowledges that it is we as individuals who invest our lives with meaning. Finally, it shares with Easter philosophy a fascination with paradox. It is paradoxical that we often say exactly the opposite of what we really mean: 'I'm perfectly relaxed' or 'It was so nice to see you again'. Apply this principle to yourself. How often do you say the opposite of what you mean? We saw examples of this problem in some of the activities in the previous chapter.

Perls' gestalt therapy combined all these influences to create a type of therapy that encouraged feelings rather than resisted them. In many other therapies, for example, the client would be helped to oppose their feelings. Thus the anxious person was encouraged to relax. Perls' method was to encourage the person to experience that anxiety and if necessary increase it. Paradoxically, as this happened the person very often relaxed and felt more comfortable. It was as though acceptance and experience of the emotion brought release. After all, what the anxious person is very good at doing is feeling anxious. Gestalt therapy, rather than fighting that inclination, allows it. Perls maintained that it is not until we fully accept ourselves as we are (and not as we would wish to be or think we ought to be) that change can come about. Further, he noted that we often blame others for our predicament ('if it wasn't for my mother I would be quite different'), or we appeal to some dubious theory about the nature of our make up ('I can't help it, it's the way I'm made!'). Gestalt therapy aims at helping the individual to experience and *own* their experiences.

As with many humanistic therapies, gestalt trainers tend to use the following 'ground rules' during practice. Gestalt trainers often prefer their clients to:

1. Use 'I' rather than 'you', 'we' or 'people'. Thus: 'I am unhappy at the moment' rather than 'you know what it's like, you tend to get unhappy at times like this'.
2. Talk to others in the first person, rather than indirectly. Thus: 'I don't agree with what you are saying' rather than 'I didn't agree with what Kevin said'.
3. Avoid asking questions, particularly 'why' questions. It is better to listen for the statement behind the question. Thus: 'I am hurt by what you say' rather than 'Why are you saying that?'
4. As far as possible, remain in the present rather than slipping into reminiscences.

These ground rules are valuable in helping the individual and the group to remain fully in the present and to take responsibility for their own thoughts, feelings and actions. These ground rules are a useful set of guidelines for clear communication in any setting. It may well be that stress is reduced through the use of such ground rules in everyday communication. If we can be more clear about what it is we want to say and how we are to say it we are likely to decrease our anxiety and tension – at least in the long term. Initially, the use of the ground rules may *increase* tension, for many of us are not used to communicating so directly.

The activities that follow are based on approaches and activities used in gestalt therapy and can be used as a means of raising awareness both to aspects of the outer environment and to the group participants' inner feelings. These activities are also very useful in helping people to develop listening and attention skills. The concentration required to do them is often found to be useful in learning how to give full attention to another person.

IMMEDIATE AWARENESS
Activity 51

Time required 30 minutes.

Aim To explore group participants' immediate field of awareness.

Group size Any number between 5 and 25.

Environment A large room with chairs of equal height. Space enough to allow participants to pair off and then to reconvene. Smaller rooms can be used for the pairs activity if required.

Equipment A whiteboard, blackboard or flipchart to allow discussion points to be jotted down. (The board should not become a focal point of the session.) Chalk or markers for the board or flipchart. Prepared handouts where necessary.

Procedure Group participants pair off and sit opposite one another. First, one member of each pair describes everything they can see. This can include considerable detail. An example of such a description might be as follows:

> 'I am aware of you sitting opposite me. I can see your face and that you are smiling. I notice that you have brown eyes and that your hair is fair but that you have some streaks of brown in it. You are sitting on a fairly old, grey chair and the carpet underneath your chair is green and has a fine pattern on it ...'

This is all that the participant is required to do. The aim is to describe as much as possible during a period of five minutes. After five minutes participants swap roles and repeat the procedure.

© P. Burnard 1992, published by Kogan Page

The trainer invites the group to reconvene. Then, a discussion is held about the activity. Two facets are discussed: the *process* of the activity (what it felt like to do it) and the *content* (what was talked about during the activity). As always, the process is more important than the content and, sometimes, the trainer may choose to discuss *only* the process. Also, the trainer helps the group to identify ways in which what has been learned from the activity can be related to the group members' professional or personal lives. The group trainer joins in wherever possible.

Evaluation The trainer invites each person in the group, in turn, to identify two things that they feel they learned from doing the activity.

Closing Participants should be encouraged to spend a few minutes talking about their plans for the immediate future: holidays, weekend trips, social events and so forth. This allows for all participants to disassociate themselves from the activity and encourages them to return to their 'normal' roles.

Notes This activity can usefully be prefaced by a short theory input on gestalt therapy (Perls 1973). In this way, the experiential learning cycle is being played out. First, the group receive some theory about the topic. Then, they test out that theory with an activity. Keep the theory input short.

This can be used as a 'warm up' activity at different points during the course of a group or workshop.

SHIFTING AWARENESS
Activity 52

Time required 30 minutes.

Aim To explore changing patterns of awareness.

Group size Any number between 5 and 25.

Environment A large room with chairs of equal height. Space enough to allow participants to pair off and then to reconvene. Smaller rooms can be used for the pairs activity if required.

Equipment A whiteboard, blackboard or flipchart to allow discussion points to be jotted down. (The board should not become a focal point of the session.) Chalk or markers for the board or flipchart. Prepared handouts where necessary.

Procedure Group participants pair off and sit opposite one another. One person in each pair sits and describes to his partner how his attention is shifting during the passage of time. He tries to verbalize what he is seeing, thinking and feeling – any change in attention or focus. An example of how this description may sound is as follows:

> 'I am aware of looking at you ... now I feel slightly embarrassed as you smile at me ... the embarrassment is fading as I say these things to you. I have just thought about another time when I was embarrassed in a workshop. Now I am looking out of the window behind you and I can see people walking about on the grass. I realize that I would quite like to be with them. Now I am focusing back on you and it looks as though you are deep in thought ...'

This process continues for five minutes, then the pairs swap roles.

© P. Burnard 1992, published by Kogan Page

The trainer invites the group to reconvene. Then, a discussion is held about the activity. Two facets are discussed: the *process* of the activity (what it felt like to do it) and the *content* (what was talked about during the activity). As always, the process is more important than the content and, sometimes, the trainer may choose to discuss *only* the process. Also, the trainer helps the group to identify ways in which what has been learned from the activity can be related to the group members' professional or personal lives. The group trainer joins in wherever possible.

Evaluation Each person in the group, in turn, says first what they liked least about the activity. Then, each person in the group says what they liked most about the activity. The group leader or trainer joins in too.

Closing Participants should be encouraged to spend a few minutes talking about their plans for the immediate future: holidays, weekend trips, social events and so forth. This allows for all participants to disassociate themselves from the activity and encourages them to return to their 'normal' roles.

Notes This activity can be used to sharpen group members' attention during the course of a group or workshop.

© P. Burnard 1992, published by Kogan Page

NOTICING

Activity 53

Time required 30 minutes.

Aim To encourage group participants to notice aspects of their environment and thoughts without necessarily labelling them or judging them.

Group size Any number between 5 and 25.

Environment A large room with chairs of equal height. Space enough to allow participants to pair off and then to reconvene. Smaller rooms can be used for the pairs activity if required.

Equipment A whiteboard, blackboard or flipchart to allow discussion points to be jotted down. (The board should not become a focal point of the session.) Chalk or markers for the board or flipchart. Prepared handouts where necessary.

Procedure Group participants pair off and sit opposite one another. One member of each pair reports on what she sees around her, with no attempt to judge or label what she sees. She is asked, merely, to describe what happens in a very literal way. Here is an example of what a description might sound like:

> 'I can see David talking to Peter. They are both engrossed in conversation. Now I can see you out of the corner of my eye and you are looking at me. Now I am aware of Peter crossing the room and going towards the door. The door is made of oak or some other sort of hard wood...'

© P. Burnard 1992, published by Kogan Page

Here is an example of what is *not* required:

> 'I can see David talking to Peter and they both seem pleased about things. Peter must be glad that the workshop is going well ...'

In the second example, the talker is adding a layer of interpretation or value to what is seen. The aim of this activity is to stick as nearly as possible to description. After a five minute period, the pairs swap roles.

The trainer invites the group to reconvene. Then, a discussion is held about the activity. Two facets are discussed: the *process* of the activity (what it felt like to do it) and the *content* (what was talked about during the activity). As always, the process is more important than the content and, sometimes, the trainer may choose to discuss *only* the process. Also, the trainer helps the group to identify ways in which what has been learned from the activity can be related to the group members' professional or personal lives. The group trainer joins in wherever possible.

Evaluation The trainer invites each person in the group, in turn, to identify two things that they feel they learned from doing the activity.

Closing Participants should be encouraged to spend a few minutes talking about their plans for the immediate future: holidays, weekend trips, social events and so forth. This allows for all participants to disassociate themselves from the activity and encourages them to return to their 'normal' roles.

Notes This activity can be used to sharpen group members' attention during the course of a group or workshop.

DESCRIBING
Activity 54

Time required 30 minutes.

Aim To encourage the further development of 'pure description'.

Group size Any number between 5 and 25.

Environment A large room with chairs of equal height. Space enough to allow participants to pair off and then to reconvene. Smaller rooms can be used for the pairs activity if required.

Equipment A whiteboard, blackboard or flipchart to allow discussion points to be jotted down. (The board should not become a focal point of the session.) Chalk or markers for the board or flipchart. Prepared handouts where necessary.

Procedure Group participants pair off and sit opposite one another. The trainer hands each person an object. Simple, everyday objects can be used, such as tin openers, cans of beans, bottles, vases and simple ornaments. Each person is invited to describe the object to their partner *without making value judgements about it nor even describing its use*. The following might be a description of a can of beans: 'This is a cylindrical object. It has a green label wrapped around it and the label has writing on it. The words are printed in brown and red...'

The aim is to make as complete and as detailed a description of the object as possible. What often happens in this activity is that people begin to see very familiar objects in different sorts of ways. This changing perception may have implications for the ways in which people see other people in everyday life and these implications can be drawn out in discussion.

© P. Burnard 1992, published by Kogan Page

The trainer invites the group to reconvene. Then, a discussion is held about the activity. Two facets are discussed: the *process* of the activity (what it felt like to do it) and the *content* (what was talked about during the activity). As always, the process is more important than the content and, sometimes, the trainer may choose to discuss *only* the process. Also, the trainer helps the group to identify ways in which what has been learned from the activity can be related to the group members' professional or personal lives. The group trainer joins in wherever possible.

Evaluation Each person in the group, in turn, says first what they liked least about the activity. Then, each person in the group says what they liked most about the activity. The group leader or trainer joins in too.

Closing Participants should be encouraged to spend a few minutes talking about their plans for the immediate future: holidays, weekend trips, social events and so forth. This allows for all participants to disassociate themselves from the activity and encourages them to return to their 'normal' roles.

Notes This activity can be used to sharpen group members' attention during the course of a group or workshop.

SELF AND OBJECT
Activity 55

Time required 45 minutes to 1 hour.

Aim To explore personal 'projections'.

Group size Any number between 5 and 25.

Environment A large room with chairs of equal height. Space enough to allow participants to pair off and then to reconvene. Smaller rooms can be used for the pairs activity if required.

Equipment A whiteboard, blackboard or flipchart to allow discussion points to be jotted down. (The board should not become a focal point of the session.) Chalk or markers for the board or flipchart. Prepared handouts where necessary.

Procedure Group members pair off. They are then encouraged to wander around the room and outside it until they come across a fairly large object such as a painting, an archway or any other architectural or decorative feature. One person then describes that object in the first person. For example, a person standing in front of a painting may say: 'I am large and oblong in shape. I am covered, mostly in green and I am divided into two parts. My lower half is darker than my top half...' This process continues until one person has described the object in some detail. Then, the pairs swap roles, find another object and the 'listener' becomes the 'describer'.

We often attribute qualities to others that are, in fact, our own. For instance, we may notice that another person is very talkative when, to others, it is clear that *we* are talkative. In this activity, however, it becomes apparent that we may attribute personal qualities of our own to *objects*. What often emerges during or after this activity is that each person realizes they have been describing aspects of *themselves*, despite the nature or appearance of the object. This can be the subject of the post-activity discussion.

The trainer invites the group to reconvene. Then, a discussion is held about the activity. Two facets are discussed: the *process* of the activity (what it felt like to do it) and the *content* (what was talked about during the activity). As always, the process is more important than the content and, sometimes, the trainer may choose to discuss *only* the process. Also, the trainer helps the group to identify ways in which what has been learned from the activity can be related to the group members' professional or personal lives. The group trainer joins in wherever possible.

Evaluation The trainer invites each person in the group, in turn, to identify two things that they feel they learned from doing the activity.

Closing Participants should be offered a five-minute period in which to raise questions, express feelings, address particular people in the group or to talk through anything else that has arisen from the activity.

Notes This activity can be used to sharpen group members' attention during the course of a group or workshop.

© P. Burnard 1992, published by Kogan Page

SELF-DESCRIPTION

Activity 56

Time required 45 minutes to 1 hour.

Aim To explore aspects of the self.

Group size Any number between 5 and 25.

Environment A large room with chairs of equal height. Space enough to allow participants to pair off and then to reconvene. Smaller rooms can be used for the pairs activity if required.

Equipment A whiteboard, blackboard or flipchart to allow discussion points to be jotted down. (The board should not become a focal point of the session.) Chalk or markers for the board or flipchart. Prepared handouts where necessary.

Procedure Group participants pair off and sit opposite one another. Each person describes themselves to their partner in the third person. A third-person description might be: 'David Smith is a tall person who is about the right weight for his height. He has light brown hair, which is greying a bit. He wears glasses and looks ..' Each person continues this description for about five minutes, then the roles are reversed.

The trainer invites the group to reconvene. Then, a discussion is held about the activity. Two facets are discussed: the *process* of the activity (what it felt like to do it) and the *content* (what was talked about during the activity). As always, the process is more important than the content and, sometimes, the trainer may choose to discuss *only* the process. Also, the trainer helps the group to identify ways

in which what has been learned from the activity can be related to the group members' professional or personal lives. The group trainer joins in wherever possible.

Evaluation A discussion is invoked by the trainer about how any learning from the activity could be carried back to the workplace.

Closing Participants should be encouraged to spend a few minutes talking about their plans for the immediate future: holidays, weekend trips, social events and so forth. This allows for all participants to disassociate themselves from the activity and encourages them to return to their 'normal' roles.

SELF-NOT SELF
Activity 57

Time required 45 minutes to 1 hour.

Aim To explore differences between self and non-self.

Group size Any number between 5 and 25.

Environment A large room with chairs of equal height. Space enough to allow participants to pair off and then to reconvene. Smaller rooms can be used for the pairs activity if required.

Equipment A whiteboard, blackboard or flipchart to allow discussion points to be jotted down. (The board should not become a focal point of the session.) Chalk or markers for the board or flipchart. Prepared handouts where necessary.

Procedure This is a variation on a meditation activity. Group participants pair off and sit opposite one another. Each person describes himself to his partner by stating a quality about himself and then acknowledging, also, that he does *not* have that quality: 'I have angry feelings and I do *not* have angry feelings... I am kind and I am *not* kind... I am a placid person and I am *not* placid...' This activity is continued for between five and ten minutes until the person has covered both poles of a wide range of personal qualities and attributes. Then roles are reversed.

The trainer invites the larger group to reconvene. Then, a discussion is held about the activity. Two facets are discussed: the *process* of the activity (what it felt like to do it) and the *content* (what was talked about during the activity). As always, the process is more important than the content and, sometimes, the trainer may choose to discuss *only* the process. Also, the trainer helps the group to identify ways in which what has been learned from the activity can be related to

© P. Burnard 1992, published by Kogan Page

the group members' professional or personal lives. The group trainer joins in wherever possible.

Evaluation Each person in the group, in turn, says first what they liked least about the activity. Then, each person in the group says what they liked most about the activity. The group leader or trainer joins in too.

Closing Participants should be encouraged to spend a few minutes talking about their plans for the immediate future: holidays, weekend trips, social events and so forth. This allows for all participants to disassociate themselves from the activity and encourages them to return to their 'normal' roles.

MEDITATION
Activity 58

Time required 45 minutes to 1 hour.

Aim To explore meditation.

Group size Any number between 5 and 25.

Environment A large room in which people can sit comfortably in a group. Chairs should be of equal height and the group should remain in a closed circle throughout. The trainer should be part of the circle. There should also be space for participants to lie full length on the floor.

Equipment Cushions or rubber mattresses.

Procedure Meditation can be used for a variety of purposes in an interpersonal skills workshop and the principles of it are related to gestalt therapy in that it encourages both a concentration on self and a detachment from it. Here is one group meditation that can be conducted by the group trainer. For the meditation, the trainer reads the script on the next page. In the early stages of meditation, it is very easy to be distracted by what Pierce calls 'roof-brain' chatter (Pearce 1982), the seemingly endless flow of thoughts and ideas that refuse to go away when we sit down to meditate. Meditation, like most things, take practice and commitment. Slowly, the roof-brain chatter dies away.

After meditation, the trainer invites the group to reconvene. Then, a discussion is held about the activity. Two facets are discussed: the *process* of the activity (what it felt like to do it) and the *content* (what was talked about during the activity). As always, the process is more important than the content and, sometimes, the trainer may choose to discuss *only* the process. Also, the trainer helps the group to identify ways in which what has been learned from the activity can be related to the group members' professional or personal lives. The group trainer joins in wherever possible.

Evaluation The trainer hands out a prepared short questionnaire about the activity. The questionnaire should ask about:

- what it was like to take part in the activity;
- what feelings were invoked by the activity;
- what elements of it would be taken back to the workplace.

Notes This activity can usefully be prefaced by a short theory input on meditation (Burnard 1990, Smith and Wilks 1988). In this way, the experiential learning cycle is being played out. First, the group receive some theory about the topic. Then, they test out that theory with an activity. Keep the theory input short.

Closing Participants should be offered a five-minute period in which to raise questions, express feelings, address particular people in the group or to talk through anything else that has arisen from the activity.

MEDITATION

1. Sit motionless, comfortably and with the eyes closed.
2. Breathe quietly and gently. Breathe in through the nostrils and out through the mouth.
3. Let your attention focus on your breathing.
4. Begin to count your breaths, from 1 to 10. One is the whole cycle of an inhalation and an exhalation. Two is the next complete cycle.
5. When the breaths have been counted from 1 to 10, begin to count again from 1 to 10 and so on.
6. If you are distracted or lose count, simply go back to the beginning and start again.

© P. Burnard 1992, published by Kogan Page

STREAM OF CONSCIOUSNESS

Activity 59

Time required 45 minutes to 1 hour.

Aim To explore the stream of thoughts and feelings that run through our heads.

Group size Any number between 5 and 25.

Environment A large room with chairs of equal height. Space enough to allow participants to pair off and then to reconvene. Smaller rooms can be used for the pairs activity if required.

Equipment A whiteboard, blackboard or flipchart to allow discussion points to be jotted down. (The board should not become a focal point of the session.) Chalk or markers for the board or flipchart. Prepared handouts where necessary.

Procedure Group participants pair off and sit opposite one another. One of each pair tries to verbalize whatever goes through her head (as long as it is not too embarrassing to be repeated). This activity mimics the free-association device used in psychoanalysis and is easy to describe but very difficult to carry out! An example of a stream of consciousness utterance might be as follows:

'I am thinking about doing this activity. Now I am thinking about being in Brighton ... walking along the beach ... my mother and father ... the pier ... going shopping on a Saturday ... Now I notice you looking at me ... back to Brighton ... the trains at the station ... Volks Railway on the seafront ... Vienna ... holiday in the mountains ... Majorca ...'

© P. Burnard 1992, published by Kogan Page

After about five minutes, roles are reversed.

The trainer invites the group to reconvene. Then, a discussion is held about the activity. Two facets are discussed: the *process* of the activity (what it felt like to do it) and the *content* (what was talked about during the activity). As always, the process is more important than the content and, sometimes, the trainer may choose to discuss *only* the process. Also, the trainer helps the group to identify ways in which what has been learned from the activity can be related to the group members' professional or personal lives. The group trainer joins in wherever possible.

Evaluation Each person in the group, in turn, says first what they liked least about the activity. Then, each person in the group says what they liked most about the activity. The group leader or trainer joins in too.

Closing Participants should be encouraged to spend a few minutes talking about their plans for the immediate future: holidays, weekend trips, social events and so forth. This allows for all participants to disassociate themselves from the activity and encourages them to return to their 'normal' roles.

Notes This can be used as a 'warm up' activity at different points during the course of a group or workshop.

HERE AND NOW
Activity 60

Time required 45 minutes to 1 hour.

Aim To explore methods of staying in the 'here-and-now'.

Group size Any number between 5 and 25.

Environment A large room with chairs of equal height. Space enough to allow participants to pair off and then to reconvene. Smaller rooms can be used for the pairs activity if required.

Equipment A whiteboard, blackboard or flipchart to allow discussion points to be jotted down. (The board should not become a focal point of the session.) Chalk or markers for the board or flipchart. Prepared handouts where necessary.

Procedure It is easy for us to live in the past or to anticipate the future. This activity encourages participants to stay firmly in the present. Group participants pair off and sit opposite one another. Each person is required to start a series of sentences beginning with the word 'Now ...' and to complete it with a phrase that says something about them. An example might be: 'Now I am feeling hungry ... Now I am wondering what we will do this afternoon ... Now I am aware that I am cold ... Now I am warming up a little ...' It is important that each person notices their changing focus of attention as they address each feeling, thought or action. After five minutes, roles are reversed.

The trainer invites the group to reconvene. Then, a discussion is held about the activity. Two facets are discussed: the *process* of the activity (what it felt like to do it) and the *content* (what was talked about during the activity). As always, the process is more important than the content and, sometimes, the trainer may choose to discuss *only* the process. Also, the trainer helps the group to identify ways in which what has been learned from the activity can be related to the group members' professional or personal lives. The group trainer joins in wherever possible.

Evaluation The trainer invites each person in the group, in turn, to identify two things that they feel they learned from doing the activity.

Closing The trainer can invite questions about any aspect of the activity.

Notes This activity can be used to sharpen group members' attention during the course of a group or workshop.

Chapter 12:
Evaluation activities

USING EVALUATION ACTIVITIES

It is necessary to evaluate interpersonal skills training at many points. For instance after an interpersonal skills activity, at the end of a day's activities, at the end of a workshop or towards the end of a course.

All the evaluation activities which follow can be used in a variety of settings and at different points during interpersonal skills training. They work best when the trainer joins in and becomes an equal member of the group.

PAIRS EVALUATION
Activity 61

Time required 45 minutes to 1 hour.

Aim To evaluate a group workshop in a pairs format.

Group size Any number between 5 and 25.

Environment A large room with chairs of equal height. Space enough to allow participants to pair off and then to reconvene. Smaller rooms can be used for the pairs activity if required.

Equipment A whiteboard, blackboard or flipchart to allow discussion points to be jotted down. (The board should not become a focal point of the session.) Chalk or markers for the board or flipchart. Prepared handouts where necessary.

Procedure The group pairs off, one as A and one as B. A then evaluates the workshop to B in terms of the following criteria:

- Content
- Teaching/learning experiences
- Things learned
- My contribution

When A has evaluated in this way, the pairs swop roles and B evaluates the workshop to A using the above criteria.

The trainer invites the group to reconvene. Then, a discussion is held about the activity. Two facets are discussed: the *process* of the activity (what it felt like to do it) and the *content* (what was talked about during the activity). As always, the process is more important than the content and, sometimes, the trainer may choose to discuss *only* the process. Also, the trainer helps the group to identify ways in which what has been learned from the activity can be related to the group members' professional or personal lives. The group trainer joins in wherever possible.

Evaluation The pairs reform at the end of the activity and discuss what they liked least and most about it. They also each give an evaluation of the other's performance.

Closing The trainer can invite questions about any aspect of the activity.

Notes This activity can be used with more than 25 participants if a certain amount of structure is used. One way of managing larger numbers is to draw up a handout that gives explicit instructions to participants. Then, sub-groups are formed from the larger group and a chairperson is elected for each of the sub-groups. The task of each chairperson is to work through the instruction sheet with their group and to ensure things run smoothly. After the activity has been completed by each of the sub-groups, the larger group reforms. The chairpeople report back to the larger group during the plenary session. Structure is essential if the serial working of sub-groups is to be effective. Make sure that everyone is clear about the aims of the activity and what it is that they are supposed to be doing. Headings for an instruction sheet might be:

- Title of the activity
- Aims
- What to do
- The role of the chairperson.

This activity can usefully be prefaced by a short theory input on evaluation. In this way, the experiential learning cycle is being played out. First, the group receive some theory about the topic. Then, they test out that theory with an activity. Keep the theory input short. On the next page is a handout for use in this activity.

© P. Burnard 1992, published by Kogan Page

EVALUATION CHECKLIST	
Content	
Training/teaching methods	
Trainer's style	
Things learned	
My contribution	
What I will take away from this workshop	
What I need to do next	

© P. Burnard 1992, published by Kogan Page

NOMINAL GROUP EVALUATION

Activity 62

Time required 45 minutes to 1 hour.

Aim To evaluate a group, workshop or course.

Group size Any number between 5 and 25.

Environment A large room in which people can sit comfortably in a group. Chairs should be of equal height and the group should remain in a closed circle throughout. The trainer should be part of the circle.

Equipment A whiteboard, blackboard or flipchart to allow discussion points to be jotted down. (The board should not become a focal point of the session.) Chalk or markers for the board or flipchart. Prepared handouts where necessary.

Procedure The group trainer invites the group to 'brainstorm' aspects of the course that they have found useful, using the brainstorming technique described in Part I. Examples of such items might be: 'the theory input on group dynamics'; 'the discussion on Tuesday, about self-awareness'; or 'the chance to work in pairs'. These items, as they are identified, are written on to a blackboard or flip-chart pad.

When the brainstorming has been completed, each person is invited to go to the board or pad and tick three items with which they most strongly agree. The most-ticked items are then discussed within the group.

Evaluation Each person in the group, in turn, says first what they liked least about the activity. Then, each person in the group says what they liked most about the activity. The group leader or trainer joins in too.

Closing The trainer can invite questions about any aspect of the activity.

SELF AND PEER EVALUATION
Activity 63

Time required 45 minutes to 1 hour.

Aim To evaluate a group, workshop or course.

Group size Any number between 5 and 25.

Environment A large room with chairs of equal height. Space enough to allow participants to pair off and then to reconvene. Smaller rooms can be used for the pairs activity if required.

Equipment A whiteboard, blackboard or flipchart to allow discussion points to be jotted down. (The board should not become a focal point of the session.) Chalk or markers for the board or flipchart. Prepared handouts where necessary.

Procedure The first part of this activity is the self-evaluation element, the second is the peer-evaluation element. One group member starts the activity by reviewing his or her contribution to the group, workshop or course, as thoroughly as possible, initially without comment from colleagues or from the trainer. Next, that person invites one of the following sorts of feedback from group colleagues about his or her role in the group, workshop or course:

- positive aspects;
- negative aspects;
- both positive and negative.

Examples of positive feedback comments might be: 'I appreciated your ability to break up arguments when they occurred in the group' or 'I liked the way you supported people . . .'; whereas 'I would have preferred you to join in some of the activities a little more . . .' is a negative comment.

Once one member of the group has undertaken both self and peer evaluation in this way, the next person goes through the same cycle until everyone in the room has completed both elements of the activity. The group trainer joins in wherever possible and undertakes both self and peer evaluation.

Evaluation Each person in the group, in turn, says first what they liked least about the activity. Then, each person in the group says what they liked most about the activity. The group leader or trainer joins in too.

Closing Participants should be offered a five-minute period in which to raise questions, express feelings, address particular people in the group or to talk through anything else that has arisen from the activity.

JOURNAL

Activity 64

Time required 45 minutes to 1 hour.

Aim To evaluate a group, workshop or course.

Group size Any number between 5 and 25.

Environment A large room in which people can sit comfortably in a group. Chairs should be of equal height and the group should remain in a closed circle throughout. The trainer should be part of the circle.

Equipment A whiteboard, blackboard or flipchart to allow discussion points to be jotted down. (The board should not become a focal point of the session.) Chalk or markers for the board or flipchart. Prepared handouts where necessary.

Procedure At the *beginning* of the group, course or workshop, each person is encouraged to keep a journal. The journal can be a note-book or ring binder with loose sheets. The following headings are used as a means of keeping notes after each meeting of the group or each day of the course or workshop:

- Things learned today
- Teaching and learning methods
- Reflections on my own contribution
- New references to journal articles or books
- Other notes.

The journal can then be used as an evaluation device in any one or more of the following ways:

© P. Burnard 1992, published by Kogan Page

- as a discussion document for use in a group meeting at the beginning of each day or a workshop or course;
- as a focus of discussion in the final hour or two of a workshop or course;
- as material for a written evaluation handed in by each participant at the end of a series of group meetings, a workshop or a course.

The group trainer joins in wherever possible and also keeps a journal.

Evaluation The trainer hands out a prepared short questionnaire about the activity. The questionnaire should ask about:

- what it was like to take part in the activity;
- what feelings were invoked by the activity;
- what elements of it would be taken back to the workplace.

Closing The trainer can invite questions about any aspect of the activity.

Notes This activity can be used with more than 25 participants if a certain amount of structure is used. One way of managing larger numbers is to draw up a handout that gives explicit instructions to participants. Then, sub-groups are formed from the larger group and a chairperson is elected for each of the sub-groups. The task of each chairperson is to work through the instruction sheet with their group and to ensure things run smoothly. After the activity has been completed by each of the sub-groups, the larger group reforms. The chairpeople report back to that larger group during the plenary session. Structure is essential if the serial working of sub-groups is to be effective. Make sure that everyone is clear about the aims of the activity and what it is that they are supposed to be doing. Headings for an instruction sheet might be:

- Title of the activity
- Aims
- What to do
- The role of the chairperson.

LEAST AND BEST
Activity 65

Time required 45 minutes to 1 hour.

Aim To undertake an instant evaluation of an activity, group, course or workshop.

Group size Any number between 5 and 25.

Environment A large room in which people can sit comfortably in a group. Chairs should be of equal height and the group should remain in a closed circle throughout. The trainer should be part of the circle.

Equipment No special equipment is required.

Procedure This activity can be used after a particular group activity, a course or a workshop. Each person, in turn, finishes two sentences, as follows:

- What I liked *least* about the (activity, day, workshop) was ...
- What I liked *most* about the (activity, day, workshop) was ...

The group trainer joins in the activity wherever possible and says what he or she liked least and most about the activity, day or workshop.

© P. Burnard 1992, published by Kogan Page

THINGS LEARNED

Activity 66

Time required 15 minutes.

Aim To evaluate an activity, group, workshop or course.

Group size Any number between 5 and 25.

Environment A large room in which people can sit comfortably in a group. Chairs should be of equal height and the group should remain in a closed circle throughout. The trainer should be part of the circle.

Equipment No special equipment is required.

Procedure Each person in turn states three things that they learned from an activity, within the group or from the workshop or course. The group trainer joins in the activity wherever possible and also offers examples of three things learned.

BRAINSTORMING
Activity 67

Time required 30 minutes.

Aim To evaluate an activity, group, workshop or course.

Group size Any number between 5 and 25.

Environment A large room in which people can sit comfortably in a group. Chairs should be of equal height and the group should remain in a closed circle throughout. The trainer should be part of the circle.

Equipment A whiteboard, blackboard or flipchart to allow discussion points to be jotted down. (The board should not become a focal point of the session.) Chalk or markers for the board or flipchart. Prepared handouts where necessary.

Procedure The trainer encourages a brainstorming activity about *all* aspects of the course, both positive and negative. Nothing is ruled out in this activity and the brainstorming is prolonged until no further items are generated. Then, a discussion is held about any items that generate interest, disagreement or emotion.

© P. Burnard 1992, published by Kogan Page

FUTURE PLANNING
Activity 68

Time required 30 minutes.

Aim To forward-plan in a group, workshop or course.

Group size Any number between 5 and 25.

Environment A large room in which people can sit comfortably in a group. Chairs should be of equal height and the group should remain in a closed circle throughout. The trainer should be part of the circle.

Equipment A whiteboard, blackboard or flipchart to allow discussion points to be jotted down. (The board should not become a focal point of the session.) Chalk or markers for the board or flipchart. Prepared handouts where necessary.

Procedure An amount of time is set aside each day (or at the end of a group meeting) for this activity. The 'quaker group' approach is used. First, members of the group are invited to state what activities they want to take part in during the next meeting of the group, workshop or course. After each item is raised by a group member, other members are allowed to 'modify' the suggestion in order to suit their own interests. If no other 'modifications' are offered, the group moves on to another suggestion. Here is an example of a proposal and its modifications, using this approach:

—'I suggest that we have a lengthy discussion, tomorrow, on the question of how we deal with anger in the group.'
—'I suggest we limit the discussion to a half-hour period.'
—'I would like to sit out on that discussion altogether.'
—'I think we should *all* take part in it.'

© P. Burnard 1992, published by Kogan Page

242   Interpersonal skills training activities

—Silence
—Trainer: 'The proposal is carried that we should all take part in a discussion about how we deal with anger.'

Evaluation A discussion is invoked by the trainer about how any learning from the activity could be carried back to the workplace.

Closing Participants should be offered a five-minute period in which to raise questions, express feelings, address particular people in the group or to talk through anything else that has arisen from the activity.

QUESTIONNAIRE
Activity 69

Time required 45 minutes to 1 hour.

Aim To evaluate a group, workshop or course.

Group size Any number between 5 and 25.

Environment A large room in which people can sit comfortably in a group. Chairs should be of equal height and the group should remain in a closed circle throughout. The trainer should be part of the circle.

Equipment A whiteboard, blackboard or flipchart to allow discussion points to be jotted down. (The board should not become a focal point of the session.) Chalk or markers for the board or flipchart. Prepared handouts where necessary.

Procedure The questionnaire (below) is given to each participant in a group, workshop or course as an aid to evaluating that activity.

Evaluation This activity is, of itself, an evaluation and requires no further evaluation procedure.

Closing The trainer can invite questions about any aspect of the activity.

Notes The items in the questionnaire can be modified to suit the exact evaluation needs of the trainer. It is important that each item addresses only *one* issue. The issues that are addressed may be clustered around the following headings:

- Course content

- Teaching and learning methods
- Enjoyment
- Trainer style
- Timing and pace
- Applicability of what is learned to 'real life'.

EVALUATION QUESTIONNAIRE

Please spend a few minutes answering the following questions about the workshop. Place a tick in the column that best represents how you feel about each item.

Key
SA = Strongly agree
A = Agree
DK = Don't know
D = Disagree
SD = Strongly disagree

Item	SA	A	DK	D	SD
1. The workshop was exactly what I hoped it would be.					
2. The content of the workshop was pitched at the right level.					
3. The teaching and learning methods suited my own style of learning.					
4. I learned new skills from the workshop.					
5. I learned new knowledge from the workshop.					
6. What I learned will be useful in my everyday work.					
7. I enjoyed the workshop.					

© P. Burnard 1992, published by Kogan Page

PERSONAL EVALUATION
Activity 70

Time required 30 minutes.

Aim To encourage each person to evaluate his or her own experience of a group, workshop or course.

Group size Any number between 5 and 25.

Environment A large room in which people can sit comfortably in a group. Chairs should be of equal height and the group should remain in a closed circle throughout. The trainer should be part of the circle.

Equipment A whiteboard, blackboard or flipchart to allow discussion points to be jotted down. (The board should not become a focal point of the session.) Chalk or markers for the board or flipchart. Prepared handouts where necessary.

Procedure Group members are invited to sit silently for a few minutes and to make notes of their own reactions to the group, workshop or course. After about ten minutes, each person in turn offers the group a summary of the points that they have jotted down. A decision must be made about whether there will be discussion after each person's contribution or whether such a discussion will be held at the end of the 'round'. The group trainer joins in wherever possible and offers a personal evaluation.

Evaluation This activity is, of itself, an evaluation and requires no further evaluation procedure.

© P. Burnard 1992, published by Kogan Page

Closing Participants should be encouraged to spend a few minutes talking about their plans for the immediate future: holidays, weekend trips, social events and so forth. This allows for all participants to disassociate themselves from the activity and encourages them to return to their 'normal' roles.

Chapter 13:
Counselling skills activities

USING COUNSELLING SKILLS ACTIVITIES

Counselling skills are used by most of the health-care professions and by large numbers of people in management, administration and customer services. Probably the most frequently encountered type of counselling is client-centred.

Client-centred counselling is based on the premise that, given the time and space, people can and do find their own solutions to their own problems. The following checklist is an attempt to identify some of the key points of the approach. Carl Rogers (1967) has developed all these concepts in depth in his book *On Becoming a Person* and if you like the sound of the approach you would be well advised to read it. This is the checklist:

- People are essentially good – they are certainly not basically evil or bad.
- People do not need and cannot be given advice about how to live their lives by experts.
- Given the time and space, people can be relied upon to find their own solutions to their own problems.
- People generally have a tendency towards growth.

- Most people can benefit from another person listening to them, being non-judgemental and supportive.
- Given this counselling climate, the most personal issues also turn out to be the most general ones.

There is also a place, of course, for a more prescriptive approach to counselling. In many walks of life there are times when people need to be given clear and appropriate advice. The point, here, is that when it comes to helping other people sort out their emotional and life problems, the client-centred approach is probably the most appropriate. On the other hand, if the term 'counselling' is interpreted more broadly, to include helping other people in fields as diverse as careers, AIDS, management, buying and selling and so on, then advice-giving becomes part of the counselling process.

Whatever style of counselling is advocated, one skill is essential: that of listening. The activities that follow, while based in the client-centred mode, all encourage listening skills. Most of us can learn to give advice and information reasonably effectively. Most of us need much more training in the area of listening.

SIMPLE LISTENING
Activity 71

Time required 30 minutes.

Aim To explore the skill of listening.

Group size Any number between 5 and 25.

Environment A large room with chairs of equal height. Space enough to allow participants to pair off and then to reconvene. Smaller rooms can be used for the pairs activity if required.

Equipment A whiteboard, blackboard or flipchart to allow discussion points to be jotted down. (The board should not become a focal point of the session.) Chalk or markers for the board or flipchart. Prepared handouts where necessary.

Procedure The group pairs off. One member of each pair is the 'listener', the other is the 'talker'. For ten minutes, the 'talker' talks to his partner while that person listens without responding. The topic for the talk can be chosen either by the trainer or by the pairs themselves. It must be emphasized that the activity is *not* a conversation. The 'listeners' are required to do just that. After ten minutes, roles are reversed.

The trainer invites the group to reconvene. Then, a discussion is held about the activity. Two facets are discussed: the *process* of the activity (what it felt like to do it) and the *content* (what was talked about during the activity). As always, the process is more important than the content and, sometimes, the trainer may choose to discuss *only* the process. Also, the trainer helps the group to identify ways in which what has been learned from the activity can be related to the group members' professional or personal lives. The group trainer joins in wherever possible.

© P. Burnard 1992, published by Kogan Page

Evaluation A discussion is invoked by the trainer about how any learning from the activity could be carried back to the workplace.

Closing Participants should be encouraged to spend a few minutes talking about their plans for the immediate future: holidays, weekend trips, social events and so forth. This allows for all participants to disassociate themselves from the activity and encourages them to return to their 'normal' roles.

Notes This activity can be used with more than 25 participants if a certain amount of structure is used. One way of managing larger numbers is to draw up a handout that gives explicit instructions to participants. Then, sub-groups are formed from the larger group and a chairperson is elected for each of the sub-groups. The task of each chairperson is to work through the instruction sheet with their group and to ensure things run smoothly. After the activity has been completed by each of the sub-groups, the larger group reforms. The chairpeople report back to the larger group during the plenary session. Structure is essential if the serial working of sub-groups is to be effective. Make sure that everyone is clear about the aims of the activity and what it is that they are supposed to be doing. Headings for an instruction sheet might be:

- Title of the activity
- Aims
- What to do
- The role of the chairperson.

This activity can usefully be prefaced by a short theory input on listening. In this way, the experiential learning cycle is being played out. First, the group receive some theory about the topic. Then, they test out that theory with an activity. Keep the theory input short. This can be used as a 'warm up' activity at different points during the course of a group or workshop.

USING OPEN QUESTIONS
Activity 72

Time required 45 minutes to 1 hour.

Aim To explore the use of open questions.

Group size Any number between 5 and 25.

Environment A large room with chairs of equal height. Space enough to allow participants to pair off and then to reconvene. Smaller rooms can be used for the pairs activity if required.

Equipment A whiteboard, blackboard or flipchart to allow discussion points to be jotted down. (The board should not become a focal point of the session.) Chalk or markers for the board or flipchart. Prepared handouts where necessary.

Procedure Open questions are those that cannot be answered with 'yes' or 'no'. Nor do they usually have a single word answer of any sort. Open questions usually start with the words 'How?', 'When?', 'Why?', 'What?' or 'Who?' Here are some examples:

- 'How did you feel when that happened?'
- 'What are your feelings about being in the group?'
- 'What did you think of the government White Paper?'

For this activity, the group pairs off. One member of each pair asks open questions of the other and listens to the answers. This process continues for about five minutes, then roles are reversed. It should be pointed out to all pairs that only open questions are to be used.

The trainer invites the group to reconvene. Then, a discussion is held about the activity. Two facets are discussed: the *process* of the

activity (what it felt like to do it) and the *content* (what was talked about during the activity). As always, the process is more important than the content and, sometimes, the trainer may choose to discuss *only* the process. Also, the trainer helps the group to identify ways in which what has been learned from the activity can be related to the group members' professional or personal lives. The group trainer joins in wherever possible.

Evaluation A discussion is invoked by the trainer about how any learning from the activity could be carried back to the workplace.

Closing Participants should be encouraged to spend a few minutes talking about their plans for the immediate future: holidays, weekend trips, social events and so forth. This allows for all participants to disassociate themselves from the activity and encourages them to return to their 'normal' roles.

Notes This activity can be used with more than 25 participants if a certain amount of structure is used. One way of managing larger numbers is to draw up a handout that gives explicit instructions to participants. Then, sub-groups are formed from the larger group and a chairperson is elected for each of the sub-groups. The task of each chairperson is to work through the instruction sheet with their group and to ensure things run smoothly. After the activity has been completed by each of the sub-groups, the larger group reforms. The chairpeople report back to the larger group during the plenary session. Structure is essential if the serial working of sub-groups is to be effective. Make sure that everyone is clear about the aims of the activity and what it is that they are supposed to be doing. Headings for an instruction sheet might be:

- Title of the activity
- Aims
- What to do
- The role of the chairperson.

© P. Burnard 1992, published by Kogan Page

USING CLOSED QUESTIONS

Activity 73

Time required 45 minutes to 1 hour.

Aim To explore the use of closed questions.

Group size Any number between 5 and 25.

Environment A large room with chairs of equal height. Space enough to allow participants to pair off and then to reconvene. Smaller rooms can be used for the pairs activity if required.

Equipment A whiteboard, blackboard or flipchart to allow discussion points to be jotted down. (The board should not become a focal point of the session.) Chalk or markers for the board or flipchart. Prepared handouts where necessary.

Procedure The group pairs off. One member of each pair asks closed questions of the other. Closed questions are those that elicit 'yes', 'no' or single-word answers and are often seen in questionnaires. Examples of closed questions are:

- 'What job do you do?'
- 'How long have you worked with your company?'
- 'Do you enjoy your work?'

The process of asking closed questions continues for five minutes. Then roles are reversed. The second phase continues for a further five minutes.

The trainer invites the group to reconvene. Then, a discussion is held about the activity. Two facets are discussed: the *process* of the

© P. Burnard 1992, published by Kogan Page

activity (what it felt like to do it) and the *content* (what was talked about during the activity). As always, the process is more important than the content and, sometimes, the trainer may choose to discuss *only* the process. Also, the trainer helps the group to identify ways in which what has been learned from the activity can be related to the group members' professional or personal lives. The group trainer joins in wherever possible.

Evaluation A discussion is invoked by the trainer about how any learning from the activity could be carried back to the workplace.

Closing Participants should be encouraged to spend a few minutes talking about their plans for the immediate future: holidays, weekend trips, social events and so forth. This allows for all participants to disassociate themselves from the activity and encourages them to return to their 'normal' roles.

Notes This activity can be used with more than 25 participants if a certain amount of structure is used. One way of managing larger numbers is to draw up a handout that gives explicit instructions to participants. Then, sub-groups are formed from the larger group and a chairperson is elected for each of the sub-groups. The task of each chairperson is to work through the instruction sheet with their group and to ensure things run smoothly. After the activity has been completed by each of the sub-groups, the larger group reforms. The chairpeople report back to the larger group during the plenary session. Structure is essential if the serial working of sub-groups is to be effective. Make sure that everyone is clear about the aims of the activity and what it is that they are supposed to be doing. Headings for an instruction sheet might be:

- Title of the activity
- Aims
- What to do
- The role of the chairperson.

USING EMPATHY-BUILDING STATEMENTS
Activity 74

Time required 45 minutes to 1 hour.

Aim To explore empathy development.

Group size Any number between 5 and 25.

Environment A large room with chairs of equal height. Space enough to allow participants to pair off and then to reconvene. Smaller rooms can be used for the pairs activity if required.

Equipment A whiteboard, blackboard or flipchart to allow discussion points to be jotted down. (The board should not become a focal point of the session.) Chalk or markers for the board or flipchart. Prepared handouts where necessary.

Procedure Counselling demands that the counsellor develops empathy with the client. In this activity, the aim is for each person to attempt to put themselves in the other person's position. The group pairs off. One member of each pair is allowed to talk to the other about any topic at all. The only interventions that the listener is allowed to make are those that indicate empathy with the talker. Examples of empathy-building statements include:

- 'It sounds as though you are quite happy to do that.'
- 'I should think that made you quite angry.'
- 'You seem to have mixed feelings about that.'

The sole aim of empathy building is to convey that the listener is on the other person's side. After ten minutes, roles are reversed.

© P. Burnard 1992, published by Kogan Page

The trainer invites the group to reconvene. Then, a discussion is held about the activity. Two facets are discussed: the *process* of the activity (what it felt like to do it) and the *content* (what was talked about during the activity). As always, the process is more important than the content and, sometimes, the trainer may choose to discuss *only* the process. Also, the trainer helps the group to identify ways in which what has been learned from the activity can be related to the group members' professional or personal lives. The group trainer joins in wherever possible.

Evaluation A discussion is invoked by the trainer about how any learning from the activity could be carried back to the workplace.

Closing Participants should be encouraged to spend a few minutes talking about their plans for the immediate future: holidays, weekend trips, social events and so forth. This allows for all participants to disassociate themselves from the activity and encourages them to return to their 'normal' roles.

Notes This activity can be used with more than 25 participants if a certain amount of structure is used. One way of managing larger numbers is to draw up a handout that gives explicit instructions to participants. Then, sub-groups are formed from the larger group and a chairperson is elected for each of the sub-groups. The task of each chairperson is to work through the instruction sheet with their group and to ensure things run smoothly. After the activity has been completed by each of the sub-groups, the larger group reforms. The chairpeople report back to the larger group during the plenary session. Structure is essential if the serial working of sub-groups is to be effective. Make sure that everyone is clear about the aims of the activity and what it is that they are supposed to be doing. Headings for an instruction sheet might be:

- Title of the activity
- Aims
- What to do
- The role of the chairperson.

© P. Burnard 1992, published by Kogan Page

CHECKING FOR UNDERSTANDING

Activity 75

Time required 45 minutes to 1 hour.

Aim To encourage the development of understanding between the counsellor and the client.

Group size Any number between 5 and 25.

Environment A large room with chairs of equal height. Space enough to allow participants to pair off and then to reconvene. Smaller rooms can be used for the pairs activity if required.

Equipment A whiteboard, blackboard or flipchart to allow discussion points to be jotted down. (The board should not become a focal point of the session.) Chalk or markers for the board or flipchart. Prepared handouts where necessary.

Procedure This is essentially a listening activity with one added dimension. The activity is based on the premise that it is essential that counsellors understand and follow what it is the client is trying to tell them. The group pairs off and one member of each pair talks to the other for about ten minutes. During that time, the only interventions that the 'listener' is allowed to make are those that involve checking that they have understood what has been said. Examples of such interventions might be:

- 'Let me just stop you ... You seem to be saying that you were happier when you were working in Doncaster and that you are not so sure about how you feel about working in London.'
- 'You are saying that you don't want to move house until house prices begin to rise again – but you want to move at *some* time.'

© P. Burnard 1992, published by Kogan Page

After ten minutes, roles are reversed.

The trainer invites the group to reconvene. Then, a discussion is held about the activity. Two facets are discussed: the *process* of the activity (what it felt like to do it) and the *content* (what was talked about during the activity). As always, the process is more important than the content and, sometimes, the trainer may choose to discuss *only* the process. Also, the trainer helps the group to identify ways in which what has been learned from the activity can be related to the group members' professional or personal lives. The group trainer joins in wherever possible.

Evaluation A discussion is invoked by the trainer about how any learning from the activity could be carried back to the workplace.

Closing Participants should be offered a five-minute period in which to raise questions, express feelings, address particular people in the group or to talk through anything else that has arisen from the activity.

Notes This activity can be used with more than 25 participants if a certain amount of structure is used. One way of managing larger numbers is to draw up a handout that gives explicit instructions to participants. Then, sub-groups are formed from the larger group and a chairperson is elected for each of the sub-groups. The task of each chairperson is to work through the instruction sheet with their group and to ensure things run smoothly. After the activity has been completed by each of the sub-groups, the larger group reforms. The chairpeople report back to the larger group during the plenary session. Structure is essential if the serial working of sub-groups is to be effective. Make sure that everyone is clear about the aims of the activity and what it is that they are supposed to be doing. Headings for an instruction sheet might be:

- Title of the activity
- Aims
- What to do
- The role of the chairperson.

EXPLORING SILENCE
Activity 76

Time required 45 minutes to 1 hour.

Aim To explore silence in the counselling relationship.

Group size Any number between 5 and 25.

Environment A large room with chairs of equal height. Space enough to allow participants to pair off and then to reconvene. Smaller rooms can be used for the pairs activity if required.

Equipment A whiteboard, blackboard or flipchart to allow discussion points to be jotted down. (The board should not become a focal point of the session.) Chalk or markers for the board or flipchart. Prepared handouts where necessary.

Procedure Counselling relies heavily on the counsellor being able to listen and to accept silence when it occurs. This activity allows participants to explore how they feel about silence. The group pairs off. Each pair sits opposite and looking at each other but silent for five minutes. No interventions of any sort are allowed during the five-minute period. Participants are encouraged to sustain eye contact with each other but are not allowed to say anything. This activity usually generates some embarrassed laughter and this, of course, is allowed. It can hardly be stopped!

The trainer invites the group to reconvene. Then, a discussion is held about the activity. Two facets are discussed: the *process* of the activity (what it felt like to do it) and the *content* (what was talked about during the activity). As always, the process is more important than the content and, sometimes, the trainer may choose to discuss *only* the process. Also, the trainer helps the group to identify ways

© P. Burnard 1992, published by Kogan Page

in which what has been learned from the activity can be related to the group members' professional or personal lives. The group trainer joins in wherever possible.

Evaluation Each person in the group, in turn, says first what they liked least about the activity. Then, each person in the group says what they liked most about the activity. The group leader or trainer joins in too.

Closing Participants should be offered a five-minute period in which to raise questions, express feelings, address particular people in the group or to talk through anything else that has arisen from the activity.

Notes This activity can be used with more than 25 participants if a certain amount of structure is used. One way of managing larger numbers is to draw up a handout that gives explicit instructions to participants. Then, sub-groups are formed from the larger group and a chairperson is elected for each of the sub-groups. The task of each chairperson is to work through the instruction sheet with their group and to ensure things run smoothly. After the activity has been completed by each of the sub-groups, the larger group reforms. The chairpeople report back to the larger group during the plenary session. Structure is essential if the serial working of sub-groups is to be effective. Make sure that everyone is clear about the aims of the activity and what it is that they are supposed to be doing. Headings for an instruction sheet might be:

- Title of the activity
- Aims
- What to do
- The role of the chairperson.

© P. Burnard 1992, published by Kogan Page

USING PROBES
Activity 77

Time required 45 minutes to 1 hour.

Aim To explore probing statements in a counselling conversation.

Group size Any number between 5 and 25.

Environment A large room with chairs of equal height. Space enough to allow participants to pair off and then to reconvene. Smaller rooms can be used for the pairs activity if required.

Equipment A whiteboard, blackboard or flipchart to allow discussion points to be jotted down. (The board should not become a focal point of the session.) Chalk or markers for the board or flipchart. Prepared handouts where necessary.

Procedure The group pairs off, one of them as the 'counsellor' and the other as the 'client'. The client then talks to the counsellor for ten minutes, about any topic, while the counsellor listens and uses occasional 'probes'. Probing statements and questions are those that encourage the person to develop a theme or to say more. Examples of such probes include:

- 'What happened when you did that ... did it turn out the way that you expected?'
- 'You sound anxious ... what happened?'
- 'Did you enjoy that ... was it what you expected?'

After ten minutes, roles are reversed.

The trainer invites the group to reconvene. Then, a discussion is held about the activity. Two facets are discussed: the *process* of the

© P. Burnard 1992, published by Kogan Page

activity (what it felt like to do it) and the *content* (what was talked about during the activity). As always, the process is more important than the content and, sometimes, the trainer may choose to discuss *only* the process. Also, the trainer helps the group to identify ways in which what has been learned from the activity can be related to the group members' professional or personal lives. The group trainer joins in wherever possible.

Evaluation The trainer invites each person in the group, in turn, to identify two things that they feel they learned from doing the activity.

Closing Participants should be offered a five-minute period in which to raise questions, express feelings, address particular people in the group or to talk through anything else that has arisen from the activity.

Notes This activity can be used with more than 25 participants if a certain amount of structure is used. One way of managing larger numbers is to draw up a handout that gives explicit instructions to participants. Then, sub-groups are formed from the larger group and a chairperson is elected for each of the sub-groups. The task of each chairperson is to work through the instruction sheet with their group and to ensure things run smoothly. After the activity has been completed by each of the sub-groups, the larger group reforms. The chairpeople report back to the larger group during the plenary session. Structure is essential if the serial working of sub-groups is to be effective. Make sure that everyone is clear about the aims of the activity and what it is that they are supposed to be doing. Headings for an instruction sheet might be:

- Title of the activity
- Aims
- What to do
- The role of the chairperson.

© P. Burnard 1992, published by Kogan Page

SUMMARIZING
Activity 78

Time required 45 minutes to 1 hour.

Aim To practise the skill of summarizing what the client has said.

Group size Any number between 5 and 25.

Environment A large room with chairs of equal height. Space enough to allow participants to pair off and then to reconvene. Smaller rooms can be used for the pairs activity if required.

Equipment A whiteboard, blackboard or flipchart to allow discussion points to be jotted down. (The board should not become a focal point of the session.) Chalk or markers for the board or flipchart. Prepared handouts where necessary.

Procedure The group pairs off. One member of each pair becomes the 'client' and the other the 'counsellor'. The clients talk to their counsellors for about five minutes while the counsellors listen to them without responding. At the end of the five-minute period, the counsellors attempt to summarize what the clients have said, as accurately as possible. Then the roles are reversed and the above process is repeated in the same two stages. An example of what a summary might sound like follows:

> You said that you were having some difficulties at home. You talked about the problems of getting the house decorated before the winter. You went on to describe the difficulties that your son had experienced when buying a car. You finished by saying that, although it had been a difficult year, you were happy that the new year would bring some changes – both at work and at home.

© P. Burnard 1992, published by Kogan Page

The trainer invites the group to reconvene. Then, a discussion is held about the activity. Two facets are discussed: the *process* of the activity (what it felt like to do it) and the *content* (what was talked about during the activity). As always, the process is more important than the content and, sometimes, the trainer may choose to discuss *only* the process. Also, the trainer helps the group to identify ways in which what has been learned from the activity can be related to the group members' professional or personal lives. The group trainer joins in wherever possible.

Evaluation A discussion is invoked by the trainer about how any learning from the activity could be carried back to the workplace.

Closing Participants should be offered a five-minute period in which to raise questions, express feelings, address particular people in the group or to talk through anything else that has arisen from the activity.

Notes This activity can be used with more than 25 participants if a certain amount of structure is used. One way of managing larger numbers is to draw up a handout that gives explicit instructions to participants. Then, sub-groups are formed from the larger group and a chairperson is elected for each of the sub-groups. The task of each chairperson is to work through the instruction sheet with their group and to ensure things run smoothly. After the activity has been completed by each of the sub-groups, the larger group reforms. The chairpeople report back to the larger group during the plenary session. Structure is essential if the serial working of sub-groups is to be effective. Make sure that everyone is clear about the aims of the activity and what it is that they are supposed to be doing. Headings for an instruction sheet might be:

- Title of the activity
- Aims
- What to do
- The role of the chairperson.

© P. Burnard 1992, published by Kogan Page

PUTTING IT ALL TOGETHER

Activity 79

Time required 45 minutes to 1 hour.

Aim To explore a range of counselling interventions.

Group size Any number between 5 and 25.

Environment A large room with chairs of equal height. Space enough to allow participants to pair off and then to reconvene. Smaller rooms can be used for the pairs activity if required.

Equipment A whiteboard, blackboard or flipchart to allow discussion points to be jotted down. (The board should not become a focal point of the session.) Chalk or markers for the board or flipchart. Prepared handouts where necessary.

Procedure The group pairs off and one member of each pair becomes the 'counsellor', the other the 'client'. The clients talk to their counsellors for a ten-minute period. During this time, the counsellors use any of the interventions from Activities 72 to 78 to help their clients develop what they have to say. Thus, the counsellors may use:

- open questions;
- closed questions;
- empathy-building statements;
- checking for understanding;
- probes;
- silence;
- summary.

© P. Burnard 1992, published by Kogan Page

After ten minutes, roles are reversed. The group trainer joins in wherever possible.

Evaluation A discussion is invoked by the trainer about how any learning from the activity could be carried back to the workplace.

Closing Participants should be offered a five-minute period in which to raise questions, express feelings, address particular people in the group or to talk through anything else that has arisen from the activity.

Notes This activity can be used with more than 25 participants if a certain amount of structure is used. One way of managing larger numbers is to draw up a handout that gives explicit instructions to participants. Then, sub-groups are formed from the larger group and a chairperson is elected for each of the sub-groups. The task of each chairperson is to work through the instruction sheet with their group and to ensure things run smoothly. After the activity has been completed by each of the sub-groups, the larger group reforms. The chairpeople report back to the larger group during the plenary session. Structure is essential if the serial working of sub-groups is to be effective. Make sure that everyone is clear about the aims of the activity and what it is that they are supposed to be doing. Headings for an instruction sheet might be:

- Title of the activity
- Aims
- What to do
- The role of the chairperson.

PERVERSE ROLE PLAY

Activity 80

Time required 45 minutes to 1 hour.

Aim To explore how *not* to counsel.

Group size Any number between 5 and 25.

Environment A large room in which people can sit comfortably in a group. Chairs should be of equal height and the group should remain in a closed circle throughout. The trainer should be part of the circle.

Equipment A whiteboard, blackboard or flipchart to allow discussion points to be jotted down. (The board should not become a focal point of the session.) Chalk or markers for the board or flipchart. Prepared handouts where necessary.

Procedure Two people volunteer to role play a counselling conversation in front of the group. The trainer may choose to be one of the volunteers. The role play consists of the counselling role being acted out *very badly*. Thus, the counsellor, purposely, does not listen very effectively, uses a large number of closed questions and does not summarize effectively. This sort of perverse role play, while initially the source of some entertainment, quickly highlights some of the difficulties of the counselling role. If it is appropriate and asked for by the group, group members can carry out perverse role plays in pairs. The trainer joins in wherever possible.

Evaluation Each person in the group, in turn, says first what they liked least about the activity. Then, each person in the group says what they liked most about the activity. The group leader or trainer joins in too.

© P. Burnard 1992, published by Kogan Page

Closing The trainer can invite the group to take part in a short 'round' in which each participant states their name, job and something they are looking forward to in the future. This allows for a 'debriefing' period to occur and for participants to disassociate themselves from the role play sufficiently to allow them to return to everyday life.

Chapter 14:
Assertiveness skills activities

USING ASSERTIVENESS SKILLS ACTIVITIES

Working in organizations can take its toll on the individual. Sometimes the person's own needs become subsumed within the demands of the organization or profession. One positive way of coping with stress in organizations and in the caring professions is to become more assertive. Assertiveness is often confused with being aggressive, but there are important differences. The assertive person is the one who can state clearly and calmly what he or she wants to say, does not back down in the face of disagreement and is prepared to repeat the point if necessary. Woodcock and Francis (1982) identify the following barriers to assertiveness:

1. *Lack of practice:* you do not test your limits enough and discover whether you can be more assertive.
2. *Formative training:* your early training by parents and others diminished your capacity to stand up for yourself.
3. *Being unclear* you do not have clear standards and you are unsure of what you want.
4. *Fear of hostility* you are afraid of anger or negative responses and you want to be considered reasonable.

5. *Undervaluing yourself:* you do not feel that you have the right to stand firm and demand correct and fair treatment.
6. *Poor presentation:* your self-expression tends to be vague, unimpressive, confusing or emotional.

Given that most professionals spend much of their time considering the needs of others, it seems likely that many overlook the personal needs identified within Woodcock and Francis' list of barriers to assertiveness. Part of the process of coping with organizational stress is learning to identify and assert personal needs and wants. The activities in this chapter are all concerned with helping people to develop the assertive side of their personalities.

YES/NO ACTIVITY
Activity 81

Time required 45 minutes to 1 hour.

Aim To explore aspects of assertive behaviour.

Group size Any number between 5 and 25.

Environment A large room with chairs of equal height. Space enough to allow participants to pair off and then to reconvene. Smaller rooms can be used for the pairs activity if required.

Equipment No special equipment is required.

Procedure People often have difficulty in saying 'no'. This activity allows for a lighthearted exploration of the problem. Group members pair off, and sit facing their partners. Then, one in each pair becomes the 'yes' person and the other the 'no' person. Partners then sit and say 'yes' and 'no' alternately. They are allowed to explore all sorts of ways of saying 'yes' and 'no', from being quiet and calm to being aggressive. The aim is to identify the circumstances in which it is easier to say 'yes' and easier to say 'no'. The 'yes/no' activity continues for about ten minutes.

The trainer invites the group to reconvene. Then, a discussion is held about the activity. Two facets are discussed: the *process* of the activity (what it felt like to do it) and the *content* (what was talked about during the activity). As always, the process is more important than the content and, sometimes, the trainer may choose to discuss *only* the process. Also, the trainer helps the group to identify ways in which what has been learned from the activity can be related to the group members' professional or personal lives. The group trainer joins in wherever possible.

© P. Burnard 1992, published by Kogan Page

Evaluation The pairs reform at the end of the activity and discuss what they liked least and most about it. They also each give an evaluation of the other's performance.

Closing The trainer can invite questions about any aspect of the activity.

Notes This can be used as a 'warm up' activity at different points during the course of a group or workshop.

© P. Burnard 1992, published by Kogan Page

SAYING NO

Activity 82

Time required 45 minutes to 1 hour.

Aim To explore situations in which it is difficult to say 'no'.

Group size Any number between 5 and 25.

Environment A large room with chairs of equal height. Space enough to allow participants to pair off and then to reconvene. Smaller rooms can be used for the pairs activity if required.

Equipment No special equipment is required.

Procedure Participants pair off. One then sits and tells the other the sorts of situations in which they find it difficult to say 'no'. Those situations may include ones at work or home and in business or social life. After ten minutes, roles are reversed.

The trainer invites the group to reconvene. Then, a discussion is held about the activity. Two facets are discussed: the *process* of the activity (what it felt like to do it) and the *content* (what was talked about during the activity). As always, the process is more important than the content and, sometimes, the trainer may choose to discuss *only* the process. Also, the trainer helps the group to identify ways in which what has been learned from the activity can be related to the group members' professional or personal lives. The group trainer joins in wherever possible.

Evaluation The trainer invites each person in the group, in turn, to identify two things that they feel they learned from doing the activity.

© P. Burnard 1992, published by Kogan Page

Closing Participants should be offered a five-minute period in which to raise questions, express feelings, address particular people in the group or to talk through anything else that has arisen from the activity.

SAYING YES
Activity 83

Time required 45 minutes to 1 hour.

Aim To explore saying 'yes' to people.

Group size Any number between 5 and 25.

Environment A large room with chairs of equal height. Space enough to allow participants to pair off and then to reconvene. Smaller rooms can be used for the pairs activity if required.

Equipment No special equipment is required.

Procedure The group pairs off. One person is nominated A and the other B. A then makes requests of B to which B always responds with a 'yes'. A is allowed to ask *any* sort of question and the aim is to experiment with questions and responses. After ten minutes, roles are reversed and B asks questions of A to which the answer is always 'yes'. The activity can encourage some hilarity but it also highlights the number of times we say 'no' when we could be saying 'yes'.

The trainer invites the group to reconvene. Then, a discussion is held about the activity. Two facets are discussed: the *process* of the activity (what it felt like to do it) and the *content* (what was talked about during the activity). As always, the process is more important than the content and, sometimes, the trainer may choose to discuss *only* the process. Also, the trainer helps the group to identify ways in which what has been learned from the activity can be related to the group members' professional or personal lives. The group trainer joins in wherever possible.

© P. Burnard 1992, published by Kogan Page

Evaluation The trainer invites each person in the group, in turn, to identify two things that they feel they learned from doing the activity.

Closing The trainer can invite questions about any aspect of the activity.

CONTRADICTORY BODY LANGUAGE

Activity 84

Time required 45 minutes to 1 hour.

Aim To explore non-verbal communication and assertiveness.

Group size Any number between 5 and 25.

Environment A large room with chairs of equal height. Space enough to allow participants to pair off and then to reconvene. Smaller rooms can be used for the pairs activity if required.

Equipment A whiteboard, blackboard or flipchart to allow discussion points to be jotted down. (The board should not become a focal point of the session.) Chalk or markers for the board or flipchart. Prepared handouts where necessary.

Procedure The group pairs off. One member of each group is nominated A and the other B. A then makes requests of B of a fairly demanding nature, to which B responds appropriately. *But*, B adopts non-verbal behaviour that is *not* assertive. Thus, B might adopt the following behaviours:

- sitting position: slightly curled up in the chair;
- eye contact: minimal;
- arms and hands: arms folded or fiddling with hands;
- expression: smiling when saying 'no' and so on.

The aim is to explore inappropriate non-verbal communication as it relates to being assertive. After ten minutes, roles are reversed.

© P. Burnard 1992, published by Kogan Page

The trainer invites the group to reconvene. Then, a discussion is held about the activity. Two facets are discussed: the *process* of the activity (what it felt like to do it) and the *content* (what was talked about during the activity). As always, the process is more important than the content and, sometimes, the trainer may choose to discuss *only* the process. Also, the trainer helps the group to identify ways in which what has been learned from the activity can be related to the group members' professional or personal lives. The group trainer joins in wherever possible.

Evaluation Each person in the group, in turn, says first what they liked least about the activity. Then, each person in the group says what they liked most about the activity. The group leader or trainer joins in too.

Closing The trainer can invite questions about any aspect of the activity.

Notes This activity can usefully be prefaced by a short theory input on non-verbal communication (Arnold and Boggs 1989). In this way, the experiential learning cycle is being played out. First, the group receive some theory about the topic. Then, they test out that theory with an activity. Keep the theory input short.

CONGRUENT BODY LANGUAGE

Activity 85

Time required 45 minutes to 1 hour.

Aim To explore appropriate use of body language in assertiveness.

Group size Any number between 5 and 25.

Environment A large room with chairs of equal height. Space enough to allow participants to pair off and then to reconvene. Smaller rooms can be used for the pairs activity if required.

Equipment A whiteboard, blackboard or flipchart to allow discussion points to be jotted down. (The board should not become a focal point of the session.) Chalk or markers for the board or flipchart. Prepared handouts where necessary.

Procedure The group pairs off. As in Activity 84, one person makes requests of the other and the partner responds appropriately to those requests. This time, however, the responders use appropriate non-verbal behaviour. Thus, they will:

- sit squarely in relation to the other person;
- sit without crossed arms or legs;
- look directly at the other person;
- use an appropriate tone of voice and so on.

After ten minutes, roles are reversed.

The trainer invites the larger group to reconvene. Then, a discussion is held about the activity. Two facets are discussed: the *process* of the

activity (what it felt like to do it) and the *content* (what was talked about during the activity). As always, the process is more important than the content and, sometimes, the trainer may choose to discuss *only* the process. Also, the trainer helps the group to identify ways in which what has been learned from the activity can be related to the group members' professional or personal lives. The group trainer joins in wherever possible.

Evaluation The trainer invites each person in the group, in turn, to identify two things that they feel they learned from doing the activity.

Closing Participants should be offered a five-minute period in which to raise questions, express feelings, address particular people in the group or to talk through anything else that has arisen from the activity.

ROLE PLAY
Activity 86

Time required 45 minutes to 1 hour.

Aim To explore assertiveness through role play.

Group size Any number between 5 and 25.

Environment A large room in which people can sit comfortably in a group. Chairs should be of equal height and the group should remain in a closed circle throughout. The trainer should be part of the circle.

Equipment A whiteboard, blackboard or flipchart to allow discussion points to be jotted down. (The board should not become a focal point of the session.) Chalk or markers for the board or flipchart. Prepared handouts where necessary.

Procedure Two people from the group are asked to volunteer to take part in a role play. One of these volunteers can be the trainer if this is desired and appropriate. The trainer then encourages the playing through of a series of situations in which assertive behaviour is called for. Examples of such situations might be:

- taking faulty goods back to a shop;
- asking for a rise in pay;
- disagreeing on a substantial issue with the boss;
- insisting on a second opinion from a GP.

The role play can be used to illustrate the player's *normal* performance in those situations and then replayed to represent the *ideal*. In this way, both the players and the group identify the elements of behaviour that go to make up an assertive performance. The group trainer joins in wherever possible.

Evaluation The trainer hands out a prepared short questionnaire about the activity. The questionnaire should ask about:

- what it was like to take part in the activity;
- what feelings were invoked by the activity;
- what elements of it would be taken back to the workplace.

Closing The trainer can invite the group to take part in a short 'round' in which each participant states their name, job and something they are looking forward to in the future. This allows for a 'debriefing' period to occur and for participants to disassociate themselves from the role play sufficiently to allow them to return to everyday life.

SUBMISSIVE ROLE PLAY
Activity 87

Time required 45 minutes to 1 hour.

Aim To explore how *not* to be assertive.

Group size Any number between 5 and 25.

Environment A large room in which people can sit comfortably in a group. Chairs should be of equal height and the group should remain in a closed circle throughout. The trainer should be part of the circle.

Equipment A whiteboard, blackboard or flipchart to allow discussion points to be jotted down. (The board should not become a focal point of the session.) Chalk or markers for the board or flipchart. Prepared handouts where necessary.

Procedure The instructions for a role play, from Activity 86 are used to set up the role-play situation. In *this* role play, however, the central player plays out a *submissive* role rather than an assertive one. This activity helps to identify the behaviours that go to make up an assertive performance by highlighting the opposite. The group trainer joins in wherever possible.

Evaluation Each person in the group, in turn, says first what they liked least about the activity. Then, each person in the group says what they liked most about the activity. The group leader or trainer joins in too.

Closing The trainer can invite the group to take part in a short 'round' in which each participant states their name, job and something they are looking forward to in the future. This allows for a 'debriefing' period to occur and for participants to disassociate themselves from the role play sufficiently to allow them to return to everyday life.

© P. Burnard 1992, published by Kogan Page

EXAGGERATED ROLE PLAY

Activity 88

Time required 45 minutes to 1 hour.

Aim To identify the elements of an assertive performance.

Group size Any number between 5 and 25.

Environment A large room in which people can sit comfortably in a group. Chairs should be of equal height and the group should remain in a closed circle throughout. The trainer should be part of the circle.

Equipment A whiteboard, blackboard or flipchart to allow discussion points to be jotted down. (The board should not become a focal point of the session.) Chalk or markers for the board or flipchart. Prepared handouts where necessary.

Procedure The previous instructions for setting up a role play are observed. In this role play, however, the role play is played through *slowly* and each player *exaggerates* his or her role. In this way, the skills of being assertive are highlighted in a dramatic (and sometimes amusing) way. The group trainer joins in wherever possible.

Evaluation The trainer invites each person in the group, in turn, to identify two things that they feel they learned from doing the activity.

Closing The trainer can invite the group to take part in a short 'round' in which each participant states their name, job and something they are looking forward to in the future. This allows for a 'debriefing' period to occur and for participants to disassociate themselves from the role play sufficiently to allow them to return to everyday life.

© P. Burnard 1992, published by Kogan Page

PSYCHODRAMA

Activity 89

Time required 45 minutes to 1 hour.

Aim To explore psychodrama as an aid to developing assertiveness.

Group size Any number between 5 and 25.

Environment A large room in which people can sit comfortably in a group. Chairs should be of equal height and the group should remain in a closed circle throughout. The trainer should be part of the circle.

Equipment A whiteboard, blackboard or flipchart to allow discussion points to be jotted down. (The board should not become a focal point of the session.) Chalk or markers for the board or flipchart. Prepared handouts where necessary.

Procedure Psychodrama is like role play but it also draws on direct, personal experience of the players. Two volunteers are called for. One of those volunteers is asked to recall a real life situation in which they should have been assertive but in which they failed. The situation is played through between the two parties. The group then offers feedback to the central player as to how they might have been more assertive. The couple then replay the psychodrama, incorporating the feedback from the group into the performance. The group trainer joins in wherever possible.

Evaluation The trainer hands out a prepared short questionnaire about the activity. The questionnaire should ask about:

- what it was like to take part in the activity;
- what feelings were invoked by the activity;

- what elements of it would be taken back to the workplace.

Closing The trainer can invite the group to take part in a short 'round' in which each participant states their name, job and something they are looking forward to in the future. This allows for a 'debriefing' period to occur and for participants to disassociate themselves from the role play sufficiently to allow them to return to everyday life.

Notes This activity can usefully be prefaced by a short theory input on psychodrama (Blatner 1988, Moreno 1969). In this way, the experiential learning cycle is being played out. First, the group receive some theory about the topic. Then, they test out that theory with an activity. Keep the theory input short.

REAL LIFE PRACTICE
Activity 90

Time required 30 minutes.

Aim To transfer assertiveness skills into everyday life.

Group size Any number between 5 and 25.

Environment A large room in which people can sit comfortably in a group. Chairs should be of equal height and the group should remain in a closed circle throughout. The trainer should be part of the circle.

Equipment A whiteboard, blackboard or flipchart to allow discussion points to be jotted down. (The board should not become a focal point of the session.) Chalk or markers for the board or flipchart. Prepared handouts where necessary.

Procedure A 'round' is conducted in which each person, in turn, identifies three situations in which they will choose to be assertive in the future. Examples might include:

- at work, with my colleagues;
- at home, with my family;
- next week, when I have to see a difficult client.

The aim is to encourage participants to offer a 'verbal contract' with themselves and with the group that will encourage them to be more assertive in real life. The group trainer joins in wherever possible.

Evaluation The trainer hands out a prepared short questionnaire about the activity. The questionnaire should ask about:

© P. Burnard 1992, published by Kogan Page

- what it was like to take part in the activity;
- what feelings were invoked by the activity;
- what elements of it would be taken back to the workplace.

Closing Participants should be offered a five-minute period in which to raise questions, express feelings, address particular people in the group or to talk through anything else that has arisen from the activity.

Chapter 15:

Interviewing skills activities

USING INTERVIEWING SKILLS ACTIVITIES

Some people loathe the prospect of interviewing almost as much as they do the process of being interviewed. A little careful planning can help here. Considerations that need to be made prior to the interview are these:

- Where will the interviewees gather and who will meet them to settle them there?
- Who will call the interviewee and will that person then introduce them to each member of the panel?
- How will the interview proceed? A traditional approach is for each of the interviewers to ask two or three questions of each person (usually the same questions). This method of interview does not allow for any real interaction between interviewer and interviewee. A more imaginative approach is to allocate a certain amount of time to each interviewer and to allow them to develop a rapport and discussion with the interviewee.
- Who will invite the interviewee to ask questions at the end of the interview and who will round off the process and thank the candidate for coming?

- If asked when the outcome of the interview will be made known to interviewees, what will be the standard response?

If these issues can be discussed and decided upon prior to the interview, the whole process will be more successful. Also, if the interview panel is to be a large one, it is important that it is chaired. The chairperson might be a contributing interviewer or may be a person who limits their interaction to the chairing process.

It is helpful if the interview follows a reasonably formal structure, even if the discussion during the interview is fairly unstructured. Typically, the following points are covered during a job interview:

- The applicant's account of their education and work prior to the application.
- Reasons for wanting the job.
- Strengths and weaknesses.
- Special qualities that the applicant can bring to the post.
- Financial and logistic issues (when the applicant would be able to start work, entry on the salary scale and so forth).

Ideally, the interview should be a two-way process. Not only does the interview panel interview the applicant but the applicant also has the chance to discuss the job and his or her suitability for it. The more formal the interview, the less likelihood of a productive discussion occurring. If only highly structured questions are asked, only 'best performance' answers will be offered. Remember that the candidate is likely to have rehearsed most of the standard interview questions prior to this moment. The more informal, open ended interviews (within a more formal outer structure) are more likely to yield in-depth anwers and insights.

All the activities in this section are concerned with enhancing people's interview skills.

PREPARING FOR AN INTERVIEW
Activity 91

Time required 45 minutes to 1 hour.

Aim To prepare participants for interviews.

Group size Any number between 5 and 25.

Environment A large room with chairs of equal height. Space enough to allow participants to pair off and then to reconvene. Smaller rooms can be used for the pairs activity if required.

Equipment A whiteboard, blackboard or flipchart to allow discussion points to be jotted down. (The board should not become a focal point of the session.) Chalk or markers for the board or flipchart. Prepared handouts where necessary.

Procedure Group participants pair off. Each pair then identifies what they need to do before they go for an interview using the following headings to order their issues:

- clothing;
- travel arrangements;
- preparation for the interview itself;
- managing stress in the interview.

The discussion can either focus around a real, anticipated interview or an imaginary one. The trainer invites the larger group to reconvene. Then, a discussion is held about the activity. Two facets are discussed: the *process* of the activity (what it felt like to do it) and the *content* (what was talked about during the activity). As always, the process is more important than the content and, sometimes, the trainer may choose to discuss *only* the process. Also, the trainer helps the group to identify ways in which what has been learned from the activity can be related to the group members' professional or personal lives. The group trainer joins in wherever possible.

Evaluation The trainer hands out a prepared short questionnaire about the activity. The questionnaire should ask about:

- what it was like to take part in the activity;
- what feelings were invoked by the activity;
- what elements of it would be taken back to the workplace.

Closing The trainer can invite questions about any aspect of the activity.

Notes This activity can be used with more than 25 participants if a certain amount of structure is used. One way of managing larger numbers is to draw up a handout that gives explicit instructions to participants. Then, sub-groups are formed from the larger group and a chairperson is elected for each of the sub-groups. The task of each chairperson is to work through the instruction sheet with their group and to ensure things run smoothly. After the activity has been completed by each of the sub-groups, the larger group reforms. The chairpeople report back to the larger group during the plenary session. Structure is essential if the serial working of sub-groups is to be effective. Make sure that everyone is clear about the aims of the activity and what it is that they are supposed to be doing. Headings for an instruction sheet might be:

- Title of the activity
- Aims
- What to do
- The role of the chairperson.

This activity can usefully be prefaced by a short theory input on interviewing. In this way, the experiential learning cycle is being played out. First, the group receive some theory about the topic. Then, they test out that theory with an activity. Keep the theory input short.

© P. Burnard 1992, published by Kogan Page

INTERVIEW CHECKLIST
Activity 92

Time required 45 minutes to 1 hour.

Aim To explore aspects of the interview process.

Group size Any number between 5 and 25.

Environment A large room with chairs of equal height. Space enough to allow participants to pair off and then to reconvene. Smaller rooms can be used for the pairs activity if required.

Equipment A whiteboard, blackboard or flipchart to allow discussion points to be jotted down. (The board should not become a focal point of the session.) Chalk or markers for the board or flipchart. Prepared handouts where necessary.

Procedure The trainer hands out the following checklist. The group pairs off and each pair fills in the checklist and discusses each other's findings. The trainer invites the group to reconvene. Then, a discussion is held about the activity. Two facets are discussed: the *process* of the activity (what it felt like to do it) and the *content* (what was talked about during the activity). As always, the process is more important than the content and, sometimes, the trainer may choose to discuss *only* the process. Also, the trainer helps the group to identify ways in which what has been learned from the activity can be related to the group members' professional or personal lives. The group trainer joins in wherever possible.

Evaluation A discussion is invoked by the trainer about how any learning from the activity could be carried back to the workplace.

© P. Burnard 1992, published by Kogan Page

Closing Participants should be offered a five-minute period in which to raise questions, express feelings, address particular people in the group or to talk through anything else that has arisen from the activity.

Notes This activity can be used with more than 25 participants if a certain amount of structure is used. One way of managing larger numbers is to draw up a handout that gives explicit instructions to participants. Then, sub-groups are formed from the larger group and a chairperson is elected for each of the sub-groups. The task of each chairperson is to work through the instruction sheet with their group and to ensure things run smoothly. After the activity has been completed by each of the sub-groups, the larger group reforms. The chairpeople report back to the larger group during the plenary session. Structure is essential if the serial working of sub-groups is to be effective. Make sure that everyone is clear about the aims of the activity and what it is that they are supposed to be doing. Headings for an instruction sheet might be:

- Title of the activity
- Aims
- What to do
- The role of the chairperson.

INTERVIEW SKILLS CHECKLIST			
	True	False	Uncertain
1. I am never stressed by interviews			
2. I have definite strategies for dealing with interview anxiety			
3. It is important to dress appropriately for interviews			
4. It is vital to read widely before you are interviewed			
5. It is better to arrive slightly before the interview time rather than 'on the dot'			
6. Interviews are a good way of assessing people's work potential			
7. There are some interviews that I have enjoyed			

© P. Burnard 1992, published by Kogan Page

IDENTIFYING KEY ISSUES

Activity 93

Time required 45 minutes to 1 hour.

Aim To identify key issues in the interview process.

Group size Any number between 5 and 25.

Environment A large room in which people can sit comfortably in a group. Chairs should be of equal height and the group should remain in a closed circle throughout. The trainer should be part of the circle.

Equipment A whiteboard, blackboard or flipchart to allow discussion points to be jotted down. (The board should not become a focal point of the session.) Chalk or markers for the board or flipchart. Prepared handouts where necessary.

Procedure Each person, in turn, identifies six things that they hold to be important about the whole process of being interviewed. The issues are written on to a blackboard or flip-chart sheet. The items are then prioritized by the group. A discussion is invoked about the relative importance of all of the issues mentioned, the aim being to finish the activity with a list of key principles about being interviewed.

Evaluation A discussion is invoked by the trainer about how any learning from the activity could be carried back to the workplace.

Closing Participants should be encouraged to spend a few minutes talking about their plans for the immediate future: holidays,

© P. Burnard 1992, published by Kogan Page

weekend trips, social events and so forth. This allows for all participants to disassociate themselves from the activity and encourages them to return to their 'normal' roles.

Notes This activity can be used with more than 25 participants if a certain amount of structure is used. One way of managing larger numbers is to draw up a handout that gives explicit instructions to participants. Then, sub-groups are formed from the larger group and a chairperson is elected for each of the sub-groups. The task of each chairperson is to work through the instruction sheet with their group and to ensure things run smoothly. After the activity has been completed by each of the sub-groups, the larger group reforms. The chairpeople report back to the larger group during the plenary session. Structure is essential if the serial working of sub-groups is to be effective. Make sure that everyone is clear about the aims of the activity and what it is that they are supposed to be doing. Headings for an instruction sheet might be:

- Title of the activity
- Aims
- What to do
- The role of the chairperson.

WRITING A CV
Activity 94

Time required 45 minutes to 1 hour.

Aim To facilitate the writing of a curriculum vitae.

Group size Any number between 5 and 25.

Environment A large room in which people can sit comfortably in a group. Chairs should be of equal height and the group should remain in a closed circle throughout. The trainer should be part of the circle.

Equipment A whiteboard, blackboard or flipchart to allow discussion points to be jotted down. (The board should not become a focal point of the session.) Chalk or markers for the board or flipchart. Prepared handouts where necessary.

Procedure Your curriculum vitae, or 'life curriculum', is often your first point of contact with another person when you are communicating through the post. It is important that your CV 'sells' you. If you produce a hurried and scruffy CV you cannot hope to impress the person that you are writing to. A CV lists your achievements to date. The following is a list of the sorts of things that are suitable for inclusion. In the activity that follows, we explore how to lay out and develop your own CV.

The group pairs off and help each other to make notes for a CV under the headings given. Particularly, they help bring order to the CV by the recalling of dates and times. If possible, each person completes a curriculum vitae outline before the full group reconvenes. The group trainer joins in wherever possible.

© P. Burnard 1992, published by Kogan Page

Evaluation The trainer hands out a prepared short questionnaire about the activity. The questionnaire should ask about:

- what it was like to take part in the activity;
- what feelings were invoked by the activity;
- what elements of it would be taken back to the workplace.

Closing The trainer can invite questions about any aspect of the activity.

Notes This activity can usefully be prefaced by a short theory input on developing a curriculum vitae. In this way, the experiential learning cycle is being played out. First, the group receive some theory about the topic. Then, they test out that theory with an activity. Keep the theory input short.

Headings for a Curriculum Vitae

- Your full name
- Your full address
- Your date of birth
- Your current job
- A brief description of your current job
- The history of your education to date
- The history of your work to date
- A list of special skills that you have
- Club and association membership
- A list of conferences at which you have given papers
- Any work published
- Other interests

ROLE-PLAY INTERVIEW

Activity 95

Time required 45 minutes to 1 hour.

Aim To explore the interview process through role play.

Group size Any number between 5 and 25.

Environment A large room in which people can sit comfortably in a group. Chairs should be of equal height and the group should remain in a closed circle throughout. The trainer should be part of the circle.

Equipment A whiteboard, blackboard or flipchart to allow discussion points to be jotted down. (The board should not become a focal point of the session.) Chalk or markers for the board or flipchart. Prepared handouts where necessary.

Procedure Two volunteers are recruited from the group. (The trainer may be one of these volunteers if this is requested and appropriate.) The pair then decide on who will be the interviewee and who will interview. They also agree about what the interview is an interview *for*. The role play is then acted out while the rest of the group look on. Afterwards, the two players invite the group to offer comments on their performances.

Evaluation The trainer hands out a prepared short questionnaire about the activity. The questionnaire should ask about:

- what it was like to take part in the activity;
- what feelings were invoked by the activity;
- what elements of it would be taken back to the workplace.

© P. Burnard 1992, published by Kogan Page

Closing The trainer can invite the group to take part in a short 'round' in which each participant states their name, job and something they are looking forward to in the future. This allows for a 'debriefing' period to occur and for participants to disassociate themselves from the role play sufficiently to allow them to return to everyday life.

© P. Burnard 1992, published by Kogan Page

PERVERSE ROLE PLAY

Activity 96

Time required 45 minutes to 1 hour.

Aim To identify key issues in the interview process.

Group size Any number between 5 and 25.

Environment A large room in which people can sit comfortably in a group. Chairs should be of equal height and the group should remain in a closed circle throughout. The trainer should be part of the circle.

Equipment A whiteboard, blackboard or flipchart to allow discussion points to be jotted down. (The board should not become a focal point of the session.) Chalk or markers for the board or flipchart. Prepared handouts where necessary.

Procedure Two volunteers are recruited from the group. (The trainer may be one of these volunteers if this is requested and appropriate.) The pair then decide on who will be the interviewee and who will interview. They also agree about what the interview is an interview *for*. The role play is then acted out while the rest of the group look on. In this role play, however, both parties act as badly as possible. The aim is, through exaggeration, to highlight the salient points of interviewing strategy. Afterwards, the two players invite the group to offer comments on their performances.

Evaluation Each person in the group, in turn, says first what they liked least about the activity. Then, each person in the group says what they liked most about the activity. The group leader or trainer joins in too.

© P. Burnard 1992, published by Kogan Page

Closing The trainer can invite the group to take part in a short 'round' in which each participant states their name, job and something they are looking forward to in the future. This allows for a 'debriefing' period to occur and for participants to disassociate themselves from the role play sufficiently to allow them to return to everyday life.

© P. Burnard 1992, published by Kogan Page

CONFIDENCE BUILDING
Activity 97

Time required 45 minutes to 1 hour.

Aim To enable participants to boost their confidence.

Group size Any number between 5 and 25.

Environment A large room in which people can sit comfortably in a group. Chairs should be of equal height and the group should remain in a closed circle throughout. The trainer should be part of the circle.

Equipment A whiteboard, blackboard or flipchart to allow discussion points to be jotted down. (The board should not become a focal point of the session.) Chalk or markers for the board or flipchart. Prepared handouts where necessary.

Procedure This activity can be used to enable participants to remember positive things about themselves. These positive thoughts can be used for confidence building prior to an interview. Each person in turn takes time in the 'hotseat'. While occupying the hotseat, other group members offer them positive comments about their performance or personality, unequivocally and without reservation; for example:

- I appreciate the way that you *listen* to people.
- I enjoy working in pairs with you.
- I like the way you dress.
- I see you as a very confident person and I like that.

Each person occupies the hotseat until every other person in the group has made a positive statement. The group trainer joins in wherever possible.

Evaluation The trainer invites each person in the group, in turn, to identify two things that they feel they learned from doing the activity.

Closing Participants should be encouraged to spend a few minutes talking about their plans for the immediate future: holidays, weekend trips, social events and so forth. This allows for all participants to disassociate themselves from the activity and encourages them to return to their 'normal' roles.

PRACTISING INTERVIEWING

Activity 98

Time required 45 minutes to 1 hour.

Aim To practise the roles of interviewer and interviewee.

Group size Any number between 5 and 25.

Environment A large room in which people can sit comfortably in a group. Chairs should be of equal height and the group should remain in a closed circle throughout. The trainer should be part of the circle.

Equipment A whiteboard, blackboard or flipchart to allow discussion points to be jotted down. (The board should not become a focal point of the session.) Chalk or markers for the board or flipchart. Prepared handouts where necessary.

Procedure The group pairs off. One member of each pair is 'interviewer' and the other 'interviewee'. Interviews are then carried out, with participants practising the skills of both roles. After 15 minutes, the interview is concluded. Then, the pairs swap roles. The group trainer joins in wherever possible.

Evaluation The trainer hands out a prepared short questionnaire about the activity. The questionnaire should ask about:

- what it was like to take part in the activity;
- what feelings were invoked by the activity;
- what elements of it would be taken back to the workplace.

© P. Burnard 1992, published by Kogan Page

Closing Participants should be encouraged to spend a few minutes talking about their plans for the immediate future: holidays, weekend trips, social events and so forth. This allows for all participants to disassociate themselves from the activity and encourages them to return to their 'normal' roles.

DEVIL'S ADVOCATE
Activity 99

Time required 45 minutes to 1 hour.

Aim To explore opposite points of view.

Group size Any number between 5 and 25.

Environment A large room in which people can sit comfortably in a group. Chairs should be of equal height and the group should remain in a closed circle throughout. The trainer should be part of the circle.

Equipment A whiteboard, blackboard or flipchart to allow discussion points to be jotted down. (The board should not become a focal point of the session.) Chalk or markers for the board or flipchart. Prepared handouts where necessary.

Procedure The group trainer sets up a role-play interview between two volunteers. During the interview, any other member of the group may play 'Devil's advocate' and call 'foul!' at any point were they feels that the interviewer or interviewee has not intervened or responded well. When foul is called, the caller states their objection and then either member of the role play must modify their behaviour according to the objection. The role play then continues until the next call. The group trainer acts as referee.

Evaluation Each person in the group, in turn, says first what they liked least about the activity. Then, each person in the group says what they liked most about the activity. The group leader or trainer joins in too.

© P. Burnard 1992, published by Kogan Page

Closing Participants should be encouraged to spend a few minutes talking about their plans for the immediate future: holidays, weekend trips, social events and so forth. This allows for all participants to disassociate themselves from the activity and encourages them to return to their 'normal' roles.

© P. Burnard 1992, published by Kogan Page

PUTTING IT ALL TOGETHER

Activity 100

Time required 45 minutes to 1 hour.

Aim To explore all aspects of interviewing.

Group size Any number between 6 and 25.

Environment A large room in which people can sit comfortably in a group. Chairs should be of equal height and the group should remain in a closed circle throughout. The trainer should be part of the circle.

Equipment A whiteboard, blackboard or flipchart to allow discussion points to be jotted down. (The board should not become a focal point of the session.) Chalk or markers for the board or flipchart. Prepared handouts where necessary.

Procedure This activity is used at the end of a training session on interviewing. The group divides into sets of three or four. The group trainer joins in wherever possible. Two of each group role play an interview in line with previous activities described above. The third and/or fourth members act as *process observers* and make notes on the progress of the interview, the interviewer's style and the interviewee's responses. After a ten-minute interview, the small group remains together and a feedback session is held in the following order:

- the interviewer briefly appraises his or her own performance,
- the interviewee briefly appraises his or her own performance,
- the process observer(s) offer both interviewer and interviewee feedback on their performances.

© P. Burnard 1992, published by Kogan Page

The trainer invites the larger group to reconvene. Then, a discussion is held about the activity. Two facets are discussed: the *process* of the activity (what it felt like to do it) and the *content* (what was talked about during the activity). As always, the process is more important than the content and, sometimes, the trainer may choose to discuss *only* the process. Also, the trainer helps the group to identify ways in which what has been learned from the activity can be related to the group members' professional or personal lives. The group trainer joins in wherever possible.

Evaluation The trainer hands out a prepared short questionnaire about the activity. The questionnaire should ask about:

- what it was like to take part in the activity;
- what feelings were invoked by the activity;
- what elements of it would be taken back to the workplace.

Closing Participants should be encouraged to spend a few minutes talking about their plans for the immediate future: holidays, weekend trips, social events and so forth. This allows for all participants to disassociate themselves from the activity and encourages them to return to their 'normal' roles.

© P. Burnard 1992, published by Kogan Page

Chapter 16:
Facilitation skills activities

DEVELOPING FACILITATION SKILLS

Heron (1989) offers a sixfold model of facilitator styles. He calls these six aspects of facilitation dimensions:

- the planning dimension,
- the meaning dimension,
- the confronting dimension,
- the feeling dimension,
- the structuring dimension,
- the valuing dimension.

The six dimensions of facilitator style may be used to make decisions about how *this* group is run at *this* time. Not all the dimensions will be used in every group. Decisions about which dimension will be used during which group will depend on the type of group that is being run, the aims of that group, the personality of the trainer and the needs of the participants. The dimensions cover most aspects of the setting up and running of groups. What follows is an adapted version of Heron's model.

The planning dimension

This dimension is concerned with the setting up of the group. Group members always need to know *why* they are in a particular group. Therefore the trainer needs to make certain decisions about how to identify the aims and objectives of the group. There are at least three options here:

- Decide upon the aims and objectives before setting up the group at all.
- Negotiate the aims and objectives with the group. In this case, the trainer will decide on some of those aims and objectives while the group will decide on others.
- Encourage the group to set its own aims and objectives. In this case, all the trainer does is to turn up on a certain day with a 'title' or name for the group. All further decisions about what the group is to achieve are made by the group.

The first example above illustrates the traditional learning group approach. The professional educator who uses this approach will have set aims and objectives for a particular lesson, planned in advance.

The second example illustrates the negotiated group approach. The professional working as a group therapist (for example), will meet the group for the first time and work with them to identify what that group can achieve in the time that they meet together.

The third example illustrates the fully client-centred or student-centred approach to working with groups. Here, the professional does not anticipate the needs or wants of the group at all. Instead, the learning, therapy or discussion group sets its own agenda. Such an approach needs careful handling if it is not to degenerate into an aimless series of meetings.

Other aspects of the planning dimension include making decisions about the number of group participants, whether or not particular 'rules' will apply to the group, and whether or not group membership will remain the same throughout the life of the group (the closed group) or if new members will be allowed to join (the open group).

Again, such planning decisions can be taken either unilaterally by the trainer or via negotiation with the group.

The meaning dimension

This aspect of group facilitation is concerned with what sense group members make of being in the group. As with the previous dimension, at least three options are open here:

- The professional can offer explanations, theories or models to enable group members to make sense of what is happening. Thus a professional running a support group for bereaved relatives may offer a theoretical model of bereavement to provide those relatives with a framework for understanding what is happening to them.
- The professional may sometimes offer 'interpretations' of what is going on. At other times, they will listen to group members' perceptions of what is happening. This may happen frequently in an open discussion group or a case conference.
- The trainer offers no explanations or theories but encourages group members to verbalize their own ideas, thoughts and theories. This is the non-directive mode of working with meaning in a group.

The confronting dimension

When people work together, all sorts of conflicts can arise. Sometimes these conflicts show themselves in arguments and disagreements; sometimes, a 'hidden agenda' is at work. Conflicts lie just beneath the surface of group life and they cannot be worked with unless the group addresses them directly. The confronting dimension of facilitation is concerned with ways in which individual members and the group as a whole are challenged. The three ways of working in this dimension are as follows:

- The professional can challenge the group or its members directly by asking questions, making suggestions or offering interpretations of behaviour in the group. The aim is to encourage the group and its members to confront what is happening at various levels.

- The professional can facilitate an atmosphere in which people feel safe enough to challenge each other (and the trainer). The following 'ground rules' for direct and clear communication can help:
    a) say 'I' rather than 'you', 'we' or 'people when discussing issues in the group;
    b) speak directly to other people, rather than about them. Thus 'I am angry with you, David' is better than 'I am angry with people in this group'.
- The professional can choose not to confront at all. In this case, two things may happen: either no confrontation takes place and the group gets 'stuck', or the group learns to challenge itself, without assistance from the trainer.

The first example of confrontation above is the traditional 'chairperson' mode of facilitation. The professional who uses this approach stays in control of the group. The negotiated style of confrontation is one that can be used in discussion groups and informal teaching sessions. The third example is one that can be used in meetings and discussions that are of a very formal kind. If it is used in therapy and self-awareness groups, the chances are that the 'hidden agenda' will not be addressed or that the group will outgrow the need for a trainer. It is arguable that *all* groups should aim to become independent of the group leader.

The feeling dimension

Therapy groups, self-awareness groups and certain sorts of learning groups, tend to generate emotion in participants. The feeling dimension is concerned with how such emotional expression is dealt with. Decisions to be made in this domain include:

- Will emotional release be encouraged? This may be appropriate in a therapy or social skills training group.
- Is there to be an explicit contract with the group about emotional release? Here, the professional may suggest at the beginning of the first group meeting that emotional release is allowed, thus giving group members permission to express emotions.

- Does the professional feel skilled in handling emotional release? If not, they may want to develop skills in coping with other people's feelings, especially when these involve the overt expression of tears, anger or fear. Training in cathartic work is needed here.

The structuring dimension

Structure is a necessary part of group life; without it, the group can fall apart. The issue, here, is how such structure is developed. Again, at least three options open up in this domain:

- The professional can decide on the total structure of the group. In a social skills group, for example, a variety of exercises and activities may be introduced that allow participants to learn how to answer the telephone, introduce themselves at parties or take faulty goods back to a shop. The trainer remains in control of the overall structure at all times.
- The professional can encourage group members to organize certain aspects of the life and structure of the group. Thus the business manager who is running a learning group may invite colleagues to read and discuss seminar papers. In this approach, some of the structure is handed over to group members.
- The professional can play a minimal role in structuring the life of the group. The extreme example of this is the 'Tavistock' approach to group therapy in which the group starts and finishes at particular times. Between those times the trainer makes no attempt to 'lead' the group. This is not for the uninitiated!

As a general rule it is probably better for the new trainer to start by imposing lots of structure. As confidence is gained in running groups, some of that structure can gradually be handed over to group members.

The valuing dimension

This aspect of group facilitation is concerned with creating a supportive and valuing atmosphere in which the group can work. No group will succeed if the atmosphere is one of distrust and suspicion. The issues, here, are:

- Is the trainer confident enough to allow disagreement, discussion and various points of view?
- Does the trainer have sufficient self-awareness to know what effect they are having on the group?
- Is the trainer skilled, positive, life-asserting and encouraging?

Learning to value other people (and oneself) comes with experience of running groups and by developing a range of therapeutic skills such as counselling, social skills and assertiveness.

Facilitation can be an exhilarating and educational experience for professionals and educators. Used effectively, such skills can have direct and indirect effects on improving the quality of education, management and care. The activities follow are all concerned with the development of facilitation skills.

IDENTIFYING FACILITATION SKILLS

Activity 101

Time required 30 minutes.

Aim To identify facilitation skills in a group setting.

Group size Any number between 5 and 25.

Environment A large room in which people can sit comfortably in a group. Chairs should be of equal height and the group should remain in a closed circle throughout. The trainer should be part of the circle.

Equipment A whiteboard, blackboard or flipchart to allow discussion points to be jotted down. (The board should not become a focal point of the session.) Chalk or markers for the board or flipchart. Prepared handouts where necessary.

Procedure The trainer leads a brainstorming session on the topic 'Group Facilitation Skills'. This session continues until no one in the group can identify any further skills. The trainer arbitrates over the question of what counts as a skill. Many people, when they do this activity for the first time, call out 'attitudes' or 'qualities'. The aim is to identify *skills*.

After the brainstorming session, the group trainer leads a discussion on how such skills might be developed. Alternatively, a theory input on facilitation skills using Heron's dimensions of trainer style, described and discussed above, may be offered.

© P. Burnard 1992, published by Kogan Page

Evaluation The trainer invites each person in the group, in turn, to identify two things that they feel they learned from doing the activity.

Closing Participants should be offered a five-minute period in which to raise questions, express feelings, address particular people in the group or to talk through anything else that has arisen from the activity.

Notes This activity can usefully be prefaced by a short theory input on group dynamics and group life. In this way, the experiential learning cycle is being played out. First, the group receive some theory about the topic. Then, they test out that theory with an activity. Keep the theory input short.

SELF-ASSESSMENT
Activity 102

Time required 45 minutes to 1 hour.

Aim To enable group participants to identify their strengths and deficiencies in group facilitation.

Group size Any number between 5 and 25.

Environment A large room in which people can sit comfortably in a group. Chairs should be of equal height and the group should remain in a closed circle throughout. The trainer should be part of the circle.

Equipment A whiteboard, blackboard or flipchart to allow discussion points to be jotted down. (The board should not become a focal point of the session.) Chalk or markers for the board or flipchart. Prepared handouts where necessary.

Procedure Following a theory input on Heron's dimensions of facilitator style, each person is given the following trainer style checklist and asked to complete it. Once all participants have completed the checklist, each, in turn, calls out their list. The trainer keeps a tally of participants scores on a 'group profile' score sheet which has been prepared earlier and displayed on a flip chart sheet (see below). By placing a tick in the appropriate box each time a participant responds it is possible to draw up a group profile of skills by totalling the number of ticks across the rows.

The resulting 'scores' from this activity can be used to determine the training needs of the group in the various dimensions of trainer-training. For example, it may be the case that most of the group feel confident in the planning and structuring dimensions but particu-

TRAINER STYLE CHECKLIST

Please fill in the following checklist. Put a tick in the column that most closely reflects your feelings about your skill level at present.

Dimension	Skilled	Unskilled	Not sure
Planning Dimension			
Meaning Dimension			
Confronting Dimension			
Feeling Dimension			
Structuring Dimension			
Valuing Dimension			

© P. Burnard 1992, published by Kogan Page

DIMENSIONS OF TRAINER STYLE : GROUP PROFILE				
Dimension	Skilled	Unskilled	Not sure	TOTALS
Planning Dimension				
Meaning Dimension				
Confronting Dimension				
Feeling Dimension				
Structuring Dimension				
Valuing Dimension				

© P. Burnard 1992, published by Kogan Page

larly unskilled in the feeling and confronting dimensions. In this case, the focus of the training group can be on the weaker aspects.

Evaluation Each person in the group, in turn, says first what they liked least about the activity. Then, each person in the group says what they liked most about the activity. The group leader or trainer joins in too.

Closing The trainer can invite questions about any aspect of the activity.

PLANNING
Activity 103

Time required 45 minutes to 1 hour.

Aim To explore the planning dimension of group facilitation.

Group size Any number between 5 and 25.

Environment A large room in which people can sit comfortably in a group. Chairs should be of equal height and the group should remain in a closed circle throughout. The trainer should be part of the circle.

Equipment A whiteboard, blackboard or flipchart to allow discussion points to be jotted down. (The board should not become a focal point of the session.) Chalk or markers for the board or flipchart. Prepared handouts where necessary.

Procedure One person is either elected or volunteers to lead the group. That person is then allowed time to organize a group activity (The focus should be *planning* a group activity.) The elected leader or volunteer then leads the group through the activity. The group trainer joins in wherever possible. Afterwards, the person practising facilitation skills invites feedback from both the trainer and the other members of the group.

Evaluation The trainer invites each person in the group, in turn, to identify two things that they feel they learned from doing the activity.

Closing The trainer can invite questions about any aspect of the activity.

© P. Burnard 1992, published by Kogan Page

MEANING
Activity 104

Time required 45 minutes to 1 hour.

Aim To explore the meaning dimension of group facilitation.

Group size Any number between 5 and 25.

Environment A large room in which people can sit comfortably in a group. Chairs should be of equal height and the group should remain in a closed circle throughout. The trainer should be part of the circle.

Equipment A whiteboard, blackboard or flipchart to allow discussion points to be jotted down. (The board should not become a focal point of the session.) Chalk or markers for the board or flipchart. Prepared handouts where necessary.

Procedure One person is either elected or volunteers to lead the group. That person then leads a group discussion and, at their own discretion, *either* invites the group to reflect on what is happening in the group at that time *or* offers an explanation of what might be happening.

By adopting the latter format, the volunteer is free to choose the theoretical framework; for example, what is happening may be explained in terms of any of the following:

- transactional analysis theory;
- group dynamics;
- psychodynamic theory;
- humanistic theory.

© P. Burnard 1992, published by Kogan Page

When the discussion has finished, the person practising facilitation invites feedback on their performance from the trainer and from other group members. The trainer joins in wherever possible.

Evaluation A discussion is invoked by the trainer about how any learning from the activity could be carried back to the workplace.

Closing Participants should be offered a five-minute period in which to raise questions, express feelings, address particular people in the group or to talk through anything else that has arisen from the activity.

CONFRONTING

Activity 105

Time required 45 minutes to 1 hour.

Aim To explore the confronting dimension of group facilitation.

Group size Any number between 5 and 25.

Environment A large room in which people can sit comfortably in a group. Chairs should be of equal height and the group should remain in a closed circle throughout. The trainer should be part of the circle.

Equipment A whiteboard, blackboard or flipchart to allow discussion points to be jotted down. (The board should not become a focal point of the session.) Chalk or markers for the board or flipchart. Prepared handouts where necessary.

Procedure One person is either elected or volunteers to lead the group, and initiates a discussion with the group on any topic. During this time as 'trainer' of the group, he or she actively challenges group members on any of the following issues:

- Their level of participation (for example, a quiet person may be invited to express their views).
- The accuracy of what they are saying.
- The evidence for what they are saying.

In these and any other appropriate ways, the volunteer trainer develops a confronting style of facilitation. When the discussion has finished, that person invites feedback on their performance from the trainer and from other group members. The trainer joins in wherever possible.

© P. Burnard 1992, published by Kogan Page

330 Interpersonal skills training activities

Evaluation A discussion is invoked by the trainer about how any learning from the activity could be carried back to the workplace.

Closing Participants should be offered a five-minute period in which to raise questions, express feelings, address particular people in the group or to talk through anything else that has arisen from the activity.

DEALING WITH FEELINGS

Activity 106

Time required 45 minutes to 1 hour.

Aim To explore the feeling dimension of group facilitation.

Group size Any number between 5 and 25.

Environment A large room in which people can sit comfortably in a group. Chairs should be of equal height and the group should remain in a closed circle throughout. The trainer should be part of the circle.

Equipment A whiteboard, blackboard or flipchart to allow discussion points to be jotted down. (The board should not become a focal point of the session.) Chalk or markers for the board or flipchart. Prepared handouts where necessary.

Procedure One person is either elected or volunteers to lead the group and initiates a discussion on any topic. During the discussion, the chosen person encourages group members to express their feelings about the topic in question. If feelings arise spontaneously, no attempt is made to stop them – indeed, their release is encouraged. When the discussion has finished, the trainee invites feedback on their performance from the trainer and from other group members. The group trainer joins in the activity wherever possible.

Evaluation Each person in the group, in turn, says first what they liked least about the activity. Then, each person in the group says

what they liked most about the activity. The group leader or trainer joins in too.

Closing Participants should be encouraged to spend a few minutes talking about their plans for the immediate future: holidays, weekend trips, social events and so forth. This allows for all participants to disassociate themselves from the activity and encourages them to return to their 'normal' roles.

STRUCTURING
Activity 107

Time required 45 minutes to 1 hour.

Aim To explore the structuring dimension of group facilitation.

Group size Any number between 5 and 25.

Environment A large room in which people can sit comfortably in a group. Chairs should be of equal height and the group should remain in a closed circle throughout. The trainer should be part of the circle.

Equipment A whiteboard, blackboard or flipchart to allow discussion points to be jotted down. (The board should not become a focal point of the session.) Chalk or markers for the board or flipchart. Prepared handouts where necessary.

Procedure One person is either elected or volunteers to lead the group. That person then leads a discussion with the group paying close attention to the *structure* of the discussion, for instance:

- the time taken to complete the discussion;
- the amount of time that each person speaks for;
- the frequency with which certain people speak (the 'leader' will attempt to obtain balance on this issue);
- the 'flow' of the discussion and any tendency for the group to wander off the topic.

The group trainer joins in the activity wherever possible. After the discussion has finished, the volunteer invites feedback on their performance from the trainer and from other group members.

© P. Burnard 1992, published by Kogan Page

Evaluation The trainer invites each person in the group, in turn, to identify two things that they feel they learned from doing the activity.

Closing Participants should be offered a five-minute period in which to raise questions, express feelings, address particular people in the group or to talk through anything else that has arisen from the activity.

VALUING

Activity 108

Time required 45 minutes to 1 hour.

Aim To explore the valuing dimension of group facilitation.

Group size Any number between 5 and 25.

Environment A large room in which people can sit comfortably in a group. Chairs should be of equal height and the group should remain in a closed circle throughout. The trainer should be part of the circle.

Equipment A whiteboard, blackboard or flipchart to allow discussion points to be jotted down. (The board should not become a focal point of the session.) Chalk or markers for the board or flipchart. Prepared handouts where necessary.

Procedure One person is either elected or volunteers to lead the group. That person leads the group in a discussion in which other group members are *encouraged* as much as possible. Thus people will be thanked for their contribution, others encouraged to join in and generally a style of facilitation will be demonstrated that values other people's contributions. The group trainer joins in the activity wherever possible. After the discussion has finished, the volunteer invites feedback on their performance from the trainer and from other group members.

Evaluation Each person in the group, in turn, says first what they liked least about the activity. Then, each person in the group says what they liked most about the activity. The group leader or trainer joins in too.

© P. Burnard 1992, published by Kogan Page

Closing Participants should be offered a five-minute period in which to raise questions, express feelings, address particular people in the group or to talk through anything else that has arisen from the activity.

LISTENING TO THE GROUP

Activity 109

Time required 45 minutes to 1 hour.

Aim To explore the range of styles of group facilitation.

Group size Any number between 5 and 25.

Environment A large room in which people can sit comfortably in a group. Chairs should be of equal height and the group should remain in a closed circle throughout. The trainer should be part of the circle.

Equipment A whiteboard, blackboard or flipchart to allow discussion points to be jotted down. (The board should not become a focal point of the session.) Chalk or markers for the board or flipchart. Prepared handouts where necessary.

Procedure One member of the group volunteers or is chosen to facilitate the group. He or she learns the six dimensions of trainer style and uses them appropriately through 'listening' to the needs of the group as it unfolds. The group trainer joins in the activity wherever possible. After the discussion, the volunteer invites feedback on their performance from the trainer and from other members of the group.

Evaluation Each person in the group, in turn, says first what they liked least about the activity. Then, each person in the group says what they liked most about the activity. The group leader or trainer joins in too.

Closing The trainer can invite questions about any aspect of the activity.

© P. Burnard 1992, published by Kogan Page

PUTTING GROUP FACILITATION INTO PRACTICE

Activity 110

Time required 45 minutes to 1 hour.

Aim To apply the principles of group facilitation 'back at base'.

Group size Any number between 5 and 25.

Environment A large room in which people can sit comfortably in a group. Chairs should be of equal height and the group should remain in a closed circle throughout. The trainer should be part of the circle.

Equipment A whiteboard, blackboard or flipchart to allow discussion points to be jotted down. (The board should not become a focal point of the session.) Chalk or markers for the board or flipchart. Prepared handouts where necessary.

Procedure Each person, in turn, states three ways in which they will practise the styles of group facilitation that have been demonstrated. This 'round' is a means of reinforcing exactly what the skills are and how they can be used in real life. If there is still any doubt about the nature of each of the dimensions of trainer style, this can be allowed to surface during this round and further elaboration can be offered by the trainer. The group trainer joins in the activity wherever possible and offers three examples of how he or she will practise the styles.

© P. Burnard 1992, published by Kogan Page

Evaluation Each person in the group, in turn, says first what they liked least about the activity. Then, each person in the group says what they liked most about the activity. The group leader or trainer joins in too.

Closing Participants should be offered a five-minute period in which to raise questions, express feelings, address particular people in the group or to talk through anything else that has arisen from the activity.

Chapter 17:

Topics for discussion

Many of the activities in this manual have called for discussions to be held, either in a pairs or a group format. It is sometimes (though not always) difficult to think of topics for such discussions. This is particularly true when you are in a hurry, under pressure or have been asked to run an activity at short notice. The following is a list of topics that can be used or modified in pairs or group discussions.

- Interests away from work
- Where I would like to live
- How I feel about my work
- What I would do if I changed job
- Which famous person I would change places with and why
- What I like and dislike about myself
- People I have known
- How I got on with my parents
- How I feel about business
- Management
- Why interpersonal skills training is important
- The difficulties of interpersonal skills training
- The nature of counselling
- The limitations of counselling
- The problem of listening
- Being assertive
- Communicating in families
- Television

Topics for discussion

- Theatre
- Music
- Coping with emotions
- Facing middle age
- Facing death
- Childhood
- Adolescence
- My political views
- My religious views
- Why I am not a Christian
- Why I am a Christian
- Things I need to learn more about
- Adult education
- The British legal system
- The debate about hanging
- Communication in the organization
- Working with other people
- Working overseas
- Being an organizational man or woman
- Coping with stress
- Sexuality
- Dealing with anger
- Writing poetry
- Being a performer
- Negotiation
- Administration skills
- The art of coping
- Talking to children
- Talking to the elderly
- Chairing meetings
- Closing sales
- Being in top management

References

Alberti, R.E. and Emmons, M.L. (1982) *Your Perfect Right: a Guide to Assertive Living*. Impact, San Luis Obispo, California.
Argyle, M. (1981) *Social Skills and Work*. Methuen, London.
Bandler, R. and Grinder, J. (1979) *Frogs into Princes: Neurolinguistic Programming*. Real People Press, Moab, Utah.
Blatner, A. (1988) *Foundations of Psychodrama: History, Theory and Practice* (3rd edn). Springer, London.
Brandes, D. and Phillips, R. (1984) *The Gamester's Handbook: Vol 2*. Hutchinson, London.
Brookfield, S.D. (1987) *Developing Critical Thinkers: Challenging Adults to Explore Alternative Ways of Thinking and Acting*. Open University Press, Milton Keynes.
Burnard, P. (1987) 'Self and peer assessment', *Senior Nurse* **6**:5; 16-17.
  (1990) *Learning Human Skills* (2nd edn). Butterworth Heinemann, Oxford.
  (1991) *Experiential Learning in Action*. Avebury, Aldershot.
Burnard, P. and Morrison, P. (1989) 'What is an interpersonally skilled person?: a repertory grid account of professional nurses' views', *Nurse Education Today* **9**:6; 384-91.
Burton, A. (1977) 'The mentoring dynamic in the therapeutic transformation', *The American Journal of Psychoanalysis* **37**; 115-22.
Campbell, A. (1984) *Moderated Love*. S.P.C.K., London.
Collins, G.C. and Scott, P. (1979) 'Everyone who makes it has a mentor', *Harvard Business Review* **56**; 89-101.
Darling, L.A.W. (1984) 'What do nurses want in a mentor?', *The Journal of Nursing Administration* October; 42-4.
Egan, G. (1990) *The Skilled Helper* (4th edn). Brooks/Cole, Pacific Grove, California.
Eliot, T.S. (1963) *Collected Poems 1909–1962*. Faber, London.

Fay, A. (1978) *Making Things Better By Making Them Worse*. Hawthorne, New York.

Gendlin, E. (1981) *Focusing*. Bantam, New York.

Gendlin, E.T. and Beebe, J. (1968) 'An experiential approach to group therapy', *Journal of Research and Developments in Education* **1**; 19–29.

Heron, J. (1973) *Experiential Training Techniques*. Human Potential Research Project, University of Surrey, Guildford.

(1977) *Behaviour Analysis in Education and Training*. Human Potential Research Project, University of Surrey, Guildford.

(1978) *Co-Counselling Teachers Manual*. Human Potential Research Project, University of Surrey, Guildford.

(1986) *Six Category Intervention Analysis* (2nd edn). Human Potential Resource Group, University of Surrey, Guildford.

(1989) *The Facilitators' Handbook*. Kogan Page, London.

(1990) *Helping the Client*. Sage, London.

Jarvis, P. (1983) *Professional Education*. Croom Helm, London.

Kalisch, B.J. (1971) 'Strategies for developing nurses' empathy', *Nursing Outlook* **19**:11; 714–17.

Kilty, J. (1983) *Experiential Learning*. Human Potential Research Project, University of Surrey, Guildford.

(1984) *Self and Peer Assessment*. Human Potential Research Project, University of Surrey, Guildford.

King, E.C. (1984) *Affective Education in Nursing: A Guide to Teaching and Assessment*. Aspen, Maryland.

Kirschenbaum, H. (1979) *On Becoming Carl Rogers*. Dell, New York.

Knowles, M.S. (1978) *The Adult Learner: A Neglected Species* (2nd edn). Gulf, Texas.

(1980) *The Modern Practice of Adult Education: From Pedagogy to Andragogy* (2nd edn). Follett, Chicago.

Knowles M. S. *et al.* (1984) *Andragogy in Action: Applying Modern Principles of Adult Learning*. Jossey Bass, San Francisco, California.

Kolb, D. (1984) *Experiential Learning*. Prentice Hall, Englewood Cliffs, New York.

Lee, H. (1960) *To Kill a Mockingbird*. Heinemann, London.

Luft, J. (1967) *Of Human Interaction: The Johari Model*. Mayfield, Palo Alto, California.

May, K.M. *et al.* (1982) 'Mentorship for scholarliness: opportunities and dilemmas', *Nursing Outlook* **30**; 22–8.

Moreno, J.L. (1969) *Psychodrama: Volume three*. Beacon House Press, Beacon, New York.

Morrison, P. and Burnard, P. (1991) *Caring and Communicating*. Macmillan, London.

Perls, F. (1969) *Gestalt Therapy Verbatim*. Real People Press, Lafayette, California.
  (1973) *The Gestalt Approach and Eyewitness to Therapy*. Science and Behaviour Books, Palo Alto, California.
Reich, W. (1949) *Character Analysis*. Simon and Schuster, New York.
Rogers, C.R. (1951) *Client-Centred Therapy*. Constable, London.
  (1967) *On Becoming a Person*. Constable, London.
Schulman, D. (1982) *Intervention in Human Services: A Guide to Skills and Knowledge* (3rd edn). C.V. Mosby, St Louis, Missouri.
Smith, E. and Wilks, N. (1988) *Meditation*. Macdonald, London.
Truax, C.B. and Carkuff, R.R. (1967) *Towards Effective Counselling and Psychotherapy*. Aldine, Chicago.
Whitehead, A.N. (1933) *The Aims of Education*. Benn, London.
Woodcock, M and Francis, D. (1982) *The Unblocked Manager: A Practical Guide to Self-Development*. Gower, Aldershot.

Bibliography

Abrami, P., Leenthal, L. and Perry, R. (1982) 'Educational seduction', *Review of Educational Research* 52; 446-64.
Adler, R. Rosenfeld, L. and Towne, N. (1986) *Interplay: The Process of Interpersonal Communication* (3rd edn). Holt, Rinehart and Winston, New York.
Argyris, C. (1982) *Reasoning, Learning and Action*. Jossey Bass, San Francisco.
Argyris, C. and Schon, D. (1974) *Theory in Practice: Increasing Professional Effectiveness*. Jossey Bass, San Francisco.
Arnold, E. and Boggs, K. (1989) *Interpersonal Relationships: Professional Communication Skills for Nurses*. Saunders, Philadelphia, Pennsylvania.
Bailey, R. (1985) *Coping With Stress in Caring*. Blackwell, Oxford.
Bailey, R. and Clarke, M. (1989) *Stress and Coping in Nursing*. Chapman and Hall, London.
Baruth, L.G. (1987) *An Introduction to the Counselling Profession*. Prentice Hall, Englewood Cliffs, New Jersey.
Belkin, G.S. (1984) *Introduction to Counselling*. Brown, Dubuque, Iowa.
Blackham, C. (1969) *Humanism*. Pelican, Harmondsworth.
Bolger, A.W. (ed) (1982) *Counselling in Britain: A Reader*. Batsford Academic, London.
Boone, E.J., Shearon, R.W., White, E.E. *et al.* (1980) *Serving Personal and Community Needs Through Adult Education*. Jossey Bass, San Francisco, California.
Boot, R. and Reynolds, M. (1983) 'Learning and experience in formal education', Manchester Monograph. Department of Adult and Higher Education, University of Manchester.
Boshier, R. (1980) *Towards a Learning Society*. Learning Press, Vancouver.

Boud, D. and Prosser, M.T. (1980) 'Sharing responsibility: staff-student cooperation in learning', *British Journal of Educational Technology* **11**: 1; 24-35.

Boud, D., Keogh, R. and Walker, M. (1985) *Reflection: Turning Experience into Learning*. Kogan Page, London.

Bower, G.H. and Hilgard, E.R. (1981) *Theories of Learning* (5th edn). Prentice Hall, Englewood Cliffs, New Jersey.

Boydel T. (1976) 'Experiential learning', Manchester Monograph No 5. Department of Adult and Higher Education, University of Manchester.

Boydel, E.M. and Fales, A.W. (1983) 'Reflective learning: key to learning from experience', *Journal of Humanistic Psychology* **23**:2; 99-117.

Brandes, D. and Phillips, R. (1984) *The Gamester's Handbook: Vol 2*. Hutchinson, London.

Brocket, R. and Hiemstra, R. (1985) 'Bridging the theory-practice gap in self-directed learning', in: *New Directions for Continuing Education No 25*. Jossey Bass, San Francisco, California.

Brown, D. and Srebalus, D.J. (1988) *An Introduction to the Counselling Process*. Prentice Hall, Philadelphia, Pennsylvania.

Brown, I.B. (ed) (1975) *The Live Classroom*. Esalen/Viking, San Francisco, California.

Brown, S.D. and Lent, R.W. (eds) (1984) *Handbook of Counselling Psychology*. Wiley, Chichester.

Brundage, D.H. and Mackeracher, D. (1980) *Adult Learning Principles and their Application to Program Planning*. Ministry of Education, Ontario, Canada.

Burnard, P. (1985) 'The teacher as trainer, *Senior Nurse* **3**:1; 34-7.

(1987a) 'Self and peer assessment', *Senior Nurse* **6**:5; 16-17

(1987b) 'Spiritual distress and the nursing response', *Journal of Advanced Nursing* **12**; 377-82.

(1988) 'The heart of the counselling relationship', *Senior Nurse* **8**:12; 17-18.

(1988b) 'Coping with other people's emotions', *The Professional Nurse* **4**: 1; 11-14.

(1988c) 'Stress and relaxation in health visiting', *Health Visitor* **61**:9; 272.

(1989) 'Role play', *Journal of District Nursing* **7**:11; 16-17.

Burnard, P. and Chapman, C.M. (1988) *Professional and Ethical Issues in Nursing: The Code of Professional Conduct*. Chichester: Wiley.

Calnan, J. (1983) *Talking With Patients*. Heinemann, London.

Campbell, A. (1984) *Paid to Care?* S.P.C.K., London.

Campbell, A.V. (1981) *Rediscovering Pastoral Care*. Darton, Longman and Todd, London.

Carkuff, R.R. (1969) *Helping and Human Relations: Vol I: Selection and Training.* Holt, Rinehart and Winston, New York.

Chene, A. (1983) 'The concept of autonomy in adult education', *Adult Education Quarterly* **32**:1; 38-47.

Clift, J.C. and Imrie, B.W. (1981) *Assessing Students and Appraising Teaching.* Croom Helm, London.

Coleman, J.S. (1982) 'Experiential learning and information assimilation', *Child and Youth Services* **14**: 3-4; 12-20.

Conrad, D. and Hedin, D. (1982) 'The impact of experiential education on adolescent development', *Child and Youth Services* **4**: 3-4; 57-76.

Corey, F. (1983) *I Never Knew I Had A Choice* (2nd edn). Brooks-Cole, Pacific Grove, California.

Cormier, L.S. (1987) *The Professional Counsellor: A Process Guide to Helping.* Prentice Hall, Englewood Cliffs, New Jersey.

Cross, K.P. (1981) *Adults as Learners.* Jossey Bass, San Francisco.

Cross-Durrant, A. (1984) 'Lifelong Education in the Writings of John Dewey', *International Journal of Lifelong Education* **3**:2; 115-25.

Davis, B (ed) (1987) *Nursing Education: Research and Developments.* Croom Helm, London.

Davis, B.D. (ed) (1983) *Research into Nurse Education.* Croom Helm, London.

Davis, C.M. (1981) 'Affective education for the health professions', *Physical Therapy* **61**:11; 1587-93.

Dixon, D.N. and Glover, J.A. (1984) *Counselling: A Problem Solving Approach.* Wiley, Chichester.

Dowd, C. (1983) 'Learning Through Experience', *Nursing Times*: 27th July.

Dowrick, P. and Briggs, S.J. (eds) (1983) *Using Video: Psychological and Social Applications.* Wiley, New York.

Edelstein, B and Eisler, R. (1976) 'Effects of modelling and modelling with instruction and feedback', *Behaviour Therapy* **4**; 382-89.

Edmunds, M. (1983) 'The Nurse Preceptor Role', *Nurse Practitioner* **8**:6; 52-3.

Egan, G. (1986) *Exercises in Helping Skills* (3rd edn). Brooks/Cole, Monterey, California.

Elias, J.L. and Merriam, S. (1980) *Philosophical Foundations of Adult Education.* Krieger, Tampa, Florida,

Ernst, S. and Goodison, L. (1981) *In Our Own Hands: A Book of Self Help Therapy.* The Women's Press, London.

Famighetti, R.A. (1981) 'Experiential Learning: The Close Encounters of the Institutional Kind', *Gerontology and Geriatric Education* **2**:2; 129-32.

Ferruci, P. (1982) *What We May Be.* Turnstone Press, Wellingborough.

Flyn, P.A.R. (1980) *Holistic Health: The Art and Science of Care.* Brady, Bowie, Maryland.

Fox, F.E. (1983) 'The spiritual core of experiential education', *Journal of Experiential Education* **16**:1; 3-6.

Frankl, V.E. (1959) *Man's Search for Meaning.* Beacon Press, New York. (1978) *The Unheard Cry for Meaning.* Simon and Schuster, New York.

Gager, R. (1982) 'Experiential Education: Strengthening the Learning Process', *Child and Youth Services* **4**:3-4; 31-9.

Geller, L. (1985) 'Another look at self-actualization', *Journal of Humanistic Psychology* **24**:2; 93-106.

Gerard, B, Boniface, W., Love, B. (1980) *Interpersonal Skills for Health Professionals.* Reston Publishing Co, Reston, Virginia.

Gibson, R.L. and Mitchell, M.H. (1986) *Introduction to Counselling and Guidance.* Collier Macmillan, London.

Gorden, D. (1982) 'The concept of the hidden curriculum', *Journal of Philosophy of Education* **16**:2; 187-8.

Gross, R. (1977) *The Lifelong Learner.* Simon and Schuster, New York.

Grossman, R. (1985) 'Some reflections on Abraham Maslow', *Journal of Humanistic Psychology* **25**:4; 31-4.

Halmos, P. (1965) *The Faith of the Counsellors.* Constable, London.

Hamilton, M.S. (1981) 'Mentorhood: a key to nursing leadership', *Nursing Leadership* **4**:1; 4-13.

Hanks, L, Belliston, L. and Edwards, D. (1977) *Design Yourself.* Kaufman, Los Altos, California.

Hare, A.P. (1976) *Handbook of Small Group Research.* Free Press, New York.

Harris, T. (1969) *I'm O.K., You're O.K.* Harper and Row, London.

Hendricks, G. and Fadiman, J. (eds) (1976) *Transpersonal Education: A Curriculum for Feeling and Being.* Prentice Hall, Englewood Cliffs, New Jersey.

Hendricks, G. and Weinhod, B. (1982) *Transpersonal Approaches to Counselling and Psychotherapy.* Love Publishing Co. Denver, Colorado.

Herinck, R. (ed) (1980) *The Psychotherapy Handbook.* New American Library, New York.

Hinchliff, S. M. (ed) (1979) *Teaching in Clinical Nursing.* Churchill Livingstone, Edinburgh.

Holt, R. (1982) 'An Alternative to Mentorship', *Adult Education* **55**:2; 152-6.

Houle, C.O. (1984) *Patterns of Learning.* Jossey Bass, San Francisco.

Hurding, R.F. (1985) *Roots and Shoots: A Guide to Counselling and Psychotherapy.* Hodder and Stoughton, London.

Hutchins, D.E. (1987) *Helping Relationships and Strategies.* Brooks-Cole,

Monterey, California.
Ivey, A.E. (1987) *Counselling and Psychotherapy: Skills, Theories and Practice*. Prentice Hall International, London.
James, M. and Jongeward, D. (1971) *Born to Win: Transactional Analysis With Gestalt Experiments*. Addison-Wesley, Reading, Massachusetts.
Jarvis, P. (1983) *Professional Education*. Croom Helm, London.
— (1987) 'Meaningful and meaningless experience: towards an understanding', *Adult Education Quarterly* **37**:3.
Jenkins, E. (1987) *Facilitating Self-Awareness: A Learning Package Combining Group*. Open Software Library, Wigan.
Jourard, S. (1971) *Self-Disclosure: An Experimental Analysis of the Transparent Self*. Wiley, New York.
Jung, C.G. (1976) *Modern Man in Search of a Soul*. Routledge and Kegan Paul, London.
Kelly, G.A. (1970) 'A Brief Introduction to Personal Construct Theory'. In: Bannister, D. *Perspectives in Construct Theory*. Academic Press. London.
Kennedy, E. (1979) *On Becoming a Counsellor*. Gill and Macmillan, London.
Kilty, J. (1978) *Self and Peer Assessment*. Human Potential Research Project, University of Surrey, Guildford.
— (1987) *Staff Development for Nurse Education: Practitioners Supporting Staff*. Human Potential Research Project, University of Surrey, Guildford, Surrey.
King, E.C. (1984) *Affective Education in Nursing: A Guide to Teaching and Assessment*: Aspen, Maryland.
Knox, A.B. (ed) (1980) *Teaching Adults Effectively*. Jossey Bass, San Francisco, California.
Kottler, J.A. and Brown, R.W. (1985) *Introduction to Therapeutic Counselling*. Brooks/Cole, Monterey, California.
Legge, D. (1982) *The Education of Adults In Britain*. Open University Press, Milton Keynes.
Levine, A (1985) 'The pollyana paradigm', *Journal of Humanistic Psychology* **25**:1; 90–3.
Levison, R.H. (1979) 'Experiential education abroad', *Teaching Sociology* **6**:4; 415–19.
Lipsett, L. and Avakian, N.A. (1981) 'Assessing experiential learning', *Lifelong Learning, The Adult Years* **5**:2; 18–22.
Lowen, A and L. (1977) *The Way to Vibrant Health: A Manual of Bioenergetic Exercises*. Harper and Row, New York.
McPeck, J.E. (1981) *Critical Thinking and Education*. St. Martins Press, New York.
Maple, F.F. (1985) *Dynamic Interviewing: An Introduction to Counsel-*

ling. Sage, Beverly Hills, California.

Marshall, L.A. and Rowland, F. (1983) *A Guide to Learning Independently*. Open University Press, Milton Keynes.

Menson, B. (ed) (1982) 'Building on experiences in adult development', *New Directions for Experiential Learning No 16*. Jossey Bass, San Francisco, California.

Merriam, S. (1984) 'Mentors and proteges: a critical review of the literature', *Adult Education Quarterly* **33**:3; 161-73.

Mezeiro, J. (1981) 'A critical theory of adult learning and education', *Adult Education* **32**:1; 3-24.

Mocker, D.W. and Spear, G.E. (1982) *Lifelong Learning: Formal, Non-formal and Self-Directed*. The ERIC Clearinghouse on Adult Career and Vocational Education, Columbus, Ohio.

Morsund, J. (1985) *The Process of Counselling and Therapy*. Prentice Hall, Englewood Cliffs, New Jersey.

Murgatroyd, S. (1986) *Counselling and Helping*. British Psychological Society and Methuen, London.

Murgatroyd, S. and Woolfe, R. (1982) *Coping with Crisis-Understanding and Helping Persons in Need*. Harper and Row, London.

Myerscough, P.R. (1989) *Talking With Patients: A Basic Clinical Skill*. Oxford Medical Publications, Oxford.

Nadler, L. (ed) (1984) *The Handbook of Human Resource Development*. Wiley, New York.

Naranjo, C. and Ornstein, R.E. (1971) *On the Psychology of Meditation*. Allen and Unwin, London.

Nelson-Jones, R. (1984) *Personal Responsibility: Counselling and Therapy: An Integrative Approach*. Harper and Row, London.

(1988) *Practical Counselling and Helping Skills: Helping Clients to Help*. Cassell, London.

Noble, P. (1983) *Formation of Freirian Facilitators*. Latino Institute, Chicago.

Nyberg, D. (ed) (1975) *The Philosophy of Open Education*. Routledge and Kegan Paul, London.

Ohlsen, A.M., Horne, A.M. and Lawe, C.F. (1988) *Group Counselling*. Holt, Rinehart and Winston, New York.

Open University Coping With Crisis Group (1987) *Running Workshops: A Guide for Trainers in the Helping Professions*. Croom Helm, London.

Patton, M.Q. (1982) *Practical Evaluation*. Sage, Beverly Hills, California.

Pearce, J.C. (1982) *The Bond of Power: Meditation and Wholeness*. Routledge, London.

Postman, N. and Weingartner, C.W. (1969) *Teaching as a Subversive Activity*. Penguin, Harmondsworth.

Procter, B. (1978) *Counselling Shop*. Deutsch, London.

Rawlings, M.E. and L. (1983) 'Mentoring and networking for helping professionals', *Personnel and Guidance Journal* **62**:2; 116-8.
Reddy, M. (1987) *The Manager's Guide to Counselling at Work*. Methuen, London.
Riebel, L. (1984) 'A homeopathic model of psychotherapy', *Journal of Humanistic Psychology* **24**:1; 9-48.
Ringuette, E.L. (1983) 'A note on experiential learning in professional training', *Journal of Clinical Psychology* **39**:2; 302-4.
Rogers, C.R. (1957) 'The necessary and sufficient conditions of therapeutic personality change', *Journal of Consulting Psychology* **21**; 95-104.
Rowan, J. (1986) 'Holistic listening', *Journal of Humanistic Psychology* **26**:1; 83-102.
Schon, D.A. (1983) *The Reflective Practitioner: How Professionals Think in Action*. Basic Books, New York.
Shapiro, E.C., Haseltime, F, and Rowe, M. (1978) 'Moving up: role models, mentors and the patron system', *Sloan Management Review* **19**; 51-8.
Shapiro, S.B. (1985) 'An empirical analysis of operating values in humanistic education', *Journal of Humanistic Psychology* **25**:1; 94-108.
Shropshire, C.O. (1981) 'Group experiential learning in adult education', *The Journal of Continuing Education in Nursing* **12**:6; 5-9.
Smith, E.W.L. (ed) (1976) *The Growing Edge of Gestalt Therapy*. Citadel Press, Secaucus, New Jersey.
Stitch, T.F. (1983) 'Experiential therapy', *Journal of Experiential Education* **5**:3; 23-30.
Tough, A.M. (1982) *Intentional Changes; A Fresh Approach to Helping People Change*. Cambridge Books, New York.
Trower, P. (ed) (1984) *Radical Approaches to Social Skills Training*. Croom Helm, London.
Truax, C.B. and Carkuff, R.R. (1967) *Towards Effective Counselling and Psychotherapy*. Aldine, Chicago.
Van Deurzen-Smith, E. (1988) *Existential Counselling in Practice*. Sage, Beverely Hills, California.
Wallace, W.A. (1986) *Theories of Counselling and Psychotherapy: A Basic Issues Approach*. Allyn and Bacon, Boston, Massachusetts.
Wheeler, D.D. and Janis, I.L. (1980) *A Practical Guide for Making Decisions*. Free Press, New York.
Wlodkowski, R.J. (1985) *Enhancing Adult Motivation to Learn*. Jossey Bass, San Francisco, California.

Index of Activities

Alternating chair **Activity number 27**

Blind walk **Activity number 6**
Body language **Activity number 30**
Brainstorming **Activities number 12, 22, 41 and 67**
Brief interviews **Activity number 2**

Centring **Activity number 32**
Checking for understanding **Activity number 75**
Childhood **Activity number 49**
Co-counselling activity **Activity number 13**
Confidence building **Activity number 97**
Confronting **Activity number 105**
Congruent body language **Activity number 85**
Contradictory body language **Activity number 84**

Dealing with feelings **Activity number 106**
Describing **Activity number 54**
Devil's advocate **Activity number 99**
Don't listen **Activity number 20**

Earliest experience **Activity number 47**
Exaggerated role play **Activity number 88**
Exaggeration **Activity number 45**
Exploration of topic **Activity number 17**
Exploring silence **Activity number 76**
Expressing feelings **Activity number 43**
Eye contact in everyday life **Activity number 38**
Eye movements **Activity number 40**

Feeling words **Activity number 42**
Fishbowl **Activity number 24**
Focusing **Activity number 48**
Formal introductions **Activity number 9**
Free for all **Activity number 26**
Future **Activity number 50**
Future planning **Activity number 68**

Giving permission **Activity number 44**
Good and new **Activity number 8**
Ground rules **Activity number 25**
Group eye contact **Activity number 34**

Here and now **Activity number 60**
Hotseat **Activity number 28**

Identifying facilitation skills **Activity number 101**
Identifying key issues **Activity number 93**
Immediate awareness **Activity number 51**
Interview checklist **Activity number 92**
Introductory handout **Activity number 4**
Introductory pairs **Activity number 11**
Inventory **Activity number 7**

Journal **Activity number 64**

Least and best **Activity number 65**
Listening **Activity number 14**
Listening to the group **Activity number 109**

Meaning **Activity number 104**
Meditation **Activity number 58**
Milling and pairing **Activity number 5**

No chairman **Activity number 23**
No eye contact **Activity number 31**
Nominal group evaluation **Activity number 62**
Noticing **Activity number 53**

Opening round **Activity number 1**

Pairs evaluation **Activity number 61**
Pairs interview **Activity number 16**

Index of activities

Pairs introductions **Activity number 3**
Paradox **Activity number 46**
Personal evaluation **Activity number 70**
Perverse role play **Activities number 80 and 96**
Planning **Activity number 103**
Practising interviewing **Activity number 98**
Prepared sheets **Activity number 10**
Preparing for an interview **Activity number 91**
Psychodrama **Activity number 89**
Putting group facilitation into practice **Activity number 110**
Putting it all together **Activities number 79 and 100**

Quaker group **Activity number 29**
Questionnaire **Activity number 69**

Real life practice **Activity number 90**
Recording **Activity number 39**
Rogerian listening **Activity number 21**
Role play **Activity number 86**
Role play interview **Activity number 95**

Saying no **Activity number 82**
Saying yes **Activity number 83**
Self-description **Activity number 56**
Self and object **Activity number 55**
Self and peer evaluation **Activity number 63**
Self-assessment **Activity number 102**
Self-not self **Activity number 57**
Shifting awareness **Activity number 52**
Silent gazing **Activity number 36**
Silent pairs **Activity number 19**
Simple listening **Activity number 71**
Snowballing **Activity number 18**
Stream of consciousness **Activity number 59**
Structuring **Activity number 107**
Submissive role play **Activity number 87**
Summarizing **Activity number 78**
Sustained eye contact **Activity number 33**

Talking and eye contact **Activity number 35**
Things learned **Activity number 66**

Using closed questions **Activity number 73**
Using empathy-building statements **Activity number 74**
Using open questions **Activity number 72**
Using probes **Activity number 77**
Using questions **Activity number 15**

Valuing **Activity number 108**

What the eyes say **Activity number 37**
Writing a CV **Activity number 94**

YES/No activity **Activity number 81**

Index

adult learning 55
advice giving 33
agenda, hidden 67
assertiveness 42–9
assertiveness skills activities 270

blind walk activity 109
body language 161
booklists 88
brainstorming 121, 145
business and administration training 11

centring 166
checking for understanding 34, 38
childhood 200
client-centred counselling 33
clients 12
climate, learning 55
closing groups 60
closing workshops 88
co-counselling 124
coaching skills 81
colleagues 12
confidence building 306
confronting dimensions 316
counselling skills 31–42
counselling skills activities 248
curriculum design 14
customer relations training 12
customers 12
CV, writing a 299

debriefing 59
dimensions of trainer style 324
discussion groups 29
dynamics, group 61

empathic understanding 24
empathy building 34, 37
evaluating interpersonal skills workshops 72
evaluation activities 228
evaluation questionnaire 245
experiential learning 26–30
experiential learning cycle 59
expressing feelings 187
eye contact, exploring 163

facial expression 46
facilitation 49
facilitation skills activities 314
facilitation, styles of group 50
feeling dimension 317
feelings 78, 183
fishbowl activity 148
flight 65
focusing 197
formal introductions 115
further education 12

games 29
genuineness 22
Gestalt exercises 29, 204

Index

gestures 46
good and new activity 114
ground rules activity 150
group dynamics 53
group facilitation 49

handouts 88
health professions 12
hidden agenda 67
higher education 12
hotseat activity 157
human potential 12
humanistic psychology 35

icebreakers 29, 99
interviewing skills activities 290
interviews, brief 101
introductory questionnaire 107
inventory, personal 113

journal, keeping a 73

knowledge, transformation of 27

labels 12
League of Gentlemen 63
learning, experiential 26–30
lifelong education 79
listening 126

management training 11
managers 12
managing interpersonal skills training 53
meaning dimension 316
meditation 29, 221, 223
mentoring 77
milling and pairing 108

nondefensiveness 21

open questions 35
opening round 100

pairing 61
pairs activities 118
pairs exercises 29
paradox 193

patients 12
peer assessment 73
personal evaluation 246
personal experience 27
personal inventory 113
personal qualities 20
personnel training 12
planning dimension 315
planning workshops 54–5
positive regard 25
project work 29
projection 63
psychodrama 29, 286

Quaker group activity 159
quality circles 12
questionnaire, introductory 107
questions 34, 129

reflection 34, 87
rescuing 67
researchers 12
residents 12
resources 57
Rogerian listening activity 143
role models 15
role play 29
running interpersonal skills workshops 83

scapegoating 62
selective reflection 34
self-assessment 73, 322
self-monitoring 22
shutting down 66
silent pairs activity 138
simulations 29
small group activities 29
snowballing 136
social skills 19
staff development 11
stream of consciousness 224
stress reduction 29
structuring dimension 318
students 12
styles of group facilitation 50
summarising 264
supervision 77

Index

therapy 13
timing 46
topics for discussion 340
trainer style checklist 323
training checklists 90
transformation of knowledge 27

unconditional positive regard 25

valuing dimension 318

warmth, personal 21
wrecking 64